Dimensions of Choice:
A Qualitative Approach to Recreation, Parks, and Leisure Research

Dimensions of Choice:
A Qualitative Approach to Recreation, Parks, and Leisure Research

Karla A. Henderson, Ph.D.

Venture Publishing, Inc.
State College, PA

Production Supervision by Bonnie Godbey
Cover Design by Sikorski Designs
Editorial Assistance by Michele Barbin
Library of Congress Catalogue Card Number 91-65915
ISBN 0-910251-44-4

Dedicated to Darlene Conover, Caroline Weiss, and Jerry Apps
who inspired me professionally when I needed each one of them most.

CONTENTS

Chapter 3 Theoretical Frameworks

Part Two *Qualitative Methods*

Chapter 4 Field Research and Participant Observation

Chapter 5 Indepth Interviewing

Chapter 6 Other Qualitative Methods

Part Three *Qualitative Techniques*

Acknowledgements

Collaboration is my preferred mode of writing. During the writing of this book I have felt rather lonely at times but I have continued to tell myself that this book reflects my personal and professional "dimensions of choice." Fortunately, I have had the encouragement of a number of individuals who have supported me professionally and personally throughout the course of this book. Professionally I would particularly like to thank the former chair of the Curriculum in Leisure Studies and Recreation Administration at the University of North Carolina-Chapel Hill, Doug Sessoms, who provided me with the time and countenance to write this book. I am most appreciative of the students with whom I have worked at UNC, Texas Woman's University, and the University of Wisconsin-Madison who asked the kinds of questions that framed the conceptualization of this book. I owe a big thanks to David Grout who persevered as my graduate assistant during the final stages of writing the book. I am also deeply professionally indebted to individuals such as Charlie Bullock, Mary Faeth Chenery, Maureen Glancy, and Chris Howe, as well as other leisure researchers, who have been pioneers in using qualitative methods and interpretive research to answer questions related to recreation, parks, and leisure. In addition, I am grateful for the "sociologist's perspective" that my friend Sherryl Kleinman has given during the writing of this book. A special thanks, however, goes to my best friends and colleagues Deb Bialeschki and Leandra Bedini who read drafts of the book and offered encouragement when I needed it most. It has been a privilege to know and to work with two such dedicated individuals. Lastly, I want to acknowledge those people who supported me personally during the writing of this book–E.J., my softball and volleyball team-mates, and my family in Iowa, all of whom were kind enough to ask from time to time, "how's it going?" and then were gracious enough to listen to what I had to say.

Karla A. Henderson

Part One

The Philosophy of Recreation, Parks, and Leisure Research

Introduction

Dimensions of Choice: A Qualitative Approach to Recreation, Parks, and Leisure Research is an introduction to the philosophy, methods, and techniques that may be applied to interpretive research and qualitative studies in recreation, parks, and leisure. The qualitative approach to research includes interpretive procedures that inductively describe, translate, and focus on the meaning rather than the frequency of occurring phenomena in the social world (Van Maanen, 1988). The qualitative approach generally uses the natural environment, focuses on determining the meaning attached to phenomena, acknowledges the researcher as the instrument in interaction with the phenomena being studied, and uses words as the primary symbols for generating grounded theory specific to the context in which the research occurs. The qualitative approach is often considered antithetical to quantitative methods which focus on deductive, statistical techniques for generating and analyzing data. These two ways of designing, discovering, and interpreting data, however, are not necessarily opposites. Both approaches can be useful in research and evaluation studies that address recreation, park, and leisure questions.

The purpose of this book is to provide a framework for using qualitative approaches in recreation, parks, and leisure research. The thesis of the book is that researchers should have enough information to make choices about what research paradigms and methods are most appropriate to use given a particular research question. As the author of this book, I am clearly biased toward qualitative methods, but the focus is not on the superiority of one paradigm over another or of one approach over another. Through reading and using this book, it is my hope that qualitative methods applied to the study of recreation, parks, leisure, and other related fields may be better understood.

This book is designed for anyone who is interested in examining the dimensions of choice pertaining to research conceptualization, design, and analysis. It is assumed that a number of graduate students, as well as some undergraduate students, may be using this book as a supplement to other texts that are frequently used in research methods courses (e.g., Babbie, 1989; Kraus and Allen, 1987; Pelegrino, 1979). It is also hoped that educators, practitioners, and researchers might be interested in continuing their own education about qualitative approaches to research. Most educators and practitioners who received graduate degrees in higher education more than five years ago received very little education in qualitative methods. Perhaps educators will be interested in acquiring a broad understanding of this qualitative approach so it might be infused in other coursework where students may be addressing research and evaluation. Finally, this book is designed for practicing professionals in a broad range of leisure services (i.e., camping and outdoor education, public parks and recreation, youth-serving agencies, clinical and community therapeutic recreation settings) who might want to consider using these qualitative techniques for "in-house" research and evaluation. For purposes of clarity, the individual reading this book or contemplating this approach to research, whether she/he is a student, educator, researcher, evaluator, or practitioner, will be referred to as the "researcher."

I would like to emphasize that a general understanding of quantitative methods precludes an understanding of qualitative methods. To have dimensions of choice in conducting research, it is necessary to have an understanding of the research paradigms, the assumptions of each approach, and how techniques and strategies may be used for various methods. While the focus of this book is on qualitative methods, it will also provide a framework for enabling the researcher to make informed choices about all research methods.

Many books and articles have been written in other disciplines over the past twenty-five years describing qualitative methods for conducting research. It is sophomoric to believe that a definitive text can be written about qualitative methods applied to recreation, parks, and leisure. One of the major parameters of interpretive research and the qualitative approach is the lack of rules and protocols for doing research. Therefore, this book is presented as an introduction, a means for getting researchers to consider additional ways of thinking and acting, and as a beginning point for helping individuals realize the many options for conducting research. The reader who becomes interested in these qualitative methods will want to pursue further reading from other authors writing about methods and techniques as well as those researchers who have applied these methods to the study of recreation, parks, leisure, and other related areas.

The text is divided into three parts that are not mutually exclusive. Just as qualitative approaches to research rely on an emerging design and necessitate the simultaneous conducting of data discovery, analysis, and interpretation, the reader is invited to explore each part of the book and reflect synchronally upon its meaning to the other two parts. The meaning of this text will be lost without contemplating how philosophy, method, and technique relate to one another.

The first part of the book describes the evolution of the use of the qualitative approach as applied to recreation, parks, and leisure research. Two models are presented addressing (a) the relationship of the world views of interpretive and positivist research to research approaches and methods, and (b) the relationship between deductive theory (theory which generally drives positivist research) and inductive theory (the grounded theory emerging from the context of interpretive research). Part One is necessarily "philosophical" and it provides a basis for why interpretive approaches might be chosen. To the individual not familiar with the philosophy of science or with the qualitative approach, the first part may seem somewhat esoteric. The reader may want to peruse Part One and then study it more thoroughly after reading the remainder of the book. It is important, however, not to discount the value of a philosophical framework for conducting research.

Part Two provides a discussion of the methods that are commonly associated with the qualitative approach. Field research/participant observation and indepth interviewing are the two most common qualitative methods used although other methods are also described. The reader is reminded that virtually any method chosen may be qualitative or quantitative depending upon how the method is used and how the assumptions surrounding the research paradigm are applied. The methods described in Part Two focus on their use in addressing interpretive research questions. If the researcher wants to fully understand how a qualitative method might be applied to a research question, Part Three must be additionally studied.

Part Three describes the techniques that are common to most qualitative methods. Chapters in this part identify specific techniques for research planning, data discovery and organization, data interpretation, and explaining the results through writing. Whether one is using field research, indepth interviewing, content analysis, or any other qualitative method, the researcher will want to consider these techniques. This last part of the book provides specific strategies to explore when using qualitative methods. The final chapter presents issues that the researcher will need to address in using qualitative methods.

I would like to caution readers that qualitative studies are not the panacea for people who are scared by the word "research." Just because statistics are generally not used in qualitative methods does not mean the research is any easier, less rigorous, or less time consuming. Qualitative research is much more than a "flying visit followed by an impressionistic essay" (Locke, 1986). The qualitative approach is appropriate and available to address questions raised about recreation, park, and leisure phenomena. Qualitative methods are more appropriate than quantitative methods for some research questions but may not be practical in other situations. The focus of this book is to provide enough information so that the researcher can make the appropriate research choices concerning paradigms, approaches, methods, and techniques.

Not everything about qualitative methods can be covered in this book, but at least the researcher can be exposed to a broad explanation of the possibilities and how choice might be applied to research and evaluation questions concerning recreation, parks, and leisure. A number of examples of excellent resources are offered to assist those individuals who would like to learn more than what this text provides. One cannot become an expert on qualitative analyses simply by reading this book but one can gain an understanding and appreciation for how and why qualitative approaches might be appropriate for certain research questions.

The best frame of mind for the reader to have in reading this book is a spirit of adventure. The use of qualitative methods in the study of recreation, parks, and leisure is only beginning to gain impetus. Much is yet to be explored and learned. This book, and particularly Part One, will provide a grounding for the potential that qualitative methods can have for better understanding leisure phenomena and the delivery of recreation, park, and leisure services.

Chapter 1

The Yin-Yang of Leisure Research

Introduction

The yin-yang is a symbol of polar energies in harmony with one another. The yin-yang has often referred to opposites such as feminine and masculine although the idea may be more broadly related to any apparent dualism one might encounter such as subjective-objective, question-answer, space-time, spontaneous-planned. Within every aspect of life, a counterforce interacts with a major force to create a balance. One concept is interdependent with the other. For example, without darkness there would be no concept for light. Thus, the Taoist Theory of Yin-Yang is a concept that unifies all opposites. I hope you will keep the yin-yang idea in mind as we begin to explore the qualitative approach to research as it harmonizes with the traditional quantitative approach.

The Yin and the Yang

The quantitative approach has predominated in social science research in general, as well as in research involving recreation, park, and leisure studies. The potential for qualitative analysis has not been acknowledged within the leisure literature and research until the past ten years. Qualitative research approaches in leisure studies, as well as other disciplines, are now "coming of age" (Taylor and Bogdan, 1984). A quiet revolution is occurring. Researchers and evaluators studying recreation, parks, and leisure now have a choice about the methods of inquiry that can be used. Either qualitative or quantitative methods or a combination of the two may be useful in addressing recreation, park, and leisure questions. Therefore, the researcher needs to know when it is appropriate to make particular method choices within qualitative and quantitative approaches.

Assumptions and Premises

It may be useful to describe some of the values and assumptions that pervade this collection of ideas that I am putting forth. In doing so, the reader can understand the thesis of the book as well as the framework in which we will operate.

First, the book will not necessarily be written in the traditional subject-object dualism that we professors were taught to use in technical writing. That subject-object dualism typically suggests that I am the teacher and you are the learner. Based on what I am saying to you from my own emerging world view, however, I will try to write in a way that is subjective, effective, open-ended with a variety of perspectives and realities, and within a context that acknowledges that research of any kind does not occur in a vacuum independent of other aspects of life. I want you to feel that we are "co-researchers" and "co-searchers" in exploring the paradigms, approaches, methods, and techniques that comprise qualitative studies. By rejecting the subject-object dualism, I am attempting to recognize the interdependence between myself and your understanding of this text. Inquiry is not value free; this book is filled with my values but I will try to acknowledge what is mine and what belongs to others and let you see what will be useful to you in putting your values into practice. I hope that I can find a context that will resonate with what you believe about the world and how we might approach research concerning recreation, parks, and leisure. Patton (1980b) suggested that in qualitative methods one must be committed to entering worlds of interaction. This book is designed to be an interaction between myself as a researcher and you as a researcher.

The qualitative approach is not clearly understood by many people. The qualitative approach is easier to describe than to define. The distinction is not as easy as saying that qualitative researchers use words while quantitative researchers use numbers, although in an oversimplified way this distinction is true. The world view or paradigm that is held (commonly referred to as either positivism or interpretive social science which will be explained in greater detail later), the general approach to research design that is chosen (qualitative verses quantitative), and the specific methods applied (i.e., participant observation, indepth interviewing) are often used to describe the ways that research is conducted. These labels and possibilities create confusion. Total agreement does not exist concerning what the qualitative approach is. Further, qualitative data discovery and interpretation, as well as the development of grounded theory, are often considered mystical processes to those accustomed to statistical analysis. I will try to present a perspective concerning how I understand the qualitative approach to research, but you must realize that this view is dynamic. One of my hesitations in writing this book is that two months after it is published, a whole new perspective may reveal itself to me. That possibility is a part of the reality of the world view that I hold; therefore, I offer my thoughts and the thoughts of other researchers as a temporary starting place so we can explore new ideas that will emerge in future literature. I will also caution the researcher to realize that in some explanations in this book, concepts are oversimplified in order to communicate the ideas more clearly.

Thirdly, I believe that the researcher needs a grounding in the philosophy of science in order to make appropriate choices in research. A researcher cannot appreciate the value of the qualitative approach without understanding the philosophical assumptions that are made surrounding methodology. Once research questions are developed, the researcher will need to find the best methods to use to discover and interpret data. Philosophically, I do not believe that interpretive research is inherently superior or inferior to positivist research. One or the other may be more appropriate for a particular individual's style or for a particular research question. Philosophical discussions about which paradigm is better than the other are not productive. Researchers need a broad philosophical base in order to enhance our understanding of the profession and of leisure behavior.

A fourth assumption is that researchers need an appreciation and understanding of both quantitative and qualitative methods. Each researcher needs to feel empowered to choose the appropriate approach to research given a particular question or problem. For me, qualitative methods of research generally fit my philosophical view of the world and offer important alternatives for the exploration of the issues of the profession as well as the study of leisure behavior. My personal bias is clearly toward the qualitative approach to research for a number of reasons that will become clearer as our discussion proceeds. I have, however, used quantitative methods in the past and will continue to do so for certain research questions in the future when those methods are most appropriate for my research question. My understanding of quantitative design and statistics has helped to provide a fuller appreciation for the value of qualitative methods. As Reinharz (1981) suggested, one must understand the dominant paradigm in order to reject it. I believe all recreation, park, and leisure researchers should know something about both paradigms and approaches and be able to make informed decisions about how best to answer the pressing questions of our discipline and field. Further, all researchers should be able to read a research study, regardless of the approach used and be able to judge its value in helping us to better understand the world. No one method can fully explain reality.

Fifth, I hope you will approach qualitative studies as an adventure. One overall assumption of the qualitative approach is that direct experiences are the way that we come to know truth (Douglas, 1976). Interacting with human beings is not necessarily predictable. While we have a lot of information about qualitative methods of research as is evident in the references used in writing this book, qualitative designs often do not follow set protocol. Some persons have suggested that even attempting to write a book on qualitative design, data discovery, and data interpretation is antithetical to the assumption of a lack of protocols for research that are inherent in the qualitative approach. Since qualitative studies are generally conducted in the natural environment (and not in laboratories) and since we are generally addressing human behavior, you really never know what data are going to emerge. If you do *not* like uncertainty, intrigue, being around humans (who are highly complex and usually not very predictable), then you will probably not be very secure in using the qualitative approach. If you are not comfortable with the methods used in qualitative studies, then you should probably not be doing them. As indicated earlier, however, your personal discomfort should not preclude your having an appreciation of the approach. Researchers using qualitative methods need to employ the techniques of adventurers, detectives, and investigative journalists (Kirk and Miller, 1986). Some of us are born with these inclinations for doing qualitative research and simply need to refine them within the qualitative approach; others of us have to learn and develop these interactive research skills.

Along with being an adventurer, the researcher using the qualitative approach should be flexible. Quantitative methods have typically had protocols associated with them. In the qualitative approach, systematic inquiry is still the framework used to identify patterns of phenomena, however, the process in using qualitative methods and techniques is generally not as linear as in applying quantitative methods. It is important not to get caught up in confusing method with rigor. In qualitative methods there is a necessary interdependency between the nature of the social world and the specific methods used to study that social world (Douglas, 1976). A strict adherence to any method or technique may become a confinement to what can be learned through the qualitative approach to research (Wax, 1971). Further, the problems that we address in the the study of recreation, parks, and leisure are boundless; therefore, we cannot deal with them only in a bounded rationality. If research problems are simplified too much, it is impossible to address them adequately.

These ambiguities in the qualitative approach may create cognitive dissonance within the researcher. It is not easy, particularly in the academic world, to be without rules. In the qualitative approach one is constantly going back and forth between developing, generating, and interpreting data so there are few hard and fast techniques or rules. It is not possible for me to write a cookbook for qualitative analysis. I will, however, offer some guidance in how you can find meaning in this type of research, how you can move ahead in examining beliefs about the world, and about how we come to know social reality through intuition and research.

Lastly, I believe that the qualitative approach to research has the power to change our lives as researchers as well as provide information that may help us to understand human behavior further. For me personally, an understanding of qualitative methods and techniques has helped me to examine some of the assumptions I make in my own life about issues of wholeness and connectedness. It has helped me develop a more inclusive view of the world. Developing an interpretive philosophy and using a qualitative "bag of tricks" has given me a broader understanding of research, the questions that need to be addressed, and the ways in which to find answers to the questions about leisure phenomena and the delivery of leisure services.

Working Definitions

Sometimes definitions are useful and sometimes they are not. By using definitions I do not wish to create limitations and set boundaries, but I do believe they can be helpful in identifying the context within which certain words are used. For you to sit and read these definitions right now may be a little boring, but I hope the definitions will provide a framework for you as you use this book.

Throughout the book I will refer to "recreation, park, and leisure studies." The focus of the book is not limited to a discussion of only leisure behavior but also the practices of the profession and the way that leisure services are delivered. The purpose of research in recreation, parks, and leisure is both to develop theory and to improve practice. The allusion to both "participant" behavior and "professional" behavior may be disconcerting to those leisure researchers concerned only with leisure behavior questions or to those practitioners who want to know only what research can tell them to help them do their jobs better. Our field of study, however, addresses both professional practice and leisure behavior; the research that has been done to date also addresses both. It is my personal belief that the separation of parks and recreation from leisure studies is not useful given the direction of programming and research today. Therefore, this book refers to both behavior and practice related to recreation, parks, and leisure. In addition, the professional field of recreation and parks is aimed at a broad range of leisure provision related to public recreation, natural resources management, tourism, therapeutic recreation, commercial recreation, organized camping, employee recreation, recreational sports, military recreation, church recreation, and so forth. Examples will be used from a variety of areas.

The study of leisure behavior, leisure studies, or leisure research will encompass a wide range of behaviors borrowing from other disciplines such as psychology, sociology, political science, history, and economics. I will not attempt to offer a definition for leisure since I believe that the qualitative approach currently is being used successfully to determine how leisure is defined and experienced. I will let the reader determine the meaning of leisure from other sources. A useful operating conceptualization for leisure research, however, might be that it is any systematic inquiry that seeks to explain the nature of free time, freedom, and enjoyment.

For purposes of clarity, research is defined as a systematic process of discovering and interpreting data to understand reality. The goal of social research is to discover, understand, and communicate truth about people in society. We might think of research as puzzle-solving. It is highly cumulative and when the research is completed we should have a picture of a particular "slice" of the world. Researchers use symbols (words or numbers) to help us make sense of the world. The purposes of research may be exploratory (what's happening), explanatory (what is shaping this behavior and why), descriptive (what are the salient behaviors), or predictive (what will occur) (Babbie, 1986a; Marshall and Rossman, 1989). A single research study might combine all of these purposes at once, but generally a study will focus on only one or two purposes. Research leads to knowledge which

Berger and Luckman (1967) described as the certainty that phenomena are real and that they possess specific characteristics. Reality is socially constructed and research provides a process for analyzing reality.

The term "evaluation" will be used to connote applied research intended to address specific problems. The same approaches, methods, and techniques that are applied to research studies can be applied to evaluation studies. The difference between research and evaluation is the use of theoretical frameworks in research and the application of the findings to specific situations in evaluation. For example, a research study might examine the motivations for participation using a particular motivational theory or develop grounded theory that could be generalized to other similar situations. An evaluation study, on the other hand, might be done by a recreation department to determine how motivations to participate could be applied to getting people to register for a particular program. Thus, while this book focuses on research rather than evaluation, the reader should keep in mind that the same methods may be applied to the conduct of qualitative evaluation studies even though the outcomes of evaluation studies may have a different application than the outcomes of research.

A paradigm is a world view. It describes ontology or the nature of the social world. A paradigm is a fundamental model or theme which organizes our view of something. It is broader than a set of rules for research. A paradigm provides the rationale for choosing a research approach. Two dominant world views or paradigms that have provided a basis for a philosophy of social and leisure science are positivism and interpretive social science. These paradigms will be defined in more detail later. For now, however, it may be useful to think of positivism as seeking facts or causes of social phenomena with the contention that truth can be obtained objectively and that it is singular and external to the individual. Positivists believe that scientists can attain objective knowledge in the study of social and natural worlds, that natural and social sciences share a basic methodology, and the natural and social worlds are mechanistic (Filstead, 1979). The interpretive paradigm allows us to look at ourselves and how our ideas reflect the social reality of the world (Schwartz and Jacobs, 1979). The interpretive paradigm allows us to view human behavior as a product of how people define their world and to see reality from others' eyes. An aspect of the interpretive paradigm is phenomenology which is the name for a philosophical movement whose primary objective is the direct investigation and description of phenomena as consciously experienced, without theories about their causal explanation and as free as possible from unexamined preconceptions and presuppositions (Spiegelberg, 1975). The assumptions of the interpretive paradigm are that meanings are what are important, social behavior can best be understood in its natural environment, reality is the meaning attributed to experience, and social reality is not the same for all people (Bullock, 1983).

In this text, "approach" is used to describe how research is conducted. Approaches are used to describe epistemology. Epistemology is the science of knowing. It encompasses how we identify problems, seek answers, and hold beliefs about how one gets information. One's approach encompasses the assumptions, interests, and purposes which will shape the methods chosen. The two approaches for research described are qualitative and quantitative. Quantitative emerges from the positivist world view and involves the testing of theory, the use of controlled data collection, and an analysis using statistics. Methods used in the qualitative approach generally have as a commonality the separation from theoretical and methodological positivism that has dominated the mainstream of American social science during the 20th century (Lidz and Lidz, 1988). The qualitative approach expropriates an emerging research design, uses the natural environment, focuses on determining the meaning attached to phenomena, acknowledges the researcher as the instrument in interaction with the phenomena being studied, and uses words as the primary symbols for generating grounded theory specific to the context in which the research occurs.

Methodology is the science of finding out (Babbie, 1986a). Methods are used to denote specific procedures. For example, field research is a method that includes systematically gathering data in a natural setting on specific aspects of social life by establishing an ongoing relationship with those studied (Manning, 1987). Indepth interviewing and field research are the most common methods used in qualitative approaches to research. Techniques involve the specific tasks undertaken to discover and interpret data within a given method.

Theory refers to an explanation of "what is." A theoretical framework is a way of looking at the world and the assumptions made about it. In the interpretive paradigm the focus is on grounded theory, theory that emerges from the specific data being examined. Researchers using the qualitative approach generally develop grounded theory but may use a number of theoretical or conceptual frameworks as a basis for the research or as a way of interpreting the outcomes of research.

Triangulation offers a means for combining methods or sources of data in a single study. Triangulation is a process by which the researcher can guard against the accusation that a study's findings are simply an artifact of a single method, a single data source, or a single investigator's bias. According to Denzin (1978), there are four types of triangulation: data triangulation which is the use of a variety of data sources, investigator triangulation which is the use of several researchers, theory triangulation which is the use of multiple perspectives to interpret data, and methodological triangulation which is the use of multiple methods. Triangulation may be used in a number of ways within qualitative studies of recreation, park, and leisure phenomena.

Background on the Qualitative Approach

The goal of social research is to discover, understand, and communicate truth about people in society. As Douglas stated, however, "A researcher's search for truth is never done and his (sic) only certainty is uncertainty" (1985, p. 158). Thus, research in any area is continually ongoing. The dimensions surrounding the goal of research are the nature of truth (ontology) and how one knows what truth is (epistemology). Social research involves both ontological paradigmatic issues as well as epistemological methodological approaches. These issues and approaches have gone through periods of questioning and metamorphosis over the years. A quote attributed to Schopenhauer (n.d.) that describes the process concerning changing ideas has been helpful to me in understanding the history of new ideas and approaches: "All truth passes through three stages. First it is ridiculed. Second it is violently opposed. Third it is accepted as being self-evident."

The dominant paradigm that has surrounded social science, and particularly the study of recreation, parks, and leisure, has been positivism. Today, some researchers are beginning to question the dominant assumptions that have been guiding their lives and research. Tuthill and Ashton (1983) have likened science to a jigsaw puzzle. The researcher attempts to put together an understanding of the world based on a predominant world view that can be likened to the "picture on the cover." Sometimes, however, problems occur in trying to piece the puzzle together if one is operating from a different cover picture than the pieces represent. A new paradigm, or a new "picture on the cover," emerges as a new approach becomes more successful in solving the problems that appear to be acute for a profession or for an area of study.

The interpretive paradigm has emerged from the sociological and anthropological tradition of inquiry. The theme of "verstehen" related to the meaning of human behavior, the context of social interaction, empathetic understanding, and the connection between subjective states and behavior is predominant in many of the qualitative methods and has provided a fruitful way to examine reality. Anthropologists have been using the qualitative approach since the discipline began, but it has only been within the past 70 years that other disciplines have begun to examine the value of qualitative methods. The Chicago School of Sociological Fieldwork, for example, has provided one of the primary models for interpretive research and the qualitative approach.

As a field of study such as recreation, parks, and leisure, begins to grow into a different conception of its subject matter, there is a need to expand research methods. When a state of confusion or crisis is reached because of the inability of the existing paradigm in its bounded rationality to help researchers understand social reality in its boundless form, a scientific revolution begins to occur (Kuhn, 1970). Just as in other disciplines, a quiet revolution is occurring in the study of recreation, parks, and leisure. A number of researchers and consumers of research have found that they are more successful with solving some of the questions about leisure by taking a different ontological and epistemological view. Leisure researchers of this "new age" are suggesting that new questions need to be asked and new methods employed to answer questions about leisure behavior and about the profession.

As noted, leisure researchers have not typically used qualitative methods in the study of leisure (Chick, 1985; Dawson, 1984). Mannell (1983) found that only nine percent of the studies appearing in *Leisurability* between 1968 and 1982 could be classified as field research (with four percent of those being case studies). Most of these field research studies that Mannell identified were applied and not basic research. In a review of the *Journal of Leisure Research* from 1978 through 1982 by Riddick, DeSchriver, and Weissinger (1984), only studies that used quantitative methods were reviewed. The authors stated that, "Such a focus was not due to a lack of appreciation for qualitative methodology... the rational... was that with the exception of 13 articles that presented models or discussed theories and three articles that summarized research or presented a research agenda on a topic, all of the articles appearing... in JLR employed quantitative methodology" (p. 312). I did a quick content analysis of the methods used in papers published by the *Journal of Leisure Research* from 1983 through 1988 and found that seven percent of the papers used typical qualitative methods such as participant observation (e.g., Roadburg, 1983; Glancy, 1986; 1988) and indepth interviews (e.g., Shank, 1986; Howe, 1988). The British journal, *Leisure Studies*, however, has published a number of articles that used the interpretive paradigm and the qualitative approach since it began in 1982 (e.g., Dixey, 1987; Fryer and Payne, 1984; Glyptis, 1985). *See Exemplar 1.1.* Within the past decade the number of research studies using qualitative approaches has gradually increased but these studies certainly do not predominate in the published recreation, parks, and leisure literature.

> Exemplar 1.1 Fryer, D. and Payne, R. (1984). Proactive behavior in unemployment: Findings and implications. *Leisure Studies*, *3*, 273-295.
>
> Fryer and Payne studied the unemployed to shed light on the deprivation hypotheses and to describe the manifest and latent consequences of unemployment. They were interested in developing a conceptual framework for successful unemployment. Their investigation used a qualitative empirical examination which included interviewing 11 unemployed people who were experiencing material but not psychological deprivation and who had adopted a proactive stance towards unemployment. The researchers described the sampling procedure of going to experienced community workers in order to identify interviewees for the study. The criterion used for interviewees was that they had to be coping well with unemployment. Semi-structured interviews were taped and transcribed. The authors described how they developed pertinent themes and using a card sorting technique to classify and group the responses. "Actual verbalization" was important in the analysis. Using the data and an extensive review of literature allowed the authors to successfully substantiate the theory that they were exploring.

A new paradigm for living in this world is being called for based on the integration of other new imperatives such as the women's movement, ecology movement, and metaphysical possibilities (Dustin, 1986). Within leisure research, a shift in the positivist paradigm of studying time, activity, and state of mind has given way to an examination of meaning associated with an interpretive paradigm. Recreation, parks, and leisure research, as it reaches its next stage, is evolving through a period of paradigmatic development, questioning, and change. Positivist views are not being rejected, but attempts are being made to include the interpretive paradigm as a viable alternative for framing research. The emergence of the qualitative approach is an indication of the maturity of the study of recreation, parks, and leisure. The emerging approach suggests that the research will be anything but stagnant. In addition, possible research questions are being expanded through the choice of either or both the qualitative and quantitative approaches.

Problems in the Study of Recreation, Parks, and Leisure

Mzorek suggested that "determining what is worth knowing is analogous to asking why life is worth living" (1983, p. 13). One of the major problems in the study of leisure and of the recreation and parks field is the inability to describe what it is that is being studied. What may be perceived as leisure to one person may not necessarily be leisure to another. Gunter and Gunter (1980) stated that the study of leisure has been a hodgepodge of ideas and methodologically weak because no consensus on its measurement and conceptualization exists. With this lack of definition, it is not unusual that commentaries have called for the improvement in the quality of leisure research both substantively and methodologically (e.g., Crandall and Lewko, 1976; Howe, 1985).

Because of the nature of leisure and play, the question is raised as to whether leisure researchers have tried to trade an awareness of the inherent value of play for more objective approaches to research and education (Robertson, 1983). Robertson suggested that by categorizing, isolating, fragmenting, and objectifying play (as has been done in the positivist paradigm), researchers have lost sight of play's "music." Mobily (1985) lamented that perhaps researchers have simplified and quantified leisure so much that the meaning has been lost. The complexity of leisure may be best maintained through a context that includes other dimensions besides traditional statistical calculations. Forcing a particular research design has not enhanced the understanding of the phenomena of work and leisure as Allison and Duncan (1987) described in their study of professional and blue-collar women. *See Exemplar 1.2*

> Exemplar 1.2 Allison, M.T. and Duncan, M.C. (1987). Women, work, and leisure: The days of our lives. *Leisure Sciences*, *9*, 143-162.
>
> Allison and Duncan used a qualitative method to identify and understand the experience of enjoyment (or lack thereof) within

the work and nonwork spheres of working women. Their focus was on a qualitative inductive strategy with a theoretical sampling of the constructs of "flow" and its antithesis. Allison and Duncan were critical of prior research approaches that used false compartmentalizing. They indicated that studies are needed that will reinforce understanding and connectedness. Allison and Duncan described how they used 20 semi-structured interviews which included a series of statements upon which the women were asked to react and reflect. Allison and Duncan's methodology, which was tied to the theoretical framework of flow and its antithesis, showed that what one experiences in work settings and leisure are not antithetical. They concluded that women may not compartmentalize their lives the way that men do and this difference creates a divergent work/leisure relationship than is normally described. Allison and Duncan made good use of direct quotes from the women that they studied. These quotes also helped to provide a way to illustrate the concept of flow that was examined.

Traditional recreation, park, and leisure research can be criticized for being methodologically myopic. There has been an excessive reliance on the survey method (Mobily, 1985) without considering other methods (Godbey, 1984). Bultena and Field (1983) suggested that researchers have reached a plateau in which only limited insights can be gained from further study that is cast in the extant theoretical and methodological modes. A further concern with method relates to how the method has dictated the problems to be studied by leisure researchers. Howe referred to this narrow approach as "the methodological cart driving the conceptual horse" (1985, p. 221). Researchers in the area of recreation, parks, and leisure are beginning to acknowledge the limitations of the traditional framework of positivism. As a community of researchers, we are moving away from the "method-idolotry" that suggested that survey research was the best (and only) way to study phenomena to an appreciation of a variety of methods that may be used to address recreation, parks, and leisure questions.

Along with research that has been focused primarily on using survey methods, recreation, park and leisure researchers have also had a particular fascination with statistics and "number crunching." In leisure behavior research, little statistical variance has been explained related to most variables studied. Therefore, researchers have learned little about the nature of the relationships of variables (Bultena and Field, 1983). Individuals such as Tinsley (1984), who have severely criticized leisure research, have suggested that it is the univariate studies that are the problem in the lack of understanding of the phenomenon and the solution to more useful research lies in more sophisticated multivariate statistics. Smith and Haley (1979) suggested that researchers have often substituted statistics for theoretical understanding. Their solution, therefore, was to combine theory and statistics by advocating factor analysis for confirmatory (theory testing) rather than discovery (theory generation) purposes. While the suggestions of Tinsley as well as Smith and Haley, are valid possibilities, other ways of thinking about leisure research outside of improved statistical procedures are also valid.

A further concern about the research that has been conducted in our field relates to the gap between the researcher and the practitioner. While some of the research addressing recreation, park, and leisure studies has only theoretical value, there is a need to continually consider how research can contribute to practice. Qualitative research offers research done within a context that may prove more directly applicable to the practice and provision of leisure services. It also has the advantage that it may be presented in a way that one does not need to know sophisticated statistical procedures in order to evaluate the validity of the results.

It is not only United States recreation, parks, and leisure researchers who have identified some of these problems in the study of leisure. Cherry (1979) commented on research in Canada and suggested that it is time to move away from correlational models and look at social processes, lifestyles, and leisure patterns from a social psychological perspective. In other words, Cherry suggested that new questions are needed. Tokarski (1983) submitted that in West Germany methods have been inadequately applied to research with the result of fragmentation and analytic dissection in handling the complexity and multidimensional nature of leisure. Agreement seems to exist among leisure researchers all over the world that complex, multi-faceted, and dynamic approaches are needed in recreation, park, and leisure research.

The qualitative approach offers an alternative for the examination of some of these issues within recreation, park, and leisure studies. For example, Bullock (1983) suggested that an intervention program such as therapeutic recreation is not static and cannot reflect a strict cause-and-effect situation. Further, the effects are not a one-time occurrence. Therefore, the qualitative approach offers an alternative way to understand therapeutic recreation and its affect on people. Shaw (1985) suggested that one reason that theoretical conceptualizations of leisure have not been more widely incorporated into empirical research is the practical difficulty of operationalizing and measuring subjective states of experiences. Studying objective states is more time-consuming (and often more expensive) than simply measuring activity participation but it gives richer and deeper information about the meaning of leisure.

An emerging paradigm that focuses on interpretive views and the qualitative approach may be a useful means for addressing some of the questions left unanswered by past recreation, park, and leisure research. The enormous complexities of leisure can no longer be simplified in positivistic and quantitative terms (Gunter, 1987). While statistics are helpful, they do not provide explanations. A diversity of researchers pursuing a multitude of topics within a variety of methodologies is needed. The past is not necessarily the prelude to future inquiry (Zukav, 1979). Researchers now have alternatives and expanding choices available for the study of recreation, parks, and leisure.

Summary

The purpose of this chapter has been to provide an introduction to the examination of the qualitative approach to research. The assumptions and premises of the book were described along with definitions, a brief background, and an examination of the problems that may result in studying recreation, parks, and leisure from only a positivist, quantitative perspective. The suggestion has not been made that qualitative methods are either superior or inferior to quantitative methods, but that qualitative methods are choices available to the recreation, parks, and leisure researcher. The researcher must know something about both the qualitative and the quantitative approach if appropriate methodological decisions are to be made. The present time is exciting for the recreation, park, and leisure researcher because of the variety of questions and options that are emerging. The researcher is encouraged to seize the moment and explore how we can best answer the questions that need to be addressed in our study of leisure behavior and the profession.

The key concepts addressed in this chapter were: research; recreation, park, and leisure studies; quantitative approach; qualitative approach.

For Further Consideration

1. Examine the past three volumes of the *Journal of Leisure Research*, *Leisure Sciences*, or *Therapeutic Recreation Journal* to ascertain the types of research questions being asked and the methods used to answer these questions.

2. Go to another research journal in a related area (special education, business, forestry) and review the past three volumes to ascertain the types of research questions being asked and the methods used to answer these questions.

3. Make a list of research questions that you have. Are these of major interest to other researchers, to students, to practitioners? How might you ask questions that would be useful to each of these groups who encounter research in various forms in their lives? What might be the best approach, qualitative or quantitative, to answering these questions?

4. Reflect upon the changes you have seen in your lifetime. Remember when you were a child and how you perceived the world in terms of such aspects as technology available and human relationships. How is the world different today? What implications do these changes have for the methods we use in the study of recreation, parks, and leisure?

For Further Reading

Individuals who would like to explore some of the issues raised in this chapter may want to begin further reading with these references:

Babbie, E. (1989). *The practice of social research.* **(5th ed.). Belmont, CA: Wadsworth Publishing Co.**
This is a textbook used by many social science students. *The Practice of Social Research* offers a useful introduction to the logic and skills that are used in social science research. The book does not address qualitative research approaches specifically but describes the importance of research, what human inquiry is all about, how theory and research are linked, and how to design, conceptualize, operationalize, and sample within the modes of experiments, survey research, field research, unobtrusive research, and evaluation research. The chapters on analysis of data will not be useful to the qualitative researcher but the textbook provides a useful beginning for examining assumptions about social science research.

Ellis, G.D., and Williams, D.R. (1987). The impending renaissance in leisure service evaluation. *Journal of Park and Recreation Administration, 5*(4), 17-29.
These authors provide a fine justification for the consideration of the use of qualitative methods. While their discussion is primarily focused on evaluation research, the points made have useful application to any type of research. These two authors understand the value of qualitative methods largely because they have done extensive research using quantitative methods in the past. Their perspective will be useful to anyone trying to clarify their own assumptions about why particular methods are chosen.

Howe, C.Z. (1985). Possibilities for using a qualitative research approach in the sociological study of leisure. *Journal of Leisure Research, 17*(3), 212-224.
Howe provided one of the first rationales for consideration of qualitative approaches in the study of the social psychology of leisure. While researchers in recreation, park, and leisure studies have used qualitative methods, Howe was one of the first to describe what the use of qualitative methods may mean in our future understanding of leisure. While the terminology used suggested that paradigms, approaches, and methods all refer to the same idea, she lays out a cogent argument for considering the possibilities for qualitative studies.

Chapter 2

Shift into Gear

Introduction

As you noted in the first chapter, a paradigm shift is occurring in the way that aspects of recreation, parks, and leisure are being understood and studied. For some of us, this shift may not be as rapid as we would like, but it is nevertheless occurring. The purpose of this chapter is to provide a model for how qualitative methods fit with our understanding of the world. This chapter is philosophical. It would be tempting to skip this chapter because it really does not address directly "how to do" qualitative studies. Without an understanding of the philosophy and beliefs that we hold about research in the social sciences and specifically leisure research, however, the studies that we do will not have the same impact. To not read this chapter and the next and then conduct research using qualitative methods may be as foolish as planning a recreation program without any recognition of the needs of the clientele or without any regard to what the objectives for the program might be. The recreation program or the research study might be successful and there might be positive outcomes, but without an initial justification and framework, it is difficult to evaluate one's success. The researcher who does not pay attention to a paradigm is really playing a game of pin the tail on the donkey. Who knows where the tail may land?

How Paradigm Shifts Occur

Kuhn (1970) identified how a new paradigm or world view gets started. Typically a new paradigm has few early supporters but these "pioneers" will improve on the ideas, explain the possibilities, and show what it is like to be guided by the new paradigm within a community of scientists. This paradigm will be clarified, more people will support it, and gradually other researchers will adopt a new mode of practicing science. People will adopt a paradigm when they see that it will resolve a problem or that it will support the problem-solving ability of a preceding paradigm. The process is far from cumulative with a certain extension of the paradigm occurring and then a period of stepping back. During paradigm shifts, there is often a period of overlap between the shifts. This overlap often creates confusion, diversity, conflict, adaption, and misunderstanding. Proponents of competing paradigms are always slightly at cross purposes. The transfer of allegiance from one paradigm to another is like a conversion experience (Kuhn, 1970). When the new paradigm is established, a profession or field of study will have changed its view of the field, its method, and its goals (Kuhn, 1970). No paradigm will solve all problems but paradigms raise the question of which problems are most significant to solve.

Many paradigms exist in the world. The interpretive and positivist views relate to research, but other aspects of life also have paradigms. A paradigm is basically a group reality. It describes a common belief about what is important in life or in the study of human behavior. New paradigms of thought in society, such as "new age" consciousness and the feminist movement, are affecting all that we do and these emerging ideas have a relationship to leisure research. For example, Howe-Murphy (1988) and Howe-Murphy and Murphy (1988) talked about reexamining the philosophical foundations of our lives and how those affect therapeutic recreation and teaching leisure studies in higher education, respectively. They described a change from the Newtonian-Cartesian (mechanistic) view of the world to an emerging consciousness (new age). This new age consciousness embodies the integration of body, mind, and spirit, a belief that life is dynamic and constantly changing, and the connection of inner consciousness to all of life. Viewing reality from a variety of perspectives is creating a new perception of art, activity, social responsibility, and ultimately leisure (McDowell, 1984). Once you begin to view the world in a different way, you start to notice changes all around you. The world does not necessarily change but we come to perceive the world differently. New views of the world, thus, underlie the need for new views of research.

Within a framework that takes world views and provides implications for conceptual thinking and methods, Lincoln (1985) summarized the work of Schwartz and Ogilvie (1980) concerning the current broader world view shifts: single to complex, hierarchy to heterarchy (no one at top of anything), mechanistic to holographic (dynamic, distributed throughout, interconnected), determinate to indeterminate, direct causality to mutual causality, assembly to morphogenesis (order emerging from disorder), objectivity to perspectivity. These changing views of the world have implications for the ways in which we live our lives and conduct our research.

Many recreation, park, and leisure researchers are currently in a "pre-paradigm debate period" (Kuhn, 1970) in the discussion of legitimate methods, problems, and standards of solution. Positivism has been the primary research paradigm but the interpretive paradigm is gaining momentum. It is unlikely that one paradigm or the other can completely define the leisure experience or the recreation and parks field. It is also unlikely that the present positivistic paradigm will fade away. The emerging interpretive paradigm is open-ended and will not create full and complete resolution for understanding recreation, parks, and leisure. Yet, most of us will need to come to some conclusion about which paradigm makes sense to us as individuals and which paradigm will guide our research. The paradigm we embrace extends beyond a set of rules for research but, at the same time, it sets a framework for the methodology that we will use. Blumer (1969) suggested that inadequate and misguided methodology and the failure to look at the obdurate character of the world has been a roadblock to the study of social behavior. A paradigm provides a framework for conceptually or theoretically looking at the world and the assumptions made about it.

A Model for Dimensions of Choice in Recreation, Park, and Leisure Research

Given the challenges associated with the study of recreation, parks, and leisure and the way in which positivism has not brought conclusive explanations of the real world (Guba and Lincoln, 1981), the following model (Figure 1, page 22) is offered as a guide for researchers who would like to have a framework for considering the paradigmatic, theoretical, and methodological options available for their research. The ultimate choice of specific research methods is based on assumptions about one's world view and epistemology.

In the model, a paradigm reflects the fundamental themes which organize one's view of social reality. Researchers "whose research is based on shared paradigms are committed to the same rules and standards for practice" (Kuhn, 1970, p. 11). The two major paradigms that have dominated scientific research are the positivist and the interpretive views. These two world views are based on different assumptions about how the world is understood. It is possible to mix qualitative and quantitative methods but it is not possible to mix these two paradigms in a research project.

Epistemology relates to one's theory of knowledge or beliefs about how one gets information. It refers to the way that individuals approach problems and seek answers. One's biases, assumptions, and perceptions of the world (one's paradigmatic world view) will affect the judgments made about ways of investigating leisure reality. In other words, the choice of approach and method comes from one's world view as a philosophical foundation (Chenery and Russell, 1987).

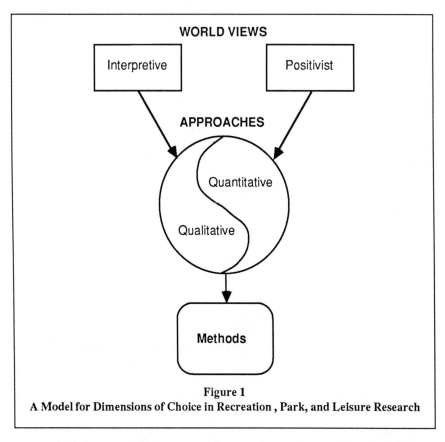

Figure 1
A Model for Dimensions of Choice in Recreation , Park, and Leisure Research

As illustrated in the model, we might think of our understanding of research as operating on three levels: paradigmatic or contextual world view (philosophy), theoretical or conceptual methodological approach, and practical applied methods. Problems occur when people confuse the level at which they are speaking and make the assumption that a method always implies a particular philosophy. A problem occurs when the researcher chooses an approach before examining the paradigmatic assumptions. For example, I may wish to research constraints to leisure participation using a qualitative method such as indepth interviewing. Once the data are collected, however, I may choose to use either a qualitative analysis or a quantitative analysis technique depending upon my initial view of whether this question about constraints should be answered deductively or inductively. Even though the method used was a qualitative method, the research may or may not embody a positivist view of reality depending on how I believe the nature of the world should be studied. As Smith and Heshusius (1986) suggested, research is more than a matter of what works. Research involves paradigms, approaches, methods, and techniques. Little compatibility exists between the two paradigms but there may be much overlap between research methods and techniques.

The difference between paradigms is not one of qualitative verses quantitative (Guba and Lincoln, 1981). Taylor and Bogdan (1984) suggested that the differences in perspective of the world (paradigm) requires differences in approaches and methods. A view of the world alone, however, does not define the method but suggests implications. Blumer (1969) reminded researchers that reality exists in the world and not in the methods. It is therefore important that leisure researchers know the explicit and implicit world views underlying research activity.

The Interpretive/Positivist Paradigm Discussion

The test of a paradigm is its utility (Guba, 1987). The study of a phenomenon like leisure or of a field like recreation and parks is complex, and thus, one perspective is not enough. More than one view of the world will enhance the puzzle-solving possibilities and will help to extend the scope and precision of scientific knowledge. Kamphorst, Tibori, and Gilgam (1984) illustrated the evolution of the dominant paradigm and the emergence of an alternate paradigm that they called phenomenology (and which I refer to as interpretive social science). They described how the world was originally governed by "divine order" and then rationality was imposed on it in the form of cause and effect or "A leads to B." This worked well until the early 20th century when some scientists decided that "A" leading to "B" was not necessarily how social reality always worked. The new view, couched in a context of symbolic interaction, suggested that "A" and "B" are constantly influencing each other and "A" and "B" are integrated elements in the totality of an interaction system. Thus, some researchers in the early 20th century concluded that nothing can really be fully explained in a critical rational sense, but much can be understood. They concluded that true understanding comes from the phenomenological or interpretive paradigm and not from the cause and effect positivist paradigm.

Followers of positivism make the assumptions that reality is:
1. External, separated, categorized, and isolated into independent parts which form a whole.
2. Approached through deduction and *a priori* (preestablished) theory.
3. Based on mechanistic processes that focus on idiographic (complete) understanding of a particular phenomena and rational cause and effect.
4. Objective and value-free.

These assumptions may be contrasted to interpretive social scientists who assume that reality includes:
1. Multiple realities, relationships, connectedness, wholeness, and inclusiveness.
2. An emphasis on induction and grounded (emerging within a context) theory.
3. Organic (contextual) processes that focus on meaning.
4. Subjectivity and perspectivity.

Each of the paradigmatic assumptions is mutually exclusive. One cannot combine the two and one cannot operate out of both paradigms at the same time. As Guba (1987) suggested, you cannot at one time believe that the world is both round and flat. You cannot believe that theory can be confirmed at the same time it is being generated. Therefore, researchers must make hard decisions about what they believe about the reality of leisure and the delivery of leisure services. No possibility exists for mixing paradigms although it has been attempted with the outcome of creating a great deal of philosophical confusion.

The positivist (often referred to as "scientific" or "rationalistic" by Guba and Lincoln, 1981) world view has been the dominant paradigm in research in general, and particularly in the short history of leisure research. Positivism assumes there is an external world and that the external world determines the singular convergent view that can be taken of it, independent of the process or circumstances of viewing (Kirk and Miller, 1986). The positivist strives for explanation, prediction, and control by dividing a phenomenon into parts that can be isolated and categorized. The emphases in positivism on the mechanistic processes for explaining social behavior have been on rigor as addressed in reliability and validity, the measurement of manifest behavior, *a priori* hypotheses testing, operationalization of concepts and procedures, verification of established *a priori* theory, generalization, scientific protocols, cause and effect, data reduction, standardization, and facts. Further, within the positivist paradigm the researcher strives to remain objective, value-free, and apart from the subjects of the research. It is assumed that these components will lead to the discovery of truth and that nothing can be accepted as truth without unbiased empirical evidence. Positivists believe that a "fuzzy" picture of reality must be sharpened with more accurate information and facts. Reality is seen by positivists as being a scientific abstraction with explanations that ought to be placed neatly into boxes labeled with grand and middle-level theories.

The interpretive paradigm (also referred to commonly as the "naturalistic" by Guba and Lincoln, 1981 or as the "phenomenological" operates from a different set of assumptions. Interpretive social scientists assume that social reality is multiple, divergent, and inter-related. We might suggest that reality to the interpretive social scientist looks like your great grandmother's crazy quilt with pieces going every which way and in every color. In the interpretive paradigm, social phenomena are understood from the actor's own perspective and human behavior is a product of how people define their world (Taylor and Bogdan, 1984); the role of the researcher is to discover and explain this reality. In the case of leisure research, for example, the ways that people come to accept an experience as leisure is the essence of interpretation or phenomenology (Dawson, 1984). Reality is the meaning attributed to experience; social reality is not the same for all (Bullock, 1983).

The interpretive view is expansionistic rather than reductionistic. Discovery of theory grounded in the context of a situation is the primary purpose of this research. Therefore, perspective, multiplicity, and recursiveness of causation are described (Ellis and Williams, 1987). Researchers operating from the interpretive view attempt to use analytic induction (Fielding and Fielding, 1986) to examine "slices of life." Interpretive social scientists believe there are multiple perspectives that can be gained from a number of data collection methods. Thus, researchers embracing the interpretive views believe that relaxing certain of the narrow definitions of the positivist model facilitates the discovery of the new and unexpected (Downing, 1983; Kirk and Miller, 1986).

The interpretive social scientist also acknowledges that data may not be sense-perceivable (Harper, 1981); that is, intuition and contextual aspects must also be included in trying to understand how people live in everyday life. A contextual view is used that examines the changing relationships among psychological and environmental aspects (Ellis and Williams, 1987). It is virtually impossible to imagine any human behavior that is not heavily mediated by the context in which it occurs. In the study of leisure behavior for example, leisure as a symbol is viewed in context with other symbols such as family and/or work. Further, the symbol of language plays an important role in interpretive social science; the aim is to discover literal as well as symbolic meanings. For the interpretive researcher, to ignore meaning is to falsify behavior. Within this paradigm, the dynamic qualities of research emerge in the course of framing questions, immersion in the discovery of evidence, and interpreting the meaning of data.

The subjectivity of interpretation results in a number of possible perspectives that help to understand and explain the meaning attached to phenomena. The combination of a low degree of imposition of constraints on antecedent variables and a low degree of imposition of constraints on possible outputs is a hallmark of this view (Guba and Lincoln, 1981). In other words, because the interpretive view allows data discovery to occur with few rules, the possibilities of uncovering meaningful conclusions are greatly enhanced. Interpretive social scientists acknowledge that it is virtually impossible to remain objective in doing research because so much interaction occurs between the researcher and those individuals being studied. The researcher as a human being is the instrument for data collection and values are admittedly a part of the analysis. Interpretive social scientists suggest that determining what specific *a priori* questions to ask biases research. No attempt is made to manipulate the environment when operating from the interpretive paradigm; the focus is only to understand subjective experiences (Guba and Lincoln, 1981).

The processes of interpretive social research are not the standard positivist steps of developing research questions based on a theory, operationalizing the theory, collecting data, and analyzing results based on the questions asked. The interpretive social scientist or phenomenologist seeks to develop a framework for research through guiding hypotheses or "sensitizing concepts" (Denzin, 1978) and then combines the development of theory with data discovery and interpretation on a simultaneous basis. The search for meaning for interpretive social scientists, thus, is a search for multiple realities, truths, and perceptions (Guba and Lincoln, 1981).

Linking Paradigms to Approaches

One's philosophy of science based on one's view of the world will bear directly on the epistemological approach and the subsequent research methods that are chosen. The paradigm is more than a methodological orientation and more than a set of rules for research (Rist, 1980a) but the paradigm also has a direct relationship to the approach. While approaches and methods are linked to paradigms and the paradigms are rigid and fixed, it is possible to mix the two approaches and the various methods although one must be cautious in doing this blending (Guba and Lincoln, 1981; Patton, 1980a).

The qualitative and quantitative approaches have several typical differences that should be emphasized. Rather than having these differences be dichotomous as was proposed concerning the two paradigms, the characteristics of the two approaches might be considered symbolically as yin-yang. Each approach may be defined in relation to the other approach and the differences serve to compliment each other. Seldom does any study exemplify all the pure characteristics of either epistemological approach. These characteristics of the quantitative and qualitative approaches, respectively, include: (a) preordinant (structural) design compared to emergent (processual) design, (b) measurement using only numbers compared to meaning using only words, (c) controlled (manipulated, impersonal) settings compared to natural (interactive, personal) settings, (d) confirming theory by analyzing variables compared to developing theory by examining patterns, and (e) rational procedures compared to intuitive processes. Table 1 provides a summary of the typical relationships between the pure qualitative and the pure quantitative approach.

Table 1		
Typical Differences between Qualitative and Quantitative Approaches*		
Category	Qualitative	Quantitative
Design	Emerging	Predetermined
Data Discovery	Ongoing	One-shot
Nature of Data	Mutually dependent	Independent
Relationship to Theory	Dynamic, Discovered	Predetermined, Confirmed
Symbols Used	Words	Numbers
Data Collection Instrument	Researcher	Physical (i.e., Paper and Pencil)
Data Summary	Rich and Deep Explanations	Statistics
Setting	Real Life or Natural	Laboratory or Controlled
Outcomes	Perspectives	Prediction
Interaction with People	Much	Limited
Values	Context dependent	Context free

* Adapted from Guba and Lincoln, 1981

The design of a research project differs between the qualitative and quantitative approaches. The quantitative approach relies on determining procedures ahead of time and generally following specific protocols with a stable treatment of the data. The qualitative approach, such as in using life history interviewing, allows for the questions to emerge as the researcher begins and may result in a variable treatment of the data. In the qualitative approach, data discovery and data analysis are ongoing processes throughout the research design. The depth and mutual dependence of qualitative data are acknowledged within a context of meaning that emerges as the data are discovered and interpreted. The qualitative approach also relies on a dynamic interchange between theory, concepts and data throughout the research.

Several generalizations about the differences in the way data are collected and measured are evident between the two approaches. Researchers using the quantitative approach have typically relied on prediction and controlled settings such as laboratories and random samples whereas researchers using the qualitative approach have focused on natural, personal settings in the "real world." The qualitative approach generally allows those people being studied to ascribe their own words and meanings to situations. Rather than controlling variables, the researcher using the qualitative approach attempts to consider as many variables as possible in the qualitative approach. Characteristically, the quantitative researcher may have little direct interaction with the subjects in a controlled environment and may be insulated from humans. The qualitative approach generally requires the researcher to have extensive interaction with people's social reality. The researcher enters their world of interaction and engages in careful observation.

The quantitative approach typically uses numbers (number crunching) for measurement and qualitative focuses on words (word crunching). Usually a physical device, such as paper and pencil, is used in quantitative studies while the instrument for qualitative studies is the researcher (Guba and Lincoln, 1981). The quantitative approach employs "hard" data with a focus on statistical procedures, while the qualitative approach focuses on "soft" (rich and deep) explanations of symbolic meaning. Ultimately the results of using the quantitative approach are based on rational numeric findings while the results of using the qualitative approach are dependent on intuition as well as the meaning of reality from a number of perspectives.

The outcomes of the research will also differ between the two approaches. In the quantitative approach, the focus is on answering specific research questions or testing hypotheses and confirming theory. In qualitative approaches the focus is on explaining, developing patterns, and developing grounded theory by using depth of analysis and detail. Qualitative approaches use descriptions to explicate experiences. As Guba and Lincoln stated, "They (qualitative researchers) empathize, describe, judge, compare, portray, evoke images, and create for the reader or listener, the sense of having been there" (1981, p. 149). These tasks are often referred to as "thick" description. The qualitative approach, however, aims to uncover the complexities of societies and of behavior and uses a technique known as theoretical sampling (Glaser and Strauss, 1967). Generally the result of the qualitative approach is discovery, but these methods may sometimes result in theory confirmation. In general, researchers using the qualitative approach analyze data beyond mere description and focus on explanation within a particular context.

The qualitative approach is not context-free and there is no attempt to control the context and the intuition needed to conduct this research. A qualitative researcher must know the context in which behavior is occurring in order to ascertain meaning. An understanding at a personal level of the motives and beliefs behind people's actions is known as *verstehen* (Weber, 1968) and the qualitative researcher strives for this. The researcher using the qualitative approach, however, must operate in both the everyday worlds of people as well as the scholarly rational world that allows for broader understanding (Denzin, 1978).

The research approach should fit the characteristics of the phenomena under study and the assumptions of the paradigm from which one is operating. It is possible, however, to mix the characteristics of the approaches in order to conduct a research study. A researcher may be a "purist" concerning the quantitative approach or a "purist" concerning the qualitative approach. This purity in approach would also relate directly to the positivist and interpretive paradigms, respectively. It is possible to mix characteristics of the approaches within a positivist view. A researcher might, for example, have a preordinant design but collect data in the form of interactive indepth interviews and then analyze the interviews using both statistics and words. Persons invested in the positivist paradigm are more likely to choose to follow the tenets of the quantitative approach but they might also choose specific qualitative methods and strategies for conducting their research. For example, Mannell (1985), who has done primarily positivist research through his "beeper" studies, has advocated for collecting both quantitative and qualitative data within the context of an individual's daily life. To be true to the assumptions of interpretive social science, however, the researcher will choose a pure form of the qualitative approach. For example, a qualitative "purist" would choose an emergent design, use words and a natural setting, focus on grounded theory, and rely on the use of intuition and the context of the setting. A problem exists when researchers use the paradigms and the approaches interchangeably and assume that because one is collecting qualitative data that she/he must be coming from the interpretive paradigm and operating out of that set of assumptions about reality. Ideally, a researcher who understands the array of methods available through both the quantitative and qualitative approaches will be able to address the ways to best study issues related to recreation, parks, and leisure.

As a final note to this discussion of the qualitative and quantitative approaches, the difference between empirical and nonempirical data are described. In general, empirical data are data that are experienced or observable. The qualitative approach generally refers to empirical data as does the quantitative approach. The qualitative approach, in its broadest sense, may also include data that are not empirical. For example, hermeneutics is the study of meaning. It is common for researchers to use existing written texts in hermeneutical research rather than to collect new data. In this case, the researcher has no interaction with people, but seeks to find meaning in the written documents that these people have produced. This is an interpretive view and uses a qualitative approach but is unlike the assumptions of phenomenologists who are concerned with empirical interaction with people in the data discovery process. Thus, the researcher exploring the qualitative approach must keep in mind that methods even within the interpretive paradigm may be quite variable. The discussion of this book is primarily on the interactive aspects of empirical qualitative data, but other nonempirical interpretive dimensions should not be overlooked.

Methods

Methods and specific techniques will emerge from the approach selected. Methods choices available to the researcher can be easily placed on a continuum. For example, observation and interviewing are methods. Neither one can be strictly categorized as a qualitative or a quantitative method. Observation can range from interpretive field research (qualitative) to sophisticated numeric checklists (quantitative) and interviewing can range from a structured close-ended telephone interviews with a random sample (quantitative) to an open-ended life history account using a theoretical sampling procedure (qualitative). Therefore, in describing methods one must examine the assumptions about the paradigm and the approach in order to know whether a particular method embodies a qualitative or a quantitative approach.

Typically, participant observation or field research and indepth interviewing have been most commonly associated with the qualitative approach while surveys and experiments are usually quantitative. All methods share several aspects in common. Description and analysis are evident in all methods. They are all concerned with the techniques of data discovery, reduction, display, interpretation, and explanation (Miles and Huberman, 1984). The strategies for using these techniques, however, are different with different methods. In general, qualitative methods tend to take longer, are more detailed, are highly variable in content, use pattern analysis, and focus on others' views more than do quantitative methods (Patton, 1980a).

Within methods there is a wide range of possible procedures that may be used. For example, a field research study might be focused on gaining indepth information about the operation of one organization or it might use a number of research sites to gather information about a more specific question. All qualitative procedures should aim to improve the researcher's ability to know and to discover, not to bring research to a single format (Blumer, 1969).

The method chosen reflects the researcher's understanding of the issues surrounding recreation, parks, and leisure. Denzin (1978) suggested that methods ought to be judged in terms of their contributions to the solution of theoretical and substantive problems of the discipline rather than in terms of abstract elegance. The methods selected will depend not only on the paradigm, the general approach, the questions asked, but also upon pragmatic issues such as the resources available, the time, limits to one's own abilities, the focus and priority of the research, and whether breadth or depth is desired (Patton, 1980b). There is no absolute method for obtaining truth about the field of recreation and parks or the study of leisure.

A term often associated with methods is triangulation. It is possible to combine methods within an approach or to combine both qualitative and quantitative methods within the positivist paradigm. Reichardt and Cook (1979) suggested that combining methods is useful particularly in evaluation because a variety of needs requires a variety of methods, one method can build upon another, and methods have biases so multiple methods can give more valid and reliable information. For example, one might do some initial field studies as Brandenburg, Greiner, Hamilton-Smith, Scholten, Senior, and Webb (1982) did in their study of why people adopt recreation activities. They used these initial field studies to determine what issues needed to be addressed in order to develop a quantitative measuring instrument. Further, a researcher might collect quantitative data through a questionnaire and then go back to a select group of people for indepth interviews to ascertain possible explanations for the results. Glyptis (1985) used both of these methods in her study concerning attitudes toward women and sports participation. Samdahl (1988) also combined quantitative and qualitative data when she studied the meaning of leisure, *See Exemplar 2.1*. Within the qualitative approach, one might use several methods in one study as Glancy did in her 1986 study of an adult softball team and her 1988 study of the play-world of auctions, *See Exemplar 2.2*, and as Howe and Keller (1988) did in their evaluation of therapeutic recreation symposia. In general, the value of multiple methods is that they lead to multiple realities (Bullock, 1982; Woodward, Green, and Hebron, 1988).

> Exemplar 2.1 Samdahl, D. (1988). A symbolic interactionist model of leisure: Theory and empirical support. *Leisure Sciences, 10(1),* 27-39.
>
> Samdahl addressed the need to strengthen the theoretical foundations of leisure research. She advocated for symbolic interaction theory as a perspective that may be useful for understanding the issues of freedom and constraint within leisure. She used a quantitative and qualitative analysis to test a typology that was created using a quantitative approach. While this study is not purely qualitative, Samdahl provided a useful and needed theoretical framework for studying leisure. The use of qualitative data shows how a positivist might use qualitative methods to assist in explaining the results of quantitative analysis. The approach that Samdahl used is hermeneutical (based on the meaning of a written text) to some extent as well. Her analysis of the previous literature provided a useful interpretation of the meaning of leisure as it has been portrayed by other researchers.

Exemplar 2.2 Glancy, M. (1988). The play-world setting of
the auction. *Journal of Leisure Research, 20* (2), 135-153.

Glancy examined commercial, personal-goods auction sales as
an adult play-world setting. She made the assumption early in her
research planning that the participant observation method was
the best way to study this auction phenomena. In this article, she
demonstrates to the reader how the participant observation method
can be successfully used in triangulation with other qualitative
methods. She used symbolic interaction theory to develop an
application of the interpretive framework of Huizinga's conception of play. Data for this study were obtained from the field
research, a personal diary the researcher kept, and purchase
records. Glancy attended over 40 auction events to obtain these
data. She talked about the specific techniques in following the
framework for analysis suggested by Bruyn. She developed
themes concerning such aspects as atmosphere, illusion-build-
ing, social bonds, and rites of membership through her analytic
induction technique of data interpretation. Glancy discussed the
ways that she used subjective and objective assessments to
control for potential bias. She did an excellent job of applying
theory back to data in order to provide a rich interpretation of the
data.

Methodological Issues

With the unique differences between positivist and interpretive paradigms and the
frameworks and guidelines surrounding the quantitative and qualitative approaches,
it is not unusual that leisure researchers have had a number of discussions
concerning the value of each approach. Qualitative researchers have often been
placed in a position of defending their assumptions and beliefs. For example, a
hierarchy has been suggested by some people in that qualitative approaches are
exploratory, secondary, or only suggestive and pave the way for the more primary
quantitative approaches. In the early years, according to Glaser and Strauss (1967),
qualitative research did not test the facts and was considered preliminary, exploratory, and ground-breaking while quantitative was the "real" research. A number of
other dualisms have been established that reflect certain hierarchical stereotypes of
qualitative and quantitative approaches such as soft/hard or navel gazers/number
crunchers (Fielding and Fielding, 1986).

  With the paradigm shift that is occurring today, most researchers now agree that
qualitative and quantitative methods can be used for either theory confirmation or
generation. While a variety of methods may be one way to address the study of
recreation, parks, and leisure better, misunderstanding has existed concerning the
assumptions about research approaches. Leisure researchers are only beginning to
agree on just exactly what these paradigms and approaches are and how they exist.

Harper (1981) has cautioned researchers that it is sometimes easier to fit reality to our method than to fit method to the reality. Therefore, the nature of the problem rather than one's predisposition should dictate the methods chosen (Howe and Keller, 1988). For example, many leisure researchers and practitioners have been educated with a heavy focus on questionnaire design as a method for research and/ or evaluation. A researcher may be interested in answering a particular question about leisure behavior but does not have the right quantitative instrument available to her or him. Depending on the situation and regardless of the background of the researcher, it may be appropriate to consider another method rather than to try to fit the data to a questionnaire that will not be valid in answering the question or solving the problem. Any information gathering device is both privileged and constrained by its structure and location and collecting one type of information usually closes off other possibilities (Fielding and Fielding, 1986). When a researcher forces a method to fit a question, she/he may be closing off other valuable information that could be discerned.

Questions have been raised concerning the criteria for measuring the quality of leisure research approaches. For example, Iso-Ahola (1986) suggested that qualitative studies are acceptable but must be equally rigorous. This need for rigor in qualitative research is imperative, but the same criteria for rigor may not be appropriate for qualitative as for quantitative studies. Method and rigor should not be confused. It is often difficult for researchers steeped in quantitative methods to accept the limits of their research. On the other hand, researchers using qualitative approaches must not employ "blitzkrieg" (hit and run) research if they wish to boost the credibility of the technique or trustworthiness of the approach (Rist, 1980).

Some energy has been spent, especially by North American leisure researchers, in debating the question of which is more appropriate, qualitative or quantitative methods. While this conflict is sure to occur in times of a paradigm shift, it is also taking energy that might be directed toward other questions about leisure behavior and the recreation and parks profession. It is just as possible for researchers using qualitative approaches to become "methodologically parochial" (Maurice, 1983) as it is for quantitative researchers to be zealots for experimental design and inferential statistics. As Maurice further explained, using only one research method is like a carpenter using only a hammer and nails for all construction. You cannot use only a hammer and nails to build a house and you cannot use only quantitative methods to build a body of knowledge.

Implications for Leisure Research

In any method of research used, the bottom line is, "Does this research make the world more understandable?" (Mobily, 1985). If leisure encompassed only the mechanical, absolute, objective, stable categories of time and activity, the positivist paradigm would continue to serve well in the study of leisure behavior. Leisure, however, is holistic, pluralistic, fluid and has "meaning," and these conceptualizations require an expanding view of appropriate research questions, as well as research methods. Some researchers have been looking for a conceptualization of "pure leisure" that fits the model of a universal operational definition necessary to conduct rigorous positivist research. A dynamic, organic, transformative concept like leisure is difficult, if not impossible, to operationally define in a way that all scientists, let alone the public, can use. A movement among leisure researchers exists toward an interpretive paradigm for the research with an emphasis on subjective states or experience (Samdahl, 1988; Shaw, 1985).

In the study of leisure behavior or the study of a leisure delivery system, the goal is to understand the meaning of the whole. This understanding can be discovered by studying the parts or studying the whole. Bultena and Field (1983) have argued for the necessity of researching the individual as well as system properties if more than a little of the variance of leisure participation is to be explained. Iso-Ahola (1980) also addressed the necessity of understanding the interaction of person with situation to understand the nature of leisure or of any kind of behavior. Mobily (1985) suggested in the study of leisure, dualism really does not exist and just as one cannot know a machine by studying one part, one can not know leisure by looking at only one dimension or looking at leisure outside the context of life in general. In addition, to really understand leisure, multiple phenomenological interpretations need to be encouraged with the combination of both empirical and philosophical input (Hunnicutt, 1986; Mobily, 1985). The qualitative approach offers new ways for understanding the whole of leisure behavior as well as the provision of leisure services.

According to Kuhn (1970), the emergence of a new paradigm with a new approach is a sign of the maturity of a scientific field. The limits of current recreation, parks, and leisure research and the problems associated with positivism require acknowledgment so that other alternatives can emerge. Kuhn (1970) presented a cogent statement about the shifting paradigms:

> The transition from a paradigm in crisis to a new one from which a new tradition of normal science can emerge is far from a cumulative process, one achieved by an articulation or extension of old paradigms. Rather, it is a reconstruction that changes some of the field's most elementary theoretical generalizations as well as many of its paradigm methods and applications. During the transition period there will be a large but never complete overlap between the problems that can be solved by the old and the new paradigm. But there will also be a decisive difference in the modes of solution. When the transition is complete, the profession will have changed its view of the field, its methods, and its goals (p. 84-85).

To understand the "meaning" of recreation, parks, and leisure, it is tacitly suggested that a choice of methods may be very important. More studies that use the interpretive paradigm or combine quantitative and qualitative methods within a positivist view may be useful for a more comprehensive understanding of leisure and the field of recreation and parks. Rigor in the research, no matter what paradigm or method, is critical for the continued understanding of the field. The philosophy of science, the philosophy of leisure research, and dimensions of methodological choice must be discussed together to help us understand the choices available in studying aspects of parks and recreation and of leisure phenomena.

Summary

Denzin (1978) suggested that all humans are involved in the process of making sense out of the social object called reality. Many leisure researchers seem to be equally involved in trying to make sense of the qualitative research approach. The fusion of theory and method is essential for research but the mixing of terminology to describe paradigms, approaches, and methods has been confusing. In this chapter, we discussed the dominant paradigms, positivism and interpretive social science, that shape the study of recreation, parks, and leisure. A model was presented regarding the assumptions that are made in using the positivist or the interpretive world view as well as how these views are linked to the yin-yang of interaction between the qualitative and quantitative approaches. The possible methods choices available to researchers were also introduced. Some of the philosophical issues surrounding methodological choices were raised and the implications of paradigms, approaches, methods, and techniques were discussed in relation to recreation, park, and leisure research.

The key concepts addressed in this chapter were: paradigm shifts, positivism, interpretive social science, qualitative approach, quantitative approach, methods.

For Further Consideration

1. Describe each one of the paradigms and apply what the assumptions of each paradigm to how you would describe the balancing of work and leisure in your own life.

2. Choose a research study from a leading leisure research journal and determine what world view the author(s) appear to have based upon the way that the author(s) conducted the study.

3. Choose an area of research inquiry and describe how you might conduct a study using a positivist view and an interpretive view.

4. From what you know at this point, describe what you might to to avoid the criticisms that might be leveled against research done using the qualitative approach and research using the quantitative approach.

For Further Reading

For those individuals interested in pursuing some of these topics further, the following readings are suggested as a starting point:

Bernstein, R.J. (1983). *Beyond objectivism and relativism: Science, hermeneutics, and praxis*. Philadelphia, PA: University of Pennsylvania Press.

Bernstein is a well known philosopher of social science. His first book, *The Restructuring of Social and Political Theory* (1976) provided the basis for post-positivist thinking. This book takes the ideas of positivism and interpretation a step further suggesting that we ought to think beyond these dichotomies. The book is most enlightening to the individual who has some background in the philosophy of science.

Blumer, H. (1969). *Symbolic interactionism: Perspective and method*. Englewood Cliffs, NJ: Prentice-Hall.

Blumer has written the "bible" of symbolic interactionism as a primary example of interpretive social science. This book explains the assumptions behind the use of symbolic interactionism as well as offers techniques that may be applied. For anyone contemplating a pure qualitative study where empirical observation is to be used, this book ought to be read.

Cook, T.C., and Reichardt, C.S. (Eds.). (1979). *Qualitative and quantitative methods in evaluation research*. Beverly Hills, CA: Sage Publications, Inc.

This compilation of papers offers a thorough look at the issue of qualitative and quantitative methods and how they are different as well as how they may be linked. A variety of approaches are presented related to how one can justify the use of the various methods for evaluation.

Denzin, N. K. (1978). *The research act*. New York, NY: McGraw Hill Book Company.

Denzin is one of the "gurus" of phenomenology. This text offers a complete look at research which is done within a phenomenological qualitative mode. He describes the justification for this research and presents information about the specific methods of field research, interviewing, and other qualitative approaches.

Lincoln, Y.S., and Guba, E. (1981). *Naturalistic inquiry.* **Beverly Hills, CA: Sage Publications, Inc.**

Lincoln and Guba provide a plethora of information about the naturalistic (interpretive) paradigm of research. They provide justification for the qualitative approach and compare naturalistic inquiry to rationalistic scientific (positivist) inquiry. Not only does the book provide a philosophical framework but it also provides an explication of how the methods can be used in research.

Rabinow, P., and Sullivan, W.M. (1987). *Interpretive social science: A second look.* **Berkeley, CA: University of California Press.**

Rabinow and Sullivan have edited a collection of essays concerning various aspects of interpretive social science. They indicate that interpretive social science is more readily accepted today but a sustained methodological debate continues. The book offers essays by several noted social science philosophers. While philosophically "heavy," the book provides a great deal of insight into what philosophers of science are thinking today.

Chapter 3

Theoretical Frameworks

Introduction

Research and theory "go together like a horse and carriage." This short chapter will provide a further explication of theory that can be confirmed or generated through the use of the qualitative approach in the study of recreation, parks, and leisure. One of the biggest criticisms leveled against research in recreation, parks, and leisure has been its lack of theoretical framework. This chapter will address what theory is, the aspects of confirming and grounding theory, theoretical frameworks for research, and the application of theory to the study of recreation, parks, and leisure.

What is Theory?

Theory is a strategy for handling data which provides conceptualizations for describing and explaining the data. Theory is a general set of statements or propositions related to a phenomena. In other words, theory is an explanation. The aim of research is either to fit the data to a theory (positivism) or fit or generate a theory from the data (interpretive science). The function of theory is to give order and insight to what is, or can be, observed. Theory, conceptualizations, and empirical activity are interwoven in qualitative studies in a contextual operation such that theory guides research while research guides theory (Denzin, 1978). Thus, in the qualitative approach, the theory is always evolving. It is NOT appropriate to use methods without thought for their theoretical implications related to the data.

Several terms are often associated with theory. Concepts are the most important elements in theoretical systems. They provide the basis for theory's operationalizing. Hypotheses are defined as specific expectations about the nature of phenomena derived from a theory. In most qualitative methods, working hypotheses or sensitizing concepts are used in the development of theory. Conceptual frameworks are used in all research whether theory is being confirmed or generated. Miles and Huberman stated that "a conceptual framework explains, either graphically or in a narrative form, the main dimensions to be studied–the key factors or variables–and the presumed relationship among them" (1984, p. 28). Concepts, hypotheses, and conceptual frameworks are the building blocks for theory.

Glaser and Strauss (1967) indicated that there are two extremes of theory which in general, but not always, describe the difference between the positivist and interpretive paradigms. The former is deductive theory, theory that is tested/confirmed, or theory that is formal and is referred to as *a priori*. The second type of theory is grounded theory or inductive theory which is developed relative to a substantive area (contextual within the place or activity) or relating to formal theory after data are discovered (conceptual ties to an area of inquiry). In grounded theory, the creation of a theory is based on observation rather than on deduction. Grounded theory could be used with both the qualitative and quantitative approaches but lends itself best to qualitative. Fielding and Fielding (1986) suggested that data are really only "rich" when they are grounded in a refined theoretical perspective.

No research procedure can at the same time generate and test theory. Therefore, it is not possible for a study to use both inductive and deductive theory as its organizational framework. A researcher may use a formal theoretical framework to help justify a qualitative study, but within an inductive study that framework must be allowed to change as grounded theory emerges. A scientific theory is usually felt to be better than its predecessors not only in the sense that it provides a better instrument for discovery and solving puzzles, but also because it is somehow a better representation of what nature is really like (Denzin, 1978). Further, researchers should be reminded that many of the great discoveries of science were not the result of hypothesis testing but were "accidents" (Kirk and Miller, 1986; Kuhn, 1970). Regardless of the outcomes, theory has a different role depending upon which paradigm and which approach to research is chosen.

Researchers must pay attention to theory and attempt to ascertain the extent to which theoretical notions are in evidence when conducting or when reviewing research. A pervasive problem in nearly any research investigation is the relationship between the theory one begins with and the data gathered to test, validate, or extend that theory. Figure 2 provides a summary of how theory and data are related comparing the deductive quantitative approach and the inductive qualitative approach. The relationship in quantitative studies is linear. The researcher generally begins with a formal theoretical framework, develops a means to collect data to test the framework, and either confirms or disconfirms the theory. As indicated above, sometimes accidents occur and new theories are generated, but these new theories then require another quantitative study.

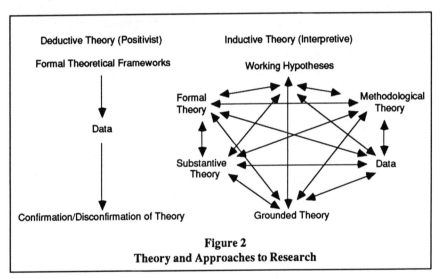

Figure 2
Theory and Approaches to Research

Qualitative researchers are usually concerned with the discovery of grounded theory which may lead to generating new substantive theory or may confirm existing formal theory. The figure emphasizes how theory and data in qualitative research are continually in interaction with one another. The qualitative approach to research is as much a process as it is a product. The relationship between theory and data is not linear but multilinear. When the researcher embarks on the study she/he does not know where the results will lead. The qualitative framework that one uses for analysis will create the systematic grounded theory (Glaser and Strauss, 1967). Grounded theory must be discovered to see if formal theories are applicable to it or whether substantive theory related to the context of the situation must be developed. Denzin (1978) suggested that theory works at different levels such as: ad hoc classificatory systems, categorical systems or taxonomies, conceptual frameworks, and empirical-theoretical systems. The qualitative researcher may generate or confirm theory on any of these levels but may not know what those levels will be until she/he works with the data.

When a researcher begins a research project, some idea of the research questions and working hypotheses generally exist. There is at the minimum a substantive area of study and perhaps some formal theoretical perspectives or a conceptual framework. For example, one might ask the question, "What is the experience of children at a summer camp?" One might suspect that this experience relates to aspects of socialization or to self-esteem. Thus, one has theoretical ideas in the form of working hypotheses, but these hypotheses or concepts are not tested as such until the data are examined. Without some sense of theory, the data are shapeless (Miles and Huberman, 1984) but one is cautioned in qualitative research not to become wedded to *a priori* frameworks too early in the investigation. The researcher is cautioned not to hold too tightly to formal theoretical assumptions because the data may not support them as the research progresses. The fit between either generating substantive theory or confirming existing formal theory and the data will emerge as the researcher proceeds back and forth between the working hypotheses, the data, the methodological assumptions, and the grounded theory generated.

The exact procedures of the research using the qualitative approach are hard to know beforehand because one does not know how the grounded theory will emerge. Glaser and Strauss (1967) suggested, also, that the researcher should not invalidate her/his own scientific intelligence in developing theory. It does not take a genius to generate grounded theory and one's intuition is often very important. The secret to developing grounded theory is to take data in the form of descriptions and anecdotes and find patterns and meaning in the data as related to the context in which they occur. As a result, formal theory may be applied and confirmed or substantive theory may be generated related to the particular context. The conclusions of a qualitative study, unlike a quantitative study, may be much different than the initial working hypotheses proposed.

Within a qualitative study, substantive theory is often generated by a process known as constant comparison. There are other data interpretation methods as well but this technique is useful in describing the relationship between theory and data. In constant comparison, the researcher allows conceptual categories and conceptual properties to emerge and then compares each piece of data for fit. New working hypotheses are generated and the categories or properties examined. The researcher may choose to confirm the emerging and changing working hypotheses with the respondents or may compare them to literature that already exists. In qualitative studies, the techniques of research design, data discovery, data interpretation, and developing theories all tend to occur simultaneously and provide a constant feedback concerning how the study is emerging.

In pure qualitative methods, the theory emerges from the data; it is not imposed on the data. When analyzing research done using the qualitative approach, one may want to pay attention to some criteria that Glaser and Strauss (1967) have proposed: Is the emphasis on verifying or generating theory? Is the focus on substantive or formal theory? To what degree is the theory grounded? How clear is the conceptual detail? What kinds of data are used? To what degree is the theory integrated? How much clarity does the author reveal? Patton (1980a) suggested that the cardinal principle of qualitative analysis is that causal relationships and theoretical statements be clearly emergent from and grounded in the phenomena studied.

It is the researcher's responsibility to convey credibility about the theory being generated or confirmed (Glaser and Strauss,1967). The canons of rigor applied to judging theory, however, may not be the same for inductive substantive theory as deductive formal theory. Rigor is addressed by explicating the theoretical framework and describing the data vividly by showing the evidence through codified procedures. For example, a study is credible if the reader gets involved in the description, understands how the researcher came to the conclusions, and sees the explicitness of important interpretations. The practical application of grounded theory must fit a substantive area, be readily understood by those working in the substantive area, be sufficiently general to be applicable to ever-changing situations, and must allow the user partial control in the interpretation (Glaser and Strauss, 1967). In other words, there are few protocols for evaluating substantive theory except that it must be guided by judgment of its propriety and fruitfulness. The conceptual frameworks considered and techniques used for analysis, however, should be made explicit if the theory is to be considered credible.

One of the values of using qualitative methods is that one may choose either an inductive or a deductive approach to theory. You may start with some theoretical assumptions about what you want to know most or first and then apply these theories to the data. Or you may be more inductive and begin to see what emerges as the study progresses. The advantage of using qualitative methods to develop grounded theory is that you can change direction and refocus data collection for the next field trip or interview based on the theory that is emerging. In essence, the conceptual framework used with the qualitative approach may be viewed as a road map. You can see the marked roads that may be taken but no one says that you have to go down a particular road or stay on it.

Theoretical Frameworks for Data Discovery

Theories used in research may relate either to the process of data discovery and interpretation as in the interpretive paradigm or may relate to the testing of formal theory as is done in the positivist paradigm. Several theoretical frameworks offer guidance for the process of conducting research using the qualitative approach. These include such cultural theories as structuralism, feminist theory, symbolic interactionism, functionalism, and ethnomethodology. Each of these cultural theories can help to confront empirical reality from the perspective of those being studied. They focus on the relationship between subjective states and human interaction. Different disciplines tend to use similar processes for interpretation but with different names. For example, anthropologists use ethnomethodology and eth-noscience, sociologists use symbolic interactionism, philosophers use hermeneu-tics, feminists use feminist theory, and political scientists may use critical theory. All processual frameworks aim to address the meaning associated with data and how researchers can best learn about social reality.

The organizing theoretical framework used will lead to different directions that the researcher may take. I would like to describe several examples of theoretical frameworks that may be applied in conducting recreation, parks, and leisure research.

Feminist Theory

Feminist theory focuses on an analysis of gender and power in society and how research can lead to social change. It generally focuses on qualitative methodology because of the notion that gender or sex is not a dichotomous variable and must be viewed in relation to the context in which interaction occurs. Feminist research is generally considered to be humanistic and concerned with the inner world. Feminist researchers focus on the need for social change and a vision of the preferred future. The goal of feminist research is to correct both the invisibility and distortion of female experience in ways relevant to social change. McCormack (1981) suggested that ultimately the justification for feminist scholarship must rest not on a special domain (women) or a special kind of empathy (sexual affinity) but on a set of principles of inquiry, a feminist philosophy of science. Feminist research does not necessarily mean a focus exclusively on women but addresses looking at women's experience from the point of view of women. It is suggested that this approach would help to understand better the male experience, as well as the whole culture.

The feminist research perspective is different from the traditional positivist research methods because it suggests that experience and feeling must be at the heart of the research (Stanley and Wise, 1983). Lather (1982) identified five tenets of feminist research: It must integrate consciousness, women must benefit from the research, it must deal with the issue of getting women to speak their own voices, it must not contribute to the ideology of sex differences, and it must be collaborative and interdisciplinary. Qualitative methods have been very useful to many feminists in their research because they often address these criteria. Further, several researchers have used feminism as a framework for their qualitative approach to the study of women and leisure (e.g., Deem, 1986; Dixey, 1987; Henderson and Rannells, 1988). *See Exemplar 3.1*

Exemplar 3.1 Dixey, R. (1987). It's a great feeling when you win. Women and bingo. *Leisure Studies, 6*, 199-214.

Dixey began with the assumption that to understand women's leisure it is necessary to start not with an activity or ways in which women spend their time, but with women's roles in our society which have resulted in particular leisure outcomes. She used an ethnomethodological approach to examine bingo in the leisure lives of working class women and to examine how reality was constructed using the actors' own words. She observed women playing bingo and talked with them about what they were doing and why. She interviewed 68 women and distributed questionnaires to another 200. Dixey described little about the methodology used but focused on the meaning of the women's experiences. She developed grounded theory concerning why these women found bingo, in relation to their daily lives, such an important activity. She found the reasons had little to do specifically with the activity but a lot to do with the context of the activity. While Dixey's analysis did not use formal theory, the study provided an example of how a qualitative data collection approach can address contextual aspects of a recreation activity through grounded theory and its substantive application.

Critical Theory

Critical theory offers a framework for integrating a post-positivist, interpretive paradigm into the study of phenomena. The objective of critical theory is to develop a theoretical framework in scientific investigations that unites the political implications of the investigations (Wuthnow, Hunter, Bergesen, and Kurzweil, 1984). Critical theory requires that the researcher take her/his own beliefs about society into account rather than attempting to suppress the beliefs in the interest of the dispassionate discovery of universal scientific laws. Critical theorists suggest that a body of knowledge should be created from which values are discussed and changes occur culturally, not just related to a specific issue or a specific research question. In other words, critical theorists, like feminist researchers, are concerned about how theory can be applied to making the world a better place to live. Habermas (1979) asserted that research questions can be better understood by focusing on how human beings reflect on their social lives for the purpose of discovering what should be done and how people should live. The focus is on how a person or group of people view themselves in the world. Critical theorists place importance on intersubjective understandings shared among people as they interact with one another. The persons under study are the center of the research and the focus is on action. Researchers using critical theory address specific reflective steps about a phenomenon, create an interaction with those who are "oppressed," and base their conclusions on larger cultural epochs.

A pragmatic framework for research that has emerged from critical theory over the past ten years is referred to as "new paradigm research." One of the criticisms of positivist research has been on how people are objectified for data collection. The focus of new paradigm research is on interacting with participants in a way that will be helpful to them rather than having an attitude of "isn't it fascinating-how-people-organize-their-weirdness?" (Reason and Rowan, 1981). Researchers following new paradigm research believe that human inquiry needs to be based on the experience that it purports to understand and on the collaboration between "researcher" and "subject." There is a commitment to a full engagement in the research on the part of the researcher. This research is cooperative in nature without a notion of "power over." The framework is for an action science and not a reflective science and may use qualitative or quantitative methods depending on the nature of the research questions asked.

New paradigm researchers operate under the premise that they ask what is of value, set criteria for research, go through the research cycle slowly and many times, see the subjects as co-researchers, allow social action to emerge from the research, and see what the research says to the participants who are the co-researchers. New paradigm researchers object to positivist orthodoxy because the traditional model isolates people from their environment, reduces actions to a set of variables, tests and quantifies variables, uses confusing language, and has a low utilization of the research (Reason and Rowan, 1981). In the new paradigm research model, intuition and feeling are important components of science. This new paradigm model can result in emancipatory, enabling, transformative, participatory, and empowering outcomes in research (Sheffield, 1988).

Phenomenology and Symbolic Interaction

Phenomenology is the name for a philosophical movement whose primary objective is the direct investigation and description of phenomena as consciously experienced, without theories about their causal explanations and as free as possible from unexamined preconceptions and presuppositions (Speigelberg, 1975). The concept of phenomenology has been around for well over a hundred years and it is finding greater applicability in relation to interpretive social science today. Bullock (1985a; 1985b) described his use of the social phenomenological method of inquiry in studying the integration of mentally retarded and nonmentally retarded children in play settings. He outlined the steps that are followed in using a phenomenological method of inquiry including deconstructing prior conceptions about a phenomenon under study, discovering multiple instances of the phenomenon, and constructing new conceptions about the phenomenon. See Exemplar 3.2. The focus of phenomenology is on understanding the internal subjective experience associated with observable reality.

Exemplar 3.2 Bullock, C.C. (1988). Interpretive lines of action of mentally retarded children in mainstreamed play settings. *Symbolic Interaction, 9,* 145-172.

This article was published from the dissertation that Bullock completed in 1985 at the University of Illinois entitled *Proving Self: The problematic imperative.* In this article, a groundwork is set for the theoretical conceptualizations that are used in this interactionist, phenomenological, interpretive study. Bullock focused on symbolic interaction and how it is used in data discovery and interpretation. He examined the various interpretive strategies used by mentally retarded persons as they attempt to comply with the mandate to prove themselves to be competent interactants in a mainstreamed play setting. The paper is a useful example of how one operates out of an interpretive paradigm to collect qualitative data that can be compared to existing data and to emerging grounded theory. Through the use of text in the article and footnotes, Bullock incorporates the methodology discussion into his assumptions about the theory which is used to guide this inductive study. Quotations are also useful in helping the reader fully understand the perceptions of the individuals with mental retardation.

Symbolic interaction is a theoretical phenomenological framework often used in interpretive research. Symbolic interactionism posits that the meanings that "things" have for human beings are central in their own right. It provides a model for studying how individuals interpret objects, events, and people in their lives and for studying how the process of interpretation leads to behavior in specific situations. To ignore meaning is to falsify behavior (Blumer, 1969). As a theoretical framework, symbolic interaction acknowledges respect for the nature of human group life and conduct. It is a common theoretical framework for bridging the gap between methods, theories, and areas of interests. The basic assumptions of symbolic interactionism, according to Denzin (1978), are that the individual defines the situation, the individual engages in self-reflexive activity, and humans interact. The meaning of an object lies in the action human beings take toward it. Blumer (1969) suggested that people act toward things on the basis of the meanings these things have for them; meaning determines action. Meanings are social patterns that arise during interaction and social actors attach meaning through a power of interpretation. Thus, interpretation by an individual determines action. Interpretation is a way to handle meaning. The meaning of any symbol (such as leisure) has its origin in interactions which are defined and changed by individuals according to the meaning that one holds. The individual being studied is the expert and the attempt is to describe their vocabularies, ways of looking, and sense of the important and the unimportant. Each action must be taken seriously as it helps to define and redefine who we are. In other words, the only real social reality is from within the individual (Schwartz and Jacobs, 1979). It is the social process in group life that creates and upholds the rules, not the rules that create and uphold group life (Blumer, 1969).

Meaning in positivist research has tended to be taken for granted or set aside. Researchers tend to become concerned with behavior and with the factors that produce it (i.e., attitudes, motives, perceptions, cognitions, rather than on social positions, social roles). In identifying factors, one may forget to examine meaning. Symbolic interaction respects the nature of the empirical world by using direct examination rather than simulated situations. Symbolic interaction can meet all the protocols of qualitative or quantitative methods. It can be used as the basis for experiments, surveys, participant observation, life history, or unobtrusive methods. Because of the focus on meaning, however, it has been most useful as a framework for the qualitative approach in research. Samdahl (1988) suggested that symbolic interaction theory may be particularly useful as a perspective for understanding the theoretical issues of freedom and constraint in leisure. Symbolic interaction places the focus on social meanings that people attach to the world, including leisure.

Leisure Theory

Very little formal theory exists that is unique to the study of recreation, parks, and leisure. This is not to say that this research is atheoretical. Rather, much of the theory associated with the content of the field has been borrowed from other disciplines and fields. The psychological literature on motivation, for example, has provided a framework for studying motivations for leisure participation. Also, according to Shaw (1985), the theoretical work on leisure meanings comes primarily from a social psychological perspective. Much leisure theory is either implicit or explicit within an interactionist framework because the individual decides subjectively whether something is leisure or not.

While formal theory for leisure behavior does not exist, a number of models have provided a framework for analyzing leisure. For example, Neulinger (1981) has developed a paradigm of leisure that divides leisure into six units based on constraint-freedom and intrinsic-extrinsic motivation. Csikszentmihalyi (1975) has conceptualized flow and anti-flow on the basis of challenge and skill that one may experience in an activity. The researcher is cautioned not to let the lack of formal leisure theory prevent her/him from continuing to use and develop theoretical frameworks for leisure in both quantitative and qualitative studies. The use of the qualitative approach may help to develop substantive leisure theory that may one day become formal leisure theory. As researchers studying recreation, parks, and leisure, it is imperative that we examine all possibilities for theory as it relates to process and conceptual frameworks. The value of the qualitative approach lies in the generation of theory but research studies will not be useful unless they build upon previous concepts and ideas and help to set a direction for further inquiry.

Summary

Using the qualitative approach is like starting on an exciting adventure in which the researcher may not know what ups and downs, twists and turns, and final destinations may be reached. Theory may help to set the course as well as to help understand where one has been. This chapter has provided an introduction to theory and selected theoretical frameworks that might be used in the qualitative approach to the study of recreation, parks, and leisure. The relationship necessary between theory and data in quantitative and qualitative studies was presented. The multilinear and reciprocal relationship between theory and data in the qualitative approach was introduced. The basis for grounded theory leading to substantive and formal theory was presented along with examples of how theoretical frameworks might be used in shaping research about recreation, parks, and leisure.

The key concepts addressed in this chapter were: theory, theoretical frameworks, feminist theory, critical theory, phenomenology, symbolic interactionism, substantive theory, formal theory, and leisure theory.

For Further Consideration

1. Describe the difference between the processual theoretical frameworks used in inductive (interpretive) studies and those predetermined frameworks used in deductive (positivist) research.

2. Find an article discussing leisure behavior in one of the leading leisure research journals. Discuss the theoretical framework that is presented concerning the concept of leisure. If no specific framework is presented, describe how you believe the author is conceptualizing leisure.

3. Criticisms from positivists are often leveled against researchers that allow "social change" to be a possible outcome of the research. Why has this been the case? Is this likely to continue to be the case in the future?

For Further Reading

Glaser, B.G., and Strauss, A. (1967). *The discovery of grounded theory: Strategies for qualitative research*. Chicago, IL: Aldine Publishing Co.

This classic text was the first to describe grounded theory and how it might be used in research. The authors present a rationale for the use of grounded theory and also show how methodologically a constant comparison method can be used to analyze data to obtain grounded theory. While much has been written about grounded theory in the past twenty years, this book provides the initial thinking for its use in social science research.

Habermas, J. (1979). *Communication and the evolution of society.* **Boston, MA: Beacon Press.**

This book, along with others that Habermas has written, makes use of critical theory as the organizing framework for helping humans reflect on their lives and make necessary changes. The text is slow reading because of the theoretical sociological approach but it offers much as a framework for understanding how research can be used to build upon theory and to lead to change in people's lives.

Stanley, L., and Wise, S. (1983). *Breaking out: Feminist consciousness and feminist research.* **Londown, England: Routledge and Kegan Paul, Ltd.**

Stanley and Wise have pulled together the thinking about feminist research, why it is important, and how it can be used to empower women. They provide a strong case for how feminist research fits into the social sciences and how research on women will not lead to social change without the application of feminist theory.

Reason, P., and Rowan, J. (Eds.). (1981). *Human inquiry: A sourcebook of new paradigm research.* **New York, NY: John Wiley and Sons Inc.**

Reason and Rowan present an edited text that answers almost everything you would ever want to know about new paradigm research. They have selected chapters that address the philosophy as well as methodology of new paradigm research. They also present several examples of new paradigm research studies. After reading this book, a researcher should feel very confident about having an understanding of how to rationalize and conduct new paradigm research.

Part Two

Qualitative Methods

Introduction

The specific methods of the qualitative approach are varied. As described before, however, the presence of emergent designs, grounded theory, words, and a natural environment tend to set the stage for empirical qualitative approach. Qualitative methods are pluralistic with a variety of possibilities. For example, such methods as direct observation, field study, participant observation, case studies, interviewing, life histories, document analysis, elite interviewing, questionnaires and surveys, audiovisuals, nonreactive or unobtrusive methods, and focus group interviews could be used within the qualitative approach. Qualitative data may be discovered and interpreted through a variety of methods.

Researchers in different disciplines have preferred one method over another. For example, anthropologists conduct ethnographies, historians use documents, and sociologists may use texts or field research. The most common method choice of leisure researchers within the qualitative approach has probably been indepth interviewing, although as was stated earlier, few examples of qualitative research existed until the 1980s. All qualitative methods share the idea of verstehen, the inner perspective, and require that the researcher understand the role of the research participant. These methods and techniques may be done singularly or triangulated. Table 2 (page 51) illustrates a chart of the major qualitative methods along with their advantages and disadvantages.

In this part of the book, the two most common methods within the qualitative approach, field research/participant observation and indepth interviewing, will be described along with several other less familiar methods that have been used in the study of recreation, parks, and leisure. The purest qualitative method is field research which is also referred to as participant observation or ethnography. The specific use of terminology for this method depends upon the academic discipline one may be pursuing. Since we do not have our own unique form of research in recreation, park, and leisure studies, we will borrow from the predominant language of others. To describe the phenomenon of observing people in their natural environment, anthropologists use the term ethnography, sociologists tend to talk about field research, and educators and evaluators are more likely to talk about participant observation. Conceptually the terms are basically all the same. I refer to field research and participant observation as being one in the same and will use the terms interchangeably to refer to this qualitative method of an observer using a face to face involvement with members of a particular social setting for purposes of scientific inquiry (Johnson, 1975).

The examination of the indepth interviewing method will be referred to as interviewing. The researcher must keep in mind, however that all research methodologies exist on a continuum related to being purely quantitative to purely qualitative. For example, interviews may be highly deductive and may be analyzed using inferential statistics. On the other hand, interviewing related to the qualitative approach is semi-structured or unstructured, indepth, and makes use of the symbols of words and not the codification of words into numbers. The major criteria for qualitative interviewing is the focus that indepth interviewing generally has on emergent designs, grounded theory, words, and data discovery in the natural environment.

Several other methods exist including case studies, content analysis, unobtrusive measures, audio-visual methods, and consensus methods that may be qualitative in nature depending on how the research is conducted. It is antithetical to interpretive research and the qualitative approach to develop hard and fast procedures and protocols, but in this section, I offer a number of ideas about how you can begin to operationalize these methods in your research in parks, recreation, and leisure studies. From this framework, it is hoped that you will develop your own style and strategies for using qualitative methods. To get the full picture of how to use a particular method it will be necessary to also address the most appropriate techniques that can be applied to the qualitative method.

Table 2 The Advantages and Disadvantages of Selected Qualitative Methods

Method	Advantages	Disadvantages
Participant Observation	Face to face encounter in natural setting Large amounts of data obtained High interaction with respondents Access to follow-up clarification Wide range of data possible Many possibilities for informants Discovery of many possible relationships and interconnections Data on nonverbal behavior and communication Data on unconscious thoughts and behaviors Useful in triangulation Possibilities for validity checks Allows for emerging designs and data Provides contextual background	Missed data Misinterpretation possible Relies on cooperation of subjects Ethical dilemmas Success depends on researcher Difficult to replicate Possible observer effects on observees Discomfort in observer Bias by researcher possible
Indepth Interviews	Face to face encounter Facilitates cooperation in research Access for probing and follow-up Discovery of possible interconnetions Useful for validity checks, triangulation Flexibility in formulation of hypotheses Provides contextual background	Misinterpretation possible Requires training Requires respondent cooperation Difficult to replicate Subject to researcher effects Discomfort to researcher Depends on interviewee honesty Highly dependent on researcher's abilities Obtrusive and reactive
Unobtrusive Measures	Data easy to analyze Wide range of types of data Easy and efficient to administer Easily quantifiable Natural setting Good for nonverbal behavior Measuring devices may exist Provides for flexibility	Possible misinterpretations Ethical dilemmas May require expensive equipment Depends on initial research question Dependent on researcher's ability
Content Analysis/ Hermeneutics	Data easy to categorize Can use large amounts of data Can be flexible with data Wide range of types of data Easy and efficient to use Easy to generalize Good for documenting major events Validity checks can be done Flexibility in hypotheses Can get at subjective side	Possible misinterpretation Depends on initial research question Minimal interaction with participants

Chapter 4

Field Research and Participant Observation

Introduction

Field research and participant observation are names given to the method that simultaneously combines observing and informal interviewing with the focus on developing an insider's view of what happened that can be described to outsiders. Patton (1980b) has argued that participant observation is the most comprehensive of the qualitative methods. Field research is research that involves social interaction between the researcher and informants in the milieu of the latter, during which data are systematically and relatively unobtrusively collected (Taylor and Bogdan, 1984). A researcher may also use other nonreactive methods such as document analysis and introspection along with field observations.

The extent to which *full* participation by the researcher in any setting is possible will vary. It is difficult to be a participant and a scientist simultaneously. A fine line exists between learning the actor's perspective and being able to transcend it with scientific perspective (Schwartz and Jacobs, 1979). The assumptions of participant observation and field research are that one can share in the subject's world, directly participate in the subject's symbolic world, and take a role in the subject's interaction. The role, however, requires both detachment and personal involvement (Bruyn, 1966). The scientific role is interdependent with the social role and reflects the social process of being in society.

From a phenomenological perspective, participant observation/field research is deliberately unstructured to maximize the discovery/verification of theory (Denzin, 1978). A constant movement between conceptualization of reality and empirical observations occurs. Douglas (1976) has described the strategies for field research initially as defocusing or immersion, maintaining an interaction, and understanding the situation. This immersion includes understanding in the subject's or member's terms, testing for understanding, member review, checking, and refocusing.

Advantages and Drawbacks

Many advantages exist for using field research or participant observation. The method is directed toward studying subtle nuances of attitudes and behaviors and for examining social processes over time. Its value lies in the depth of understanding as evident in the interaction occurring in everyday experiences. Other advantages of the method are its flexibility, relatively inexpensiveness (you only need a pen and notebook, but lots of time), and superior validity. Blumer used the metaphor of describing participant observation as, "Lifting the veils that cover the area of group life that one wishes to study." (1969, p. 39). Lifting those veils requires a great deal of creativity on the part of the field researcher; thus, the method may be both extremely exciting and incredibly frightening.

Ellis and Williams described the value of this method of research compared to experiments and traditional correlational studies by stating that it "permits the investigator to focus more closely on change across time, the context within which the change occurs, and the nature of the causes or conditions associated with the change" (1987, p. 20). Glancy (1986) used participant observation in her studies of adult play behavior. She felt the value of the method was in determining meaning structures, how they develop, and how they influence behavior in a comprehensive and objective fashion. *See Exemplar 4.1*

> Exemplar 4.1 Glancy, M. (1986). Participant observation in a recreation setting. *Journal of Leisure Research, 18*(2), 59-80.
>
> Glancy reports the exploratory use of participant observation as a direct method of scientific observation for examining the social-psychological context of recreational sport group membership. The article focuses primarily on the techniques used in the participant observation method. The bibliography that is presented is comprehensive and would be very useful to anyone wishing to use participant observation in a study in the area of recreation, parks, and leisure. Her justification for using this method along with an explication of the limitations were clear and informative. Glancy described how she started out with a guiding hypothesis that ended up being rejected by the end of the study. She described in some detail how she became a member of the group and how her field data were recorded in an unobtrusive manner. Glancy also described how she learned to be a participant observer by trial and error in this study. She shared a variety of techniques used to summarize data, locate patterns, trace conceptual links, and adjust or reform her working models. Glancy suggested that the participant observation method may be useful particularly in answering lifestage, family, and peer-group questions.

Another advantage of field research/participant observation is that the persons studied are the experts, not merely the subjects (Spindler, 1982). These experts, which are also referred to as "members," are the sources of all data. They do not realize the extent of their own cultural knowledge and social behavior; therefore, the researcher helps them to understand where this knowledge is unclear or ambiguous so that it can be better described and interpreted by the researcher.

Participant observation should allow the field researcher to step outside her/his own narrow cultural background and ethnocentricism to apprehend the world from the viewpoint of other human beings who live by different meaning systems (Spradley, 1979). This setting aside of one's cultural background was clearly true for us in the study we did of the meaning found in a Women's Week camp (Henderson and Bialeschki, 1987). We spent a week at a camp in northern Wisconsin with 100 women, many of whom had little background in camping and who felt their primary role in life was wife/mother except for that week at camp. To hear them speak about their lives and the meaning of the experiences they were having at camp provided a whole new insight to the leisure and lives of women that was certainly outside my background of being an avid outdoor participant with few day to day familial obligations. *See Exemplar 4.2*

> Exemplar 4.2 Henderson, K.A. and Bialeschki, M.D. (1987). A qualitative evaluation of a women's week experience. *The Journal of Experiential Education, 10*(2), 25-28.
>
> Henderson and Bialeschki described the study they undertook of a five day Women's Week where they used primarily participant observations to analyze the experiences of the women at the camp. The information about method and the data presented in this article are not extensive due to the nature of the *Journal of Experiential Education*. The article does, however, provide some insight concerning how data may be collected and how they may be presented as evaluation information. The observations in this study were triangulated with precamp telephone interviews and three month follow-up questionnaires. The authors described the values of participant observation as they used the method in this outdoor setting. They also presented findings concerning the perceptions that the women had of this camp and the aspects that made the experience a success.

Disadvantages also exist in the field research/participant observation method. The closeness to people involves attention to the minutia of daily life through direct contact over a period of time. This method of research requires a lot of time. Patton's analogy said it best: "A couple of nights of fieldwork is to a full qualitative study what a 'one-night stand' is to mutually satisfying and deeply intimate lovemaking" (1980b, p. 223). Participant observation is no quick and easy study.

Limitations exist in choosing field research just as with any other method. It is simply not suited for some problems. For example, I may wish to examine the pervasiveness of "sex as leisure" within a committed relationship. It would be very difficult to conduct field research on such a topic. While the validity and reliability of other methods might also be questioned, obviously one cannot conduct field research to answer this question. Some problems have a limited domain of analysis and can be better answered by a mailed questionnaire or by document analysis than by field research.

Field research also has been criticized for not yielding precise descriptions, providing suggestive rather than definitive conclusions, having questionable reliability, and lacking generalization. Hopefully, the researcher will see the ways that these criticisms can be mitigated through the application of appropriate research techniques, but it is important to realize that for some positivists, field research may seem antithetical to the traditional understanding of scientific method.

Criteria for Field Research

A graduate student at the University of Wisconsin used the metaphor of swimming to describe how he felt about participant observation (Turner, 1983). He noted that as a field researcher you undertake participant observations by swimming out into the lake of everyday life. Sometimes the water feels warm and sometimes it is very cold. As you get further from the shore, you feel like there may be no bottom to the water. You need to swim fast enough to keep your head above water but not too fast that you become exhausted. Various strokes may affect you differently. You are all alone except for the lake. After awhile it is necessary for you to conclude your swim and you wonder, did I swim long enough? Did I go far enough away from the shore? Field research/participant observation is like taking a swim or a series of swims and then determining when it is time to move on to something else.

Field researchers use a variety of data sources including field notes, tape recordings, artifacts, records, and anything else that will be helpful in understanding the culture or activity that is being studied. Field research/participant observation is not a single method and is not used to gather a single kind of information; researchers use multiple sources and multiple resources (Patton, 1980b). Researchers are concerned with what people say, why people act, the artifacts people use (Spradley, 1979), and how these data converge (Fielding and Fielding, 1986). Researchers study "social occasions" by seeing what people do and use informal interviews for contriving other occasions that one may not be able to see (Denzin, 1978).

Gorden (1975) reminded researchers that the type of field settings may vary greatly from hostile to friendly, open to guarded, and single to multiple contacts which all affect what we "learn" in the research. Rather than studying people, field researchers are actually learning from them. The actual doing of the field work is really a process of the researcher being socialized. The researcher adopts the role as "learner" (Lofland and Lofland, 1984) and being a learner is one of the aspects that makes field research/participant observation so interesting and exciting.

Spindler (1982) suggested several criteria that can set the stage for doing field research or ethnographies: direct observation, sufficient time, volume of recorded data, evolving character of the study, instrumentation, quantification, object of study, and selective holism and conceptualization.

Direct observation is the most important component of field research. The specific techniques of observation will be discussed later in this chapter but the criteria suggests that field researchers have opportunities for prolonged observation and interaction. The researcher should keep in mind that many dimensions of people's behavior and interactions must be considered. The data are broad and diverse and need to be collected in a face-to-face manner. In direct observation, the researcher must also be aware of the influence she/he may have on the actions and behaviors of others.

As was mentioned earlier, but cannot be stressed enough, sufficient time is necessary to spend in conducting a field research/participant observation study. Spindler (1982) suggested the time spent should be at least a year but depending upon the problem, this amount of time may not be necessary. The researcher must stay long enough to get a complete picture, and must reach the point where no new data are being generated and when enough consistency exists that grounded theory may emerge. For example, Smith (1985) spent three months visiting a "rough" working class pub to help him understand the leisure of the people there. In other cases, the amount of time spent may be reflective of a phenomenon. For example, Glancy (1986) observed an adult softball team for a season. This seemed to be long enough to gather data, but in this case, if data had not been sufficient, it might have been necessary for her to return to the same team or a similar team the following season. The validity of the qualitative approach is also dependent on the quality of time spent in the field. Those field researchers who stay at a site longer are generally able to get more sensitive and indepth information.

Related to time spent is the volume of recorded data. Data in the form of field notes are collected by the researcher on the site and then organizing and examining off the site. One of the problems of qualitative research can be the overwhelming amount of data that are discovered. Various techniques exist for managing the data as are described in Chapter 8, but it must first be appropriately collected. In discovering the data, deep access is needed. The data do not consist of just a few questions or talking to a couple of people. Observing and talking to different people and using different types of data will enable the researcher to get the greatest volume of data to use for interpretation. Triangulation may be used to check the consistency of the data sources, theories, or researchers. Not only does triangulation provide more data, but it is a plan of action that will raise researchers above personal biases that stem from single methodologies. Thus, using triangulation may help to increase generalizability of the interpretation as well as assure that the appropriate data in sufficient amounts have been collected.

Field research/participant observation is as much a style of inquiry as a method. Therefore, the evolving character of the research study is essential. In one sense, as Schwartz and Jacobs suggested (1979), the field researcher needs to make a familiar world look strange. At the same time, it is necessary to help the informants understand their world better. All observations are contextual and this is a primary dimension of this research method. The hypotheses emerge from the situation being studied. Roadburg (1980) had the experience of helping people to contextualize their situation. Roadburg studied the meanings of work and leisure held by amateur and professional soccer players in Scotland. Through his observations and informal interviewing, he helped these players to understand their attitudes and so they could then make their perceptions more clear to Roadburg. *See Exemplar 4.3*

Exemplar 4.3 Roadburg, A. (1983). Freedom and enjoyment: Disentangling perceived leisure. *Journal of Leisure Research,* *15*(1), 15-26.

Roadburg used the participant observation method with professional and amateur soccer players and gardeners to identify why something is work or leisure. He followed this with open-ended interviews with elderly people to test the working hypotheses developed in the participant observation. He hypothesized about why an activity is leisure to some people and work to others. He felt the use of people's own words would provide the most information about what is work and what is leisure. Roadburg described little about his methodology but he has written other articles that describe in more detail how his data were collected (cf. Roadburg, 1980). He described his method of participant observation as it was clearly linked to the findings. The conclusions developed suggested that freedom is a necessary but not sufficient condition for leisure. To experience leisure, Roadburg found that one must experience enjoyment.

The instrumentation used in participant observation is primarily the researcher although some paper and pencil instruments or checklists may be developed for the specific site or may be used to collect information more efficiently. Because the researcher is the instrument, it is necessary to develop trust in order to get the most valid information from those being observed. This attention to validity raises the question of bias in the research. Does empathy result in sympathy (Johnson, 1975), and does this create problems? The validity of the data hinges on achieving that delicate balance of distance and closeness that characterizes effective interaction between the researcher and the member or subject. Technical devices such as tape recordings or video recordings may help the researcher, but they will be no substitute for the researcher as the primary data collection instrument.

Quantification may be used in field research to analyze some data, but numbers are supplementary to words which are the primary symbols for qualitative interpretation. For example, a researcher may count the occurrences of certain types of behavior from time to time. One must, however, be careful to use counting in appropriate ways and not to let quantification become the only means of observing or reporting data.

The object of study must also be kept in mind. The member or the "native" is the primary focus of the research and that individual's knowledge is referred to as "emic" knowledge. For the study to be useful as more than just a great story about a group of people, however, the "etic" knowledge of the researcher must be applied to develop grounded theory and to test and generate theoretical propositions. For example, in the study of a women's week at a camp with which I was involved, the emic knowledge from several of the women was that they were very anxious about the whitewater raft trip that was to be taken. They were able to describe a number of reasons why. In observing many of them on the river that day, the researchers were able to develop etic knowledge about how the women coped with the anxiety and how it appeared to relate back to how they, in fact, coped with anxiety in other aspects of their lives (Henderson and Bialeschki, 1987). The researcher must always be careful to distinguish between emic and etic data especially when recording field notes as well as when reporting the conclusions of the research to others. The researcher should keep in mind that this field observation method goes beyond journalistic reporting and anecdotal or impressionistic story-telling, although these aspects are also components of the method. As Werner and Schoepfle (1987) suggested, the difference between ethnography/field research and journalism is that journalists look for the unusual whereas ethnographers are focused on the "everyday" experience.

A field researcher must always be concerned about the member's view of reality or the inner perspective. The best field research uses care in using the native's language and not putting words in the individual's mouth. Spoken language occupies a large part of human experience and language is the tool used for field research. Sometimes the behavior or language is implicit or tacit and it is the researcher's role to try to make it explicit. One must be careful to observe between facts and interpretation and must use the emic as well as the etic.

Selective holism and conceptualization are used to make sense of the field work. In an everyday situation, obviously everything can not be observed or reported. Thus, the researcher must learn to focus on the emerging design. The use of a transcultural, comparative perspective is evident in well done field research. This perspective adds to the focus on the whole, and what meaning exists in a particular context.

Observation in General

It takes practice to become a good observer. Many of us take observation for granted or do not realize the extent to which we have learned to be selective in what we observe. To be a good field researcher, one has to overcome years of selective inattention and learn all over again how to watch, listen, concentrate, and above all, how to interpret data apart from gathering data. Observation is a skill that requires training and supervision. Just as most of us were not inherently blessed with the ability to do statistics without being taught and given chances to improve upon our mathematical and analytical abilities, field researchers must also be taught observational techniques and given opportunities to practice them.

In observation, the researcher as the instrument, must be the reliable and valid measurer. An effective observer must be trained to notice events and actions that are relevant to one's conceptions as well as those that contradict the conceptions. Field research takes enormous amounts of energy to look beyond one's ordinary day to day observations to apply the rigor of scientific inquiry and interpretation.

Part of good observation is learning what to observe. It is impossible to observe everything and even if one could, it would result in total sensory overload. Therefore, observation becomes more and more focused as the field researcher continues with her/his work on a particular study. The purposes of collecting observation data are to describe the setting observed, the activities, the people, and the meaning. For example, Bullock (1985a, 1985b) employed participant observation effectively in describing the overall experience of mentally retarded children who were put in a play situation with nonmentally retarded children.

The observations must be factual, accurate, and thorough. In observing descriptively, one may want to acknowledge the context which includes the setting, the human social environment, and the units of activity. Everything that goes on around an activity are data that may be useful (Patton, 1980b). The successful observer will be able to observe aspects that have escaped conscious awareness. Ultimately, the observations should result in a written report that will allow the reader to actually enter the situation and understand what was happening based on detailed descriptions. All observations are ultimately observations of theoretical constructs but it is essential that the researcher relates these constructs directly to the actual observations.

The value of observations are obvious. They build on direct experiences, give the sense of "I was there," are especially helpful when subjects are not as verbal as we would like them to be, do not necessarily require the cooperation of subjects, and the researcher can be used as a data source in her/his own reaction to an event that is observed (Guba and Lincoln, 1981). Little (1985) for example, used direct observation along with interviews to describe the conflict resolution that occurred in the planning of a community recreation event. Campbell (1970) used observation for several weeks in a campground to examine depreciative behavior (i.e., littering, nuisance violations, vandalism).

Cautions also surround pure observation. Concerns such as reactivity to the setting, the manifestation of too much personal interpretation, biases associated with becoming too "native", deceptive observations, and the researcher taking meanings for granted are possible in any type of observation. Without prolonged observation in a setting, it is difficult to see all that one needs to see. There is also the possibility that through observation the researcher may be changing the nature of the setting in which she/he becomes a part. The researcher's mere presence may create a changed situation; therefore, it is imperative that observations continue over a prolonged time to improve the validity of the study. One also must be in touch with how a particular study may have changed the biases of the researcher over time. When the researcher spends a great deal of time with individuals, they may become friends and this may affect the interpretations the researcher will make concerning the study. Despite these cautions, the field research/participant observation method which uses observation as well as informal interviews and other means, provides a way to integrate words and deeds and to get useful information from observing recreation, parks, and leisure settings.

Kinds of Observations

Observation may occur in different ways. A number of researchers have identified some of these kinds of observations. Spradley (1980) described grand tour observation in which one identifies the major features of a phenomena compared to mini-tour observations where a smaller unit of experience is observed. For example, Glancy (1988) employed mini-tour observations in her examination of auctions where she specifically focused on the concept of play as it related to other facets that might be examined related to auctions. Another way to think about observation is as a funnel or an inverted funnel. In the funnel, one takes in many observations and then narrows the focus. In the inverted funnel, one may observe one type of behavior and then broaden it to examine the context in which it is occurring. The direction of the funnel may depend on whether discovery or verification is desired, the cooperation of the members, and the *a priori* structures that exist (Guba and Lincoln, 1981). In general, observation usually begins with a wide focused descriptive observation, moves to focused observation, and then, finally, to selective observations. In Hutchinson's deductive (1987) study of 13 neighborhood and regional parks in Chicago to examine the racial variation in leisure and recreation activities, he moved from broad observations to more focused observations as the research questions began to narrow.

The most common kinds of observation falls on continua from nonreactive to reactive, unobtrusive to obtrusive, complete observer to complete participant, and covert to overt (Patton, 1980b). Depending on the extremes of each continuum, the research outcomes may be affected. A nonreactive observer might remove herself/ himself completely from involvement. An example of nonreactive observation might be someone analyzing the way the leisure behavior of women is portrayed on

TV by watching TV or someone observing behavior from behind a one-way mirror. Unobtrusive observers, similarly, try to be as invisible as possible and seek to elicit very little reaction to the researcher from the individuals being observed.

A complete participant systematically reflects on her/his involvement after an activity is over and writes a diary or reaction. For example, Dustin (1988) as a complete participant finished a 100 mile run and then described his experience and his new found understanding of himself as a result of that experience. Most field research, however, is conducted by using some dimension of observer as participant or participant as observer. In the observer as participant, the role may be infused with watching and engagement in discussion, indepth interviews, and eavesdropping.

The type of observer ranges from unknown observer (covert) to known (overt) observer. The covert observer becomes a group member and in essence is posing as a spy. The overt observer is an outsider who makes her/his intentions clear. The known researcher does not try to pass as anything but known. It is difficult to say which type of observation is best. Covert research may get better results because the researcher may have less effect on the situation, but there is the issue of ethics which is important to consider. As noted above, overt and covert research is on a continuum. For example, a researcher may make herself/himself known to a group but may not inform the group fully as to what is being researched. In many cases, the extent of disclosure by the researcher may be minimal but in other cases the researcher may be better to give as much information as possible. The problems of covert research are discussed more fully in Chapter 11. For now, the researcher may want to acknowledge the possible problems with unknown observation including the invasion of privacy of people and what may happen to the research if one is "found out" and the observed individuals are unhappy about having been observed.

What behaviors are observed and how they are observed are also components of observation. Stumbo (1983) has identified four types of observational techniques that can be used in addition to ethnographic notetaking: checklists, rating scales, anecdotal records, and critical incidents. Checklists and rating scales tend to be more quantitative than qualitative. They also assume a priori factors to be identified. Other similar methods include frequency counts and duration recordings. These may be useful, for example, in observing activities done in classrooms, in therapeutic recreation settings, or for the recording of specific behaviors in the outdoors. Stumbo (1983) believes that in therapeutic recreation there is a great need to develop systematic observation instruments in order to more reliably assess behaviors. The systematic observations usually include a checklist or a standardized form with a unit of analysis identified. The more structured an observation, the more likely analysis will involve scoring and statistical analysis (Denzin, 1978).

Anecdotal records and critical incidents provide an ongoing chronicle of behaviors. In some cases the researcher may be able to take notes as an event occurs and in other cases the notes will have to be taken in one's head and recorded as soon as possible. These incident observations must be specific, systematic, and accurate.

Anecdotal records provide factual descriptions which are separate from interpretations. In field work, these are the primary data used. Critical incidents are situations recorded that provide unusual or significant data. An interpretation based on the observation is used to analyze the antecedent framework and the consequences of behavior (Stumbo, 1983). The challenge of critical incident observations is that one must spend a lot of time in a setting in order to know what is usual verses what is unusual; therefore, anecdotal records or field notes in the long run may be just as useful as critical incident reports. Critical incident reports must be grounded in the interaction that occurs within a particular context. Levy (1982) and Avedon (1984) described the need for observations in therapeutic recreation settings related to interaction processes. Lewko, Bullock, and Austin (1978), for example, observed the relationships between counselors and children with disabilities in an organized camp setting in order to analyze the interactions.

Observing involves nonverbal behavior, as well as verbal interactions. The study of signification whereby objects related to nonverbal behavior connote meaning may be useful and may greatly add to the understanding of social contexts. Guba and Lincoln (1981) described several branches of nonverbal behavior: kinesics (body movement), proxemics (spatial relationships), synchrony (rhythmical relation of sender and receiver), chronemics (use of time such as pacing, pausing), paralinguistics (extraverbal elements of speech such as volume, quality, accent, tone), and haptics (touching). Researchers are cautioned not to use nonverbal behavior only in most types of observations, but aspects of nonverbal behavior can provide useful data. Nonverbal behavior can be described and related to verbal behavior and may be interpreted based on awareness levels and the immediacy, status, and importance that may be attributed to verbal interactions.

We have alluded to the types of data that may be collected in observations. In all cases the researcher is looking for accurate, reliable, valid data. Denzin (1978) suggested that a reliable observation is one that is not biased by idiosyncrasies of either the observer, the research instrument, the subject, or by the constraints of time and place. A valid observation is one that is theoretically directed and is grounded in the actual behavior of interacting individuals.

In making observations within the qualitative approach, one may want to consider noting a short biographical history, the dress of participants, the particular speech or behavior patterns, nonverbal gestures, the period of observation, situation or settings, salient social objects acted upon, relationship of one actor to another, and/or the rules of conduct displayed (Denzin, 1978). The observational units may include time and its passage, social situations, social occasions, social relationships, attitudes, and the interactions that occur around these aspects. What one wishes to study will determine the appropriate observations.

All observations have in common, therefore, descriptive note-taking, gathering a variety of information, cross-validating emerging patterns, representing people on their own terms, reporting objective experiences, and separating description from interpretation (Patton, 1980b). As mentioned before, it takes practice to become good at observation and conducting field research. Practicing descriptive recording and note-taking, learning how to separate detail from trivia, and using rigorous methods to validate data are all ways that we become better observers and thus, better qualitative researchers.

What Does a Field Researcher Do?

The best way to learn to do participant observation is "just do it." While there are a number of excellent examples of field research that a novice researcher ought to read, the only way that one becomes accomplished as a field researcher and participant observer is by actually trying it. Each field situation will be different and each individual will have a different experience. Patton described what a field researcher does using Halcom's Evaluation Laws:

> A field researcher should be able to sweep the floor, carry out the garbage, carry in the laundry, cook for large groups, go without food and sleep, read and write by candlelight, see in the dark, see in the light, cooperate without offending, suppress sarcastic remarks, smile to express both pain and hurt, experience both pain and hurt, spend time alone, respond to others, take sides, stay neutral, take risks, avoid harm, be confused, care terribly, become attached to nothing...the nine-to-five set need not apply (1980b, p. 119).

Being a participant observer or a field researcher in not an easy task. It is difficult to play the role of a group member without becoming involved at some point. Although more details are covered about taking notes and sampling in Chapter 8, a few strategies for the field researcher to consider will be described here.

Getting Established at a Site

The field researcher generally has in mind a site where the participant observation will be conducted. It is necessary to gain permission to do the investigation from the "gatekeeper" of the site. This permission may involve a disclosure of the research in a thorough way. The issue of ethics concerning disclosure will need to be addressed. The known investigator is able to move about, observe, and or ask questions in a relatively unrestricted way and note-taking is not problematic. Different levels of explanation of a participant observer's presence, however, may be necessary in order to facilitate the potential for observation (Fine, 1980). In other words, the researcher may fully disclose the project to the gatekeeper but may provide only partial explanation to the members to be observed if their full knowledge may affect the outcomes of the study.

The beginning period for a field researcher is often a difficult time. Fear is often associated with the field experience. The researcher will sometimes feel stupid and anxious and frequently wonder why in the world she/he ever embarked upon such a research study. Some fear is grounded while other fears are baseless. The best field researchers tell about their initial fears in getting started (e.g., Wax, 1971), so you should not worry if you are not sure initially that you can do all that may be required of you as a field researcher. Immersing oneself, gaining membership, assuming a native identity, and role playing are not necessarily daily activities with which most of us are familiar.

At the field site, it will be necessary to establish some sort of role. You may choose to be a participant, a staff member, or something in between. For example, Hunter (1987) described how he collected data on the wilderness experience of adolescent boys. He chose neither to be a leader nor a participant, but just someone who was along for the trip. His role seemed relatively normal and little mention was made of his role because he never demanded anything from the particpants, he performed the normal tasks that everyone else did, and he was unobtrusive in his observation and interviewing roles. Many roles are possible to choose in most any situation including those of supervisor, leader, observer, or friend. The role may affect one's ability to gain acceptance within a group or with particular individuals so the role should be carefully chosen. No matter what role is used, as an observer one must be explicitly aware, use a "wide-angle viewing lens," take the insider/outsider perspective, be introspective oneself, and keep good records of both one's objective and subjective feelings. Patton (1980b) suggested that what the researcher does rather than what the researcher says will determine how people will respond.

Establishing rapport in the field site will be an important early aspect of the field research. Taylor and Bogdan (1984) offered several tips for establishing social interaction including: Remain passive in the first few days, put people at ease in whatever ways you can such as doing favors or helping out, collect data as secondary to getting to know people, act naive, pay attention to people's routines, explain who you are to the people, explain what will be done with the data (people are often particularly sympathetic to graduate students working on a thesis), try to figure out what being at the right place at the right time means, begin with small amounts of time and then increase the time at the site, and keep your overt notetaking to a minimum initially and adjust to more visible notetaking as you and the participants feel comfortable later. Above all, the field researcher should act interested and the people being observed will see that she/he is serious about them and the project being undertaken. The researcher needs to try to be open to everything and forget her/his preconceived notions. The field researcher should initially strive to identify with the lives, hopes, and pain of the individuals from whom she/he is learning.

Doing Field Research/Participant Observation

Once you, as the researcher, have established rapport or developed trust, which may take a little or a lot of time depending on the situation, then you can begin the systematic data collection. As will be discussed in Chapter 8, however, the "serious" data collection should begin the moment you decide on a site as you document the process and the procedure that you use to make contact and to get started. Data discovery will involve getting close enough to the people, perceiving the facts of the situation, getting pure description with little interpretation initially, and collecting direct quotations.

Beware, however, of getting too close to the participants and especially to one or two people early on. This idea of getting too close is referred to as "going native." It is important to become a "regular" but the research should not be invalidated because of biases that may develop in becoming too close. If too much time is being spent as a participant and not as an observer, perhaps the research should be restructured. While the value of this qualitative method is the analysis of interaction that can occur, a drawback is the possibility of losing some sense of objectivity in data collection and analysis. In some situations, becoming too close to some people may alienate others or put one in a competitive situation. You do not want to take sides if there are factions within an organization. On the other hand, it is impossible to treat everyone equally and the researcher has to do the best job that she/he can to remain objective in data collection. It is best to try to adopt the perspective of those being studied and to use the degree of participation that will yield the most meaningful data about the phenomena being studied given the characteristics of the situation. It is sometimes difficult to be a complete participant as Campbell (1970) found in studying camping behavior. Campbell found it was difficult to let the depreciative behavior in the park (i.e., vandalism and littering) that was being observed go on, let alone participate in it. As a field researcher one does need to know where to draw the line in terms of involvement.

Field research is an ongoing process of data discovery and interpretation. The researcher may go to the field with some general questions in mind but these will change and become redefined as one observes and interacts with people. As a researcher, you may find yourself becoming resocialized as you participate (Wax, 1971). In other words, you will develop new insights and new ways of obtaining information as you discover new data. It is important that this resocialization is allowed to happen. The researcher must also keep in the mind the effect that she/he is having on the nature of the interactions that are occurring. One should be continually aware of not only the words and actions at the site but be sensitive as well to the possible value of a wide range of supplementary information which may become evident (Lofland and Lofland, 1984).

Field research requires a high level of concentration to pay attention to what is happening. If the researcher cannot take notes immediately, it really requires concentration to imprint the notes in mental photography. The observer must look for key words in people's remarks, concentrate on the first and last remarks of each conversation because those are generally the most important, and be able to play back the observation or conversation easily in one's mind.

If note-taking is not possible on the spot, it may be a good rule of thumb to leave the field setting as soon as you have observed as much as you can remember.

Always record your notes as soon as possible after observing. In recalling, walk through the experience in your mind and reconstruct the conversations and comments. Use a tape recorder if that helps you remember, but be sure to transcribe as soon as possible. It is quite appropriate to add in snippets of data that may occur to you after the initial writing of the field notes.

Key Informants

A final, but not unimportant, aspect of field research is the utilization of key informants. Respondents are people who answer questions with no particular rapport necessarily having been established, actors are those persons that we observe, but key informants are people who provide more indepth information about what is occurring because the researcher has established an element of trust with them. Information is usually obtained from key informants by either formal or informal interviews. One way to regard these informants is as "research collaborators." They help to interpret the research and give us the emic language of the participants as opposed to the etic language of the social scientist. The value of key informants is in helping the researcher see if people say what they mean and mean what they say. The key informants should be "veterans" of the organization, currently involved, unfamiliar with the academic theoretical cultural scene, have adequate time, and be nonanalytical (Spradley, 1979).

Key informants may be used in several ways and, as is true in other aspects of the qualitative approach, firm rules for general situations can not be standardized. Some informants may have general information about the past and their perceptions of the present, others may be representative of a group of people, and others may serve as observers when one is not there and may report events at a later date to the researcher. Taylor and Bogdan (1984) suggested that the researcher should develop a key informant relationship with half the people observed. These relationships will help the researcher develop a deeper understanding of the setting and she/he can use these people as a reality check for emerging themes, hunches, and hypotheses. It is important that key informants are not selected too soon in the field research process but that one has a good sense of the setting before establishing these relationships. One must avoid letting the informants control the research.

Sometimes the researcher will run into hostile respondents and informants. These people should be given a chance to "come around." The researcher needs to be friendly but not pushy. The researcher may want to employ some additional investigative skills to determine why the lack of cooperation is occurring. At times it may feel like you as the researcher are walking a tightrope, but that is the nature of this method of research. It is often common that the field researcher must talk to people that she/he dislikes, distrusts, or despises. It is necessary to talk to all types and not just to the people that one likes. Talking to only people that you like will result in an elite bias or an overconcentration on some respondents (Fielding and Fielding, 1986). The researcher needs to try to understand even those things that she/he may not want to hear. The researcher needs to make the initial questions broad and give people a chance to discuss what is on their minds. One must discern what not to ask until it is appropriate and how to ask sensitive questions. The field researcher's questions will become more focused and directive as she/he becomes more comfortable in the field situation.

Field research/participant observation requires a complete commitment to the task of understanding. The researcher may never be the same again as a result of the field experience. In field work, many serendipitous, unanticipated discoveries occur not only about the data but also about oneself and social interactions.

Summary

This chapter has provided an introduction to the qualitative method of field research which is also referred to as participant observation and sometimes ethnography. The method consists of going into the field and learning about social reality through observation, participation, and informal interviewing. The advantages and disadvantages of the method are described along with principles of observation and how one goes about doing field research. Field research is really not one method but a combination of techniques that are applied to obtaining data in a natural setting.

The key concepts discussed in this chapter were: field research, ethnography, participant observation, emic, etic, anecdotal records, critical incidents, nonverbal behavior, key informants.

For Further Consideration

1. Practice observation skills by unobtrusively observing people involved in some recreational activity. Write down everything that you notice for a period of 20 minutes.

2. Engage someone in a conversation for 10-15 minutes. Try to concentrate on everything that is being said. Then write down, in as much detail as possible, what was said. Practice listening and observing the details and not just making interpretations from what people say. You may wish to tape record the conversation so that you can go back and check the accuracy of what you heard.

3. Describe the advantages and disadvantages of conducting a research study using field research.

4. Think of three research problems that could be answered by the use of the field research method. How would you go about designing a study to answer any one of these questions? How will you "get in" to do the field research.

For Further Reading

For those researchers who would like further information about this method, consult the following literature:

McCall, C.J., and Simmons, J.L. (Eds.) (1969). *Issues in participant observation.* **Reading, MA: Addison-Wesley.**

McCall and Simmons provide a variety of chapters that address some of the techniques and issues that arise in doing participant observation. While many researchers since 1969 have applied the techniques suggested in this text, this book still provides a basis and justification for participant observation.

Patton, M. Q. (1980). *Qualitative evaluation methods.* **Beverly Hills, CA: Sage Publications.**

Patton provides a useful reference for anyone considering any number of methods of qualitative research and evaluation. He provides a thorough discussion of how to conduct field research (evaluation) and interviews. Useful examples of a practical nature are provided as well. The reader will want to refer to Patton's book for a number of topics relevant to the discussion of qualitative methods.

Spradley, J.P. (1980). *Participant observation.* **New York, NY: Holt, Rinehart, and Winston.**

Spradley has devoted an entire book to how to do participant observation. He provides some justification for the method but spends most of the time developing the steps that are involved from getting into the situation to the final writing of a report. Spradley offers a useful perspective on data analysis and provides a rigorous approach to conducting field research.

Taylor, S.J., and Bogdan, R. (1984). *Introduction to qualitative research methods: The search for meaning* **(2nd ed.). New York, NY: John Wiley and Sons.**

Taylor and Bogdan have had numerous opportunities to conduct qualitative research studies in sociological areas. They offer a useful practical approach to the methods that a researcher will want to use in doing field research or indepth interviewing. The examples from their own research provide the reader with a basis for seeing how methods can be applied.

Whyte, W.F. (1984). *Learning from the field.* **Beverly Hill, CA: Sage Publications.**

Whyte has sometimes been referred to as the father of field research. In this book he summarizes his 50 years of work and offers strategies that have worked for him. He addresses such topics as the rationale and roles of participant observation, planning the project, field relations, observational methods, team research, using social history, and ethics. Whyte's use of personal recollections from his research makes the opportunities and challenges of doing field research come to life.

Chapter 5

Indepth Interviewing

Indepth interviewing has many exciting possibilities for discovery of qualitative data. Interviewing is the best method for pursuing a subject indepth, operating in a discovery mode, and creating interaction with an individual. Leisure researchers frequently rely on verbal accounts to learn about social life since it is impossible to "be there" for some individual or community events that may occur. The interview may take on many forms ranging from highly structured questions to open-ended questions. Interviewing may occur as a part of field research as in interviewing key informants or it may be used as a singular qualitative method to obtain general data. Interviews may be focused on a particular topic or may, as in the case of life history, involve hours and hours of conversation. The focus of this chapter is on the use of indepth interviewing as a qualitative method. The guidelines pertaining to asking questions, however, may also be useful in the interviewing of key informants in participant observation. While specific suggestions are given for interviewing, the researcher must keep in mind what Dexter suggested, "to reduce interviewing to a set of techniques is ... like reducing courtship to a formula (1970, p. 110). Many ways exist for conducting interviews.

The purpose of interviews is to find out what is on people's minds and to access the perspective of others. A researcher, according to Patton (1980b), cannot observe feelings, thoughts, and intentions, previous behaviors, or how people organize the world. We cannot always be there to observe what happens, so we rely on people's accounts. The indepth interview also provides data for translating research hypotheses into grounded theory.

Choosing to Use Interviewing

Indepth interviewing can be expensive, time consuming, biased, and sometimes inefficient, but the method also provides some of the richest data that we can find. Indepth interviews are hard to pretest, have unpredictable results because different people tend to respond differently, and are difficult to standardize and replicate. On the other hand, they also offer many advantages in allowing the researcher to have a greater understanding of the complexities of social reality from a number of perspectives. For example, Woodward, Green, and Hebron (1988) provided a thought-provoking rationale for how interviewing was one of the most effective ways to learn about the meaning of leisure in women's lives. *See Exemplar 5.1*

> Exemplar 5.1 Woodward, D., Green, E., and Hebron, S. (1988). The Sheffield study of gender and leisure: Its methodological approach. *Leisure Studies*, 7, 95-101.
>
> Woodward and her colleagues suggested that since women have been underrepresented in the leisure literature, a variety of methods might be applied to studying them. They described their study done for the Sports Council of Great Britain. In this study both quantitative questionnaires and semi-structured interviews were used to gain breadth and depth in the research. The individuals selected for interviewing had originally completed mailed surveys. The interviews with women were intensive one hour conversations about leisure histories, daily routines, definitions of leisure, impact of childcare, sexuality, and social control. The interviews with men addressed questions concerning their partner's leisure. The interviews were followed with small discussion groups of women who volunteered from among those who had been interviewed. The authors felt this combination of methods, and particularly the use of qualitative interviews, provided important information. One of the interesting ethical questions raised was how a researcher operating from a feminist perspective was able to explain how the women interviewed could be so sure their oppression was right and justifiable.

Like other methods of research, interviewing is not an easy task. Some people have assumed interviewing is simply common sense so little really needs to be learned about it. While common sense is certainly important, one can learn how to use specific strategies and can practice becoming a better interviewer. The initial establishment of rapport is crucial if the interview is to be successful. The researcher must provide a way for people to respond comfortably, accurately, and honestly. The researcher has to work hard to keep the interviewee motivated and to encourage a flow of useful information. The challenge of interviewing is to unlock the internal perspective of every interviewee (Patton, 1980b).

The researcher, as interviewer, is the research instrument. A bad interview is the fault of the interviewer. If ethnographic indepth interviewing (Spradley, 1979) or qualitative interviewing (Taylor and Bogdan, 1984) are used, the researcher will likely be returning to the interviewee a number of times for face-to-face encounters to check and refocus the data as interviewees describe their lives, experiences, or situations in their own words. This indepth interviewing may take many hours over the course of time and will require focused effort.

As was stated earlier, the choice of the qualitative or quantitative approach is determined by researcher interests, the circumstances of the setting, and practical constraints. The researcher might choose to use indepth interviews if the research interests are relatively clear and well-defined, the setting or people are not otherwise accessible, the researcher has some time constraints, the researcher is depending on a broad range of settings or people, and if the researcher wants to illuminate subjective human experience. As a guided conversation, the researcher tries to elicit from interviewees rich and detailed accounts. The technique requires a great deal of creativity on the part of the interviewer and aims at optimizing cooperation, mutual disclosure, and a search for mutual understanding (Douglas, 1985).

Variations of Interviews

A number of forms of interviewing exist. Patton (1980b) has identified four variations on interview instrumentation that range from purely quantitative to purely qualitative. These include at one end, closed-ended quantitative interviews that are determined in advance with fixed responses. A second variation, called standardized open-ended interviews, uses the exact wording and sequence of questions for each interview although the interviewee may respond in what ever way she/he wishes. The assumption in these interviews is that the researcher already has a sense about the types of information that is to be discovered. Boothby, Tungatt, and Townsend (1981) used standardized open-ended questions along with probes to examine why people ceased participation in sports. *See Exemplar 5.2, page 74.* The interview guide approach, as a third form, uses topics and issues to be covered but does not specify any particular way that the questions should be asked. It provides general areas of questioning but no specific protocol for asking those questions. It can be expanded as additional interviews are conducted and is often useful in team research. Henderson and Rannells (1988) used an interview guide in their study of the meaning of work and leisure for farm women. They had a series of questions that they wanted to cover but asked them as they were appropriate to the progression of the interview. *See Exemplar 5.3, page 74.* The final purely qualitative form is informal conversational interviews in which the questions emerge from the immediate context and are asked in the natural course of the interaction. This interview form sounds more like a conversational exchange than a question and answer exchange and may offer the opportunity to deal with more sensitive issues as those naturally emerge in a conversation. This informal conversational approach requires a lot of time spent with an individual and the interviewer must be able to interact easily. The questions emerge from the interaction (Schwartz and Jacobs, 1979). Aside from the quantitative structured interview, any of the other three would be included as methods within the qualitative approach. The informal conversational form would most likely be used in field research .

> Exemplar 5.2 Boothby, J., Tungatt, M.F. and Townsend, A.R. (1981). Ceasing participation in sports activity: Reported reasons and their implications. *Journal of Leisure Research*, *13*(1), 1-14.

> Boothby and his colleagues used indepth interviews to ascertain why people ceased participation in sports activities. These researchers believed that a focus on understanding constraints from the reference of the participant was needed. They felt the key to understanding was the subjective experience of the individual as described in his/her own words. The researchers were highly systematic in the use of probed open-ended questions free of interviewer or respondent bias, leading questions, and self-fulfilling predictions. In collecting the data, they used the respondents' own words as much as possible. A category sorting technique was used for a content analysis for data interpretation. While the data were analyzed quantitatively to reduce their complexity, the qualitative method of indepth interviewing provided a richness of data concerning people's recreation and leisure life histories. Boothby et al. concluded that the reason why people ceased participation was because of changes in physical ability and changes in the relationshis between the individuals and their sport environments.

> Exemplar 5.3 Henderson, K.A. and Rannells, J.S. (1988). Farm women and the meaning of work and leisure: An oral history perspective. *Leisure Sciences*, *10*(1), 41-50.

> This research used the life history method and the oral history data collection technique. The purpose of the study was to determine the "leisure" experience of farm women over their lifespan. The authors provide a framework of symbolic interaction for studying the lives of women and a justification for the oral history perspective. Henderson and Rannells described how twenty-seven women between the ages of 62-95 years were selected for a two to three hour life history interview. The interviews were transcribed and analyzed using a form of constant

comparison to determine the meaning that was associated with work and leisure. Several major conclusions about the patterns concerning work and leisure were identified in the oral life histories that the women provided.

These four variations range in strengths from the informal being very context specific to the closed quantitative being easily aggregated and generalized with the use of appropriate sampling techniques. The weaknesses of any of the variations depend upon the type of information gathered. Clearly the close-ended interview would be focused primarily on predetermined ideas of the researcher while the informal would be less systematic with frameworks emerging in data analysis. The remainder of this chapter will address primarily the interview guide, which Denzin (1978) refers to as the nonscheduled standardized interview, and the standardized open-ended interview which is sometimes called the scheduled standardized interview.

Getting Started

Criteria for a good interview includes securing the respondent's interest, ensuring clarity, making intentions precise, relating each question to the overall intent, and handling problems of fabrication (Denzin, 1978). In the qualitative approach, the interview is a two-way communication so the interviewer is not just acting as the interrogator. The interviewee needs to know the purpose of the interview. The initial rapport building may be slow but is essential for data to emerge in a useful and honest manner. The interviewer may be perceived in a number of different ways. According to Massarik (1981), the interviewee may see the interviewer as hostile, automated, friendly, trustworthy, as a peer, or as a caring individual. Obviously, the best interview will probably be the one where the interviewer is perceived as caring by being an equal and committed co-researcher with the interviewee.

Interviewers may feel they are imposing on people. Yet handled appropriately, what could be more flattering to an individual than to be asked to talk about one's own life? People can easily become enthralled with themselves and the interviewer can help them feel that way. On the other hand, the interviewee is giving a gift of time and emotion so she/he should be respected for that contribution as well.

The researcher should be aware of the problems that can be associated with interviewing. Sometimes language presents a problem. This language problem was particularly true for us in our interviews about leisure with rural farm women (Henderson and Rannells, 1988). The farm women tended to laugh when we asked questions about their leisure and proclaimed they had none. Yet, when we asked what they did on holidays or with their families, they could describe activities that were meaningful and enjoyable to them which seemed to exemplify traditional ideas about leisure, although these experiences were not termed "leisure" by the women. It became clear to us in the process of interviewing that we needed to use a different term like "free time" or "fun activity" in order to get the information that we needed.

Language may also present a problem if interviewees cannot articulate some feelings and attitudes. This inability to communicate emotions may result in a bias by choosing only people who are articulate. If an unclear terminology is being used between the interviewer and interviewee, then the researcher may need to learn the "right words" from the interviewee, may need to teach the interviewee what the researcher's questions mean, or may need to use some type of translation procedure (Schwartz and Jacobs, 1979).

Interviewees do not always tell the interviewer what she/he wants to know until a considerable amount of trust has developed. Subjects may also tend to exaggerate, distort and/or protect themselves. A discrepancy may exist between what they say and do. People may also say and do different things in different situations. Since the interviewer is deprived of the context of the interviewee's daily life, some statements may be taken for granted or the researcher may have to make certain kinds of assumptions about what is being said. Many of these drawbacks can be mitigated by indepth, sensitive contact over a period of time.

Finding interviewees is highly dependent on the research question. The researcher needs to determine who might be appropriate respondents based on who has information. The interviewer might want to consider aspects such as high or low status in a community, active or passive involvement, insider or outsider, mobility verses stability, as well as who is accessible and who is willing to give information (Gorden, 1975). Interviewees may be found in a number of ways. You may get recommendations from others who serve as brokers or you may try to convince interviewees on your own. Depending on the issues, friends and acquaintances may help as interviewees or may suggest persons. As you begin interviewing, the interviewees themselves may be able to offer some suggestions of others to interview.

Theoretical sampling is also a part of interviewing that is discussed further in Chapter 8. Sampling done in the qualitative approach generally does not focus on numbers of interviewees but the contribution each interviewee makes to developing grounded theory. The more basic the phenomena, the fewer people the researcher will need to study but the interviews must have more depth. The researcher needs to keep interviewing people until she/he stops getting new information and starts to see the same issues emerge over and over. The researcher must also be attuned to "minority opinions" as well as those recurring ideas that reflect the majority views. Thus, the number of interviewees and the length of time of the interviews are highly dependent on the research questions and the theoretical sampling. Lofland and Lofland (1984) suggested that major data management problems may occur in indepth interviews and 20-50 interviewees may be all the researcher can handle. An exact number is hard to determine. Douglas (1985) suggested that the researcher will need to interview as many people as possible to explore the truth one is seeking, although he did also suggest that twenty-five was a common number used in an indepth interviewing study.

In setting up the interview, one needs to evaluate each potential contact to see if it will lead to developing the theoretical sampling model that is desired. In the case of the study of farm women, we chose as our criteria: women over age 60 who lived on a farm the majority of their lives and who were relatively verbal (Henderson and Rannells, 1988). Each potential interviewee was screened for these characteristics before the interview time was set.

Contact should be made with interviewees by mail or phone. The time, place, and other logistics of the interview should also be described and discussed. Usually an indepth interview will often take two hours so a place should be scheduled where privacy is possible. Enough time and the proper place can greatly effect the nature of the interview. It is useful to let the interviewee know whether or not the conversation will be taped. The researcher must be clear about the research intentions and assure the anonymity of the respondents. It is useful if the researcher explains the general topics that will be covered. It is also useful to offer the interviewee an opportunity to find out what you are going to write for publication, but as a researcher you must also reserve the right to have the final say. It is usually best to avoid issues of money when you are setting up interviews.

Not all individuals will be willing or able to be interviewed. Some will not be willing because of competing demands for time or because of the ego threat. Others may not be able to be interviewed because of forgetting, chronological confusion, and unconscious emotional behavior. The researcher must accept these limitations and try to offer realistic expectations, use altruistic appeals, be sympathetic, offer a new experience or a chance for catharsis, and express the importance of the research (Gorden, 1975). The interviewee must be aware of the mutual benefits. Beyond that, it is up to the individual to decide whether or not to be involved.

Establishing Rapport

Interviewing is highly individualistic and does not involve a set of specific rules. There are, however, strategies that the interviewer may want to acknowledge in setting the tone, climate, and stage for the interview. The two processes of developing rapport and eliciting information should be going on simultaneously (Spradley, 1979). Rapport is the degree to which the interviewer and the respondent are able to understand one another. It may be necessary for the researcher to tell the interviewer some of her/his background and the sponsorship of the study as well as to give the interviewee a chance to ask questions at the beginning of the interview process. The interviewee will probably be interested in how she/he was selected.

The interviewer should be on time, courteous, and establish eye contact immediately. It may be useful to just chat initially for 10-15 minutes until the individual, as well as the interviewer, feels at ease. Creative interviewing is concerned with truth and not business, therefore you must get to know someone first (Douglas, 1985). The researcher should exhibit value-neutral behaviors and may set the rhythm of the interview as lively or leisurely depending on the situation. The interviewer can make the interviewee feel interesting by being interested (Babbie, 1989). According to Spradley (1979), the interview progresses through several stages including rapport building, apprehension, exploration, cooperation, and participation. The interviewer will want to be flexible but also must maintain control of the interview by asking the right questions, giving encouraging feedback, and wording the questions in a way that will affect the nature and the quality of the responses. Warmth is the way one gives signs of positive emotion and entreats others to share with her/him (Douglas, 1985). The researcher should, however, be careful to avoid instant intimacy and should share about herself/himself only as appropriate. Some situations will lead to more sharing than others. The researcher should realize that information of the past may be information that people relate to emotionally so the interviewer should be prepared to respond to both positive and negative emotions.

In general, an interviewer who is similar to the interviewee in age, sex, ethnicity, speech, and dress is likely to get better results. The interviewer generally needs training in how to establish rapport and must have complete familiarity with the interview questions.

Asking Questions

The questions asked of interviewees will have a great deal of variability depending on the structure of the interview and the research problem. Specific questions may be addressed followed with peripheral questions to get more information or probing questions used for clarification, amplification, refocusing, or getting more intensity of feelings. Silence may also be a way to indicate to the interviewee that more information is wanted. Moments of silence, however, are seldom written into the interview schedule.

The key to successful interviewing is to get people to talk. Questions may be asked in the time frame of past, present, or future and may explore issues of experience/behavior, opinion/values, feelings (emotional responses), knowledge/ facts, senses (what was seen, heard, touched), or background/demographics (Patton, 1980b). According to Guba and Lincoln (1981), the questions may be direct, indirect, personal, impersonal, retrospective, introspective, or prospective. The range of questions may be hypothetical "what if," may pose an ideal for the response, may use "supposing that . . . ," may play devil's advocate, ask for an interpretation, or ask reasons. Other types of questions are "give me an example of" and "recall an experience when" questions. Some questions may be filters to determine what other questions to ask. Some questions may be asked to try to get people to bring back memories. Interviewers should avoid questions that imply a close-ended response and questions that can be phrased as a "yes-no" dichotomy.

Patton (1980b) also suggested that "why" questions be avoided because they presume a cause and effect, suggest an ordered world, intimate perfect knowledge, imply rationality, and may threaten the interviewee. The answers to "why" questions are also very broad and the analysis may be difficult.

Good questions should be open-ended, neutral, singular, and clear. A good example of an open-ended question might be, "Tell me what it was like to be a high school athlete?" Precision is necessary no matter what kind of structure the interviewer uses. It is also important to keep the individual on track as the interview proceeds which may mean bringing her/him back to the topic at hand. In addition, prefatory statements may be used in making a transition from one type of question to another. Sample 1 gives examples of questions used in an interview guide prepared by the author of this book.

The sequencing of the questions may be important. Usually noncontroversial questions are asked at the beginning of the interview. These questions may also provide a context for determining attitudes and knowledge. The interviewer may

---

Sample 1
Examples of Interview Questions

The following is an example of an interview guide used by Karla A. Henderson and M. Deborah Bialeschki in a study of "Women and Entitlement to Leisure" conducted during the summer of 1989:

1. Tell me a little about yourself.
2. Describe a typical weekday.
3. What is a typical weekend like for you?
4. Tell me a little bit about the importance of leisure in your life. (Probe–How do you define it? Do you feel you have enough, not enough, or too much leisure?)
5. What activities do you enjoy doing at home?
6. What activities do you enjoy doing away from home?
7. Describe an experience that you would call "true leisure." What was happening, who were you with, how did you feel?
8. How would you compare your leisure to most other women that you know? How would you compare it to most other men that you know?
9. How do your roles as wife, mother, daughter, friend, etc. affect your leisure?
10. Tell me about the priorities in your life you have concerning work, leisure, and family. (Probe about these responses)
11. What constraints prevent you from having more leisure or enough leisure?
12. If you could change some things about your life, what would they be?
13. What else is important for me to know in order to understand the role of leisure in your life?

start with very general questions and proceed to more specific or she/he may begin specific and proceed to more general questions. One may become more directive as time goes on in the interview. Certain props may be useful in helping people to talk such as asking them to use a diary, calendar, memorabilia, or pictures to tell about experiences. It may actually help the interviewer to "play dumb" sometimes in order to get a full explanation from the interviewee. The demographic and background questions should be asked at the end because they are often boring and the interviewee may not see their usefulness in the very beginning.

During the interview, the researcher needs to be nonjudgmental and just let people talk. The researcher doing the interviewing should pay attention, be sensitive, and not take anything for granted. Neutrality can be established by reinforcing that the individual being interviewed can say anything and it will not elicit a positive or negative response. The interviewer should probe for clarification and elaboration so one has clear picture of what is being said. The interviewer should be prepared to provide a shoulder to cry on or be a confidant if that is the role that the interviewee wants the interviewer to take. For less chatty people, the interviewer will have to be more of the guide. Creativity in getting people to talk will certainly be necessary. Establishing rapport, reciprocity, generosity, and responsibility with the informants is critical.

The use of mechanical recording devices is an issue that must be addressed in any discussion of in-depth interviewing. The tape recorder may serve as both a reassurance of the seriousness of the interview as well as a technological reminder of human separateness (Douglas, 1985). Generally tape recording is a requirement for interviewing because it is extremely difficult to write extensive notes and give full attention to the interview. On the other hand, the use of a tape recorder should not be an excuse to "take a nap" while the interview is occurring. If people are really ill at ease with a tape recorder, perhaps the recorder should not be used. Usually, however, a small tape recorder does not create a problem and people generally forget it is running after a period of time.

It is wise to make no big issue about the recorder but mention it casually and matter-of-factly as you begin the interview. The use of battery operated recorders is most convenient so the interviewer will not have to worry about plug-ins. Always make sure, however, the batteries are working. Let the interviewee know that the tape may be paused at any time and assure her/him continuously that the recording will be kept confidential. Use quality mikes and make sure the tape recorder is working properly beforehand. As an added reminder, do not forget to label the tapes and make tape back-ups if transcription will not be done immediately.

The tape recordings should be transcribed as soon as possible. It is useful if the person doing the interviewing does the transcribing but this recommendation may not always be possible. The tapes should be transcribed in the order they were done. From the transcriptions, data analysis can be started and the basis for future questioning can be developed. The researcher should make duplications of the interview transcriptions. Chapters 8 and 9 explain more detail about interview data organization and interpretation.

The interviewer may also want to use an interviewer's journal. In this journal the researcher will keep track of the topics covered and can record information about what was said in the interview and what the researcher thought about the interview. One might keep track of puzzlements and thoughts, probe questions that were useful, and evaluative comments about the interviews that may be useful later. The journal may also provide a basis for reinterviewing. If an interview guide is being used, the interviewer is advised to use a fresh copy of the questions each time so notes may be taken briefly on the guide for each individual.

Life History Interviews

One variation of the indepth interview method is life history interviewing. This is also referred to as historiography which is the reconstruction of the past from data obtained from collecting, recording, and analyzing documents that are woven into a meaningful set of explanations (Denzin, 1978). Life history materials include any records or documents that provide insight on the behavior of individuals or groups. Life histories represent the experiences and definitions held by one person, one group, or one organization as this person, group, or organization interprets their experiences (Denzin, 1978).

Two of the major issues raised in life history interviews are the genuineness and credibility of the data. These issues concern the interviewee's ability to tell the truth, willingness to tell the truth, accurate reporting, and corroboration. Generally life history interviews are conducted over a period of time and the interviewer gets to know an interviewee quite well. According to Schwartz and Jacobs (1979), life histories ought to be autobiographical, cover as much of the life history as possible, be detailed, and give attention to dates of events. The outcome of the life history is a story that is put together describing how people view their world. In doing this kind of interviewing, it is important to just let the interviewee go and keep the questions open-ended. The interviewer must assume that everything said is important initially.

Some questions have been raised about the reliability of memory and retrospective interpretation. What people believed happened, however, is important because people think, act, and react according to what they believe is the way something occurred. Therefore, it is important to listen carefully to what feelings and emotions underlie what is being said. Many people take aspects of their lives for granted so it is important that the life history interviewer use the same techniques to get people to talk as for any interview.

The data from the life history interview method may be analyzed based on individual case studies or may be generalized to a whole group. The data analysis is similar to the interpretation techniques used for other qualitative data. In addition to the interview data, other forms of information such as public archival records (i.e., media accounts, government documents) and private archival records (i.e., diaries, memoirs, logs, letters, verbatim reports) might be used in triangulation with the interviews.

Another form of life history interviewing is the oral history where the data are recorded so others might listen to the tapes as well as see the transcripts. This method is distinctive in that it presents the ideas of people in their own words. While a retrospective study is acknowledged to be no substitute for a longitudinal one, it does offer information which helps to link the past and the present. According to Gluck (1979) there are three types of oral histories: topical, biographical, and autobiographical. A complete or autobiographical oral history surveys the life of a person. A biographical oral history has an interviewee talking about someone else's life. The topical looks at only one phase of the person's life from that individuals' perspective. In its purest form, the oral history is presented exactly as it is said by the interviewee. An edited oral history may also be written which intersperses the monologue with comments and explanations. In summary, all oral and life histories have the following central features: They provide the person's own story, address a social and cultural circumstance, and provide a sequence of the past experience and situation.

Group Interviews

One other variation of qualitative interviewing is group interviews. A common way that group interviews are conducted today is in the form of "focus groups." According to Krueger (1988), the characteristics of a focus group include people who possess certain characteristics and who provide qualitative data through a focused discussion. Generally, the focus groups consists of 7-10 participants selected based on some established criteria such as possessing certain characteristics like being new adopters of a product. The researcher using focus groups tries to get a relatively homogeneous group of individuals. A discussion is carefully designed to get the perceptions of the participants about the issues being addressed.

These groups have been used most frequently and successfully in an applied situation such as in doing marketing research. The focus group may be used to obtain information to use for a quantitative study, may be used at the same time a quantitative study is done, may follow other procedures, or may stand by itself as a qualitative study. In marketing or evaluative research, focus groups may be used before a program begins, during a program, or after a program. The major requirement is that a suitable problem is chosen that lends itself to the group interview. Richardson, Long, and Perdue (1988) used focus groups to identify the importance of recreation economic impact issues within local communities. They then conducted a more extensive quantitative study based on the data obtained from the focus group. *See Exemplar 5.4*

Exemplar 5.4 Richardson, S.L., Long, P.T., and Perdue, R.R. (1988). The importance of economic impact to municipal recreation programming. *Journal of Park and Recreation Administration, 6*(4), 65-78.

These authors used focus group interviews as one phase in an assessment of the identification of economic impact in recreation programming. The focus groups were used as the initial part of a two phased project. The second phase involved questionnaires sent to professionals. Each focus group had six interviewees. The focus groups were used to refine the research questions and to develop hypotheses. The authors provided little detail about the focus groups they used but suggested that the typical procedures used in any focus group were followed. Richardson, Long, and Perdue concluded from both phases of their study that high revenue dependent agencies were very concerned about economic impacts.

In designing a focus group one must determine the purpose and whom to study. Appropriate questions must be developed. These questions are similar to a structured interview in that they are open ended, avoid dichotomous answers, do not ask why, are carefully prepared, are presented within a background, and are logically focused.

Krueger (1988) stated that the advantages of the focus group are that it is a socially oriented research procedure, allows the moderator to probe, is relatively low cost, can provide speedy results, and can use fairly large samples if several small groups are combined in data analysis. The limitations of the focus group are that there is less control in a group interview, data are sometimes difficult to analyze, the interviewer must be carefully trained, groups may vary considerably, groups may be difficult to assemble, and the discussion must be in an environment conducive to conversation.

The interviewer is the moderator in a focus group. In addition to moderating, this individual also listens, observes, and analyzes what is happening. The moderator must take an unobtrusive position, must be good listener, and must be able to make people feel at ease. The general pattern for a focus group is the welcome, overview of the topic, presentation of ground rules, and the questions for discussion. The usual interview techniques of pausing and probing are useful in this group method.

The focus group should be recorded in some way. A video tape is one of the best ways. The moderator should also be taking notes as the discussion occurs. A transcript of the tape may be done or one may simply run the tape several times to ascertain the key issues. Analysis is similar to other qualitative methods. Raw data are used to examine descriptive statements and then interpretations are made from the data. Numbers and percentages are generally not used. The analysis results in finding the "big ideas" and reflecting upon those ideas for the final report. The final report should answer the original questions and should be geared to the audience for which it is intended.

Several variations of the focus group may be used including the use of the telephone conference call, the same people coming together over a period of time, multiple moderators, or the use of an already established group as the focus group. The purposes of the focus group may be for research but they also may be for providing therapy, resolving differences, achieving consensus, and obtaining information.

Summary

This chapter has focused on indepth interviewing as a method used commonly for collecting qualitative data. Indepth interviews may be used as a formal method or may be triangulated with field research techniques and done informally. The general aspects of interviewing such as setting up an interview and developing interview questions were discussed in detail. In addition to qualitative interviews, special uses of interviews such as life history and group interviews also were discussed.

The key concepts addressed in this chapter are: interview instrumentation, rapport building, communication, questions, life histories, oral histories, group interviews, and focus groups.

For Further Consideration

1.   Choose a topic that interests you. Set up an interview schedule and practice interviewing by interviewing a classmate or colleague. Practice using probes and asking questions for clarification.

2.   You may want to tape record the interview you did above so you analyze how the questions were asked. It may be necessary to transcribe some of the interview and then see where you might have asked questions or probed differently.

3.   Not everyone will be an excellent interviewer at first try. What could you do to become a better qualitative interviewer?

4.   Plan a training workshop that you might organize if you were to teach others how to become better interviewers. What do they need to know and what skills do they need to develop?

For Further Reading

Researchers interested in learning more about qualitative interviewing may want to consult the following literature along with some of the others that have already been mentioned.

Douglas, J.D. (1985). *Creative interviewing.* **Beverly Hills, CA: Sage Publications.**

Douglas presents a thorough, clever analysis of how one ought to conduct interviews. The examples he uses are helpful in understanding how one goes about getting interviewees and how one establishes rapport with them. He presents a number of tips that will be helpful to anyone who wants to become proficient at indepth interviewing.

Krueger, R. (1988). *Focus groups.* **Beverly Hills, CA: Sage Publications.**

The most up-to-date compilation of information about focus groups is presented in this short text. Krueger does an excellent job of synthesizing the literature about focus groups and how these groups can be used for a variety of research questions. The bibliography in this text will provide a springboard for researchers that want to apply this group interview technique.

Schwartz, P., and Jacobs, J. (1979). *Qualitative sociology: A method to the madness.* **New York, NY: Free Press.**

This text offers a comprehensive look at the rationale and methods for conducting qualitative studies in sociology. Schwartz and Jacobs describe a number of methods and offer insights into how they can best be applied. Since interviewing is such an integral part of qualitative sociology, they incorporate the use of formal and informal interviewing easily into the entire text.

Spradley, J.P. (1979). *The ethnographic interview.* **New York, NY: Holt, Rinehart and Winston.**

Spradley devotes an entire book to the interviewing method. He provides a step-by-step guide to how to get interviewees, ask questions, and analyze the data. In the ethnographic interview, Spradley suggests that one may have to go back to people several times in order to get the information needed and to develop patterns and themes in the qualitative analysis.

Chapter 6

Other Qualitative Methods

Introduction

While field research/participant observation and indepth interviewing are the primary qualitative methods, there are several other methods which the recreation, park, and leisure studies researcher might want to consider. These other methods may be either quantitative or qualitative depending on how the research is structured. In addition, the methods described in this chapter may be used alone or may be used in triangulation with either or both of the two major qualitative methods of interviewing and participant observation. The methods addressed will be case studies and single subject designs, unobtrusive methods, content analysis (hermeneutics), audio-visual analysis, and consensus models. The purpose of this chapter is to introduce how these less familiar methods may be used qualitatively with a focus on emergent designs, grounded theory, and meanings.

Case Studies and Single Subject Designs

Case studies and single subject designs are quite different methods from one another but they do share the commonality of using a small sample or a single sample with a number of sources of data. In general, case studies and single subject designs are particularistic in that they portray events in one situation or for one subject, holistic in that as many variables as possible are examined within the specific context of the situation or individual, semi-longitudinal in that they occur over a period of time, and either or both qualitative using prose and literary styles for descriptions about the case or subject being studied or quantitative using summary statistics (Wilson, 1979). The usefulness of the case study or single subject design will depend on the purpose of the study, the depth of the study, the generalizability of the study to other similar situations, and the theoretical orientations proposed. Case studies and single subject designs are most often used to explain, describe, and explore particular questions or issues.

Some confusion has existed surrounding the term called "case study." A case study is an intensive investigation of a particular unit. It includes an analytic description of a group as observed over a period of time. It includes the indepth study of the background, current status, and/or interactions of a given unit and may employ a variety of other methods to obtain data pertaining to the case. Using one site as an example to examine a research question is really not a case study if the focus is not on the context of the interactions within the particular setting. A more appropriate term for many case studies might be "case history."

Yin (1984) suggested six main sources of evidence used for case studies: documentation such as letters, agendas, and reports; archival records; interviews; direct observation; participant observation; and physical artifacts. This list sounds very similar to the types of data that are often used in field research. However, in case studies a unit such as an organization, a person, or a specific phenomena is frequently studied and the boundaries between the context and the phenomena are inseparable. One may study an entire unit, multiple case units, or one may study only a specific aspect of one case site or one aspect of multiple sites.

Case studies have sometimes been criticized for their lack of rigor, sloppiness, and lack of generalization and comparisons (Campbell, 1979). They often take a long time to complete and may result in massive, difficult to read documents. Yin (1984) suggested that good case studies are difficult to do. Exemplary case studies are significant, complete, consider alternative perspectives, display sufficient evidence, and engage the reader in an understanding of the case being studied. According to Yin (1984), it is essential that multiple sources of evidence are used, a case study data base is created, and that one maintains a chain of evidence concerning the data that are collected. The researcher should keep a record of where all information comes from as one begins collect data and to draw conclusions.

The analysis for a case study consists of examining, categorizing, tabulating, and recombining evidence, just as is done in other forms of qualitative data interpretation. Any number of techniques are available for data interpretation. A good case study makes use of theoretical propositions and case descriptions just like any other study using qualitative methods. The case study analysis uses pattern making, explanation building, and will be conducted over a period of time. The writing is also similar to what is done in other forms of qualitative data reporting. Saunders and Turner (1987) were successful in using off-track betting offices as case studies to examine gambling as a leisure pursuit. Their report of the case studies was written like one is reading a story. *See Exemplar 6.1*

> Exemplar 6.1 Saunders, D.M. and Turner, D.E. (1987). Gambling and leisure: The case of racing. *Leisure Studies*, 6, 281-299.
>
> Saunders and Turner used five case studies in South Wales to analyze gambling as a leisure pursuit. They were interested in studying those individuals who were "having a bet" and not in studying compulsive gamblers. The setting they used was off-track betting offices to examine customers and staff concerning groupings, career patterns, and lifestyles. They used observations, records, and informant interviews. Little information was included about the techniques used in analyzing the case studies. The conclusions, however, were written as a story and provided a good example of putting data into a broader context in order to understand the phenomenon of betting.

The single subject design is similar to the case study except only one person or a very small number of people are used as the sample for the research. The data collected may be quantitative or qualitative. The single subject design offers a viable method for making informed decisions about the quality of a program, such as a recreation program, and provides a context for understanding behavior dynamics (Dattilo, 1986a; 1986b). The focus in the single subject design is on an individual; a series of measurements or observations occur over a period of time to determine how an individual may be changing as a result of a particular recreation program or as in therapeutic recreation, a particular treatment plan or intervention. Some subjects, such as those those served by therapeutic recreation where average performance is sometimes the exception rather than the rule, can be studied using this method to see if and how recreation as a treatment may improve the individual's leisure functioning. The technique allows the researcher to learn the details of how treatment is working for an individual rather than averaging the effects across a number of cases (Kennedy, 1979).

A single subject design will often address the rate and level of attainment of objectives, program strengths and weaknesses, standards of individual performance, validity of innovations and trends, and cost benefits. The method does not lack precision and sensitivity. As in other methods, however, the results of single subject design can be compromised by inadequate assessment tools and measurement procedures (Dattilo, 1986a). While most of the studies using the single subject design in therapeutic recreation have used quantitative data, qualitative data could also be used. Whatever form of data, it is essential, as in the case study, that multiple sources of data are used.

In the single subject design as well as the case study, there is a problem with the lack of generally accepted rules for drawing causation and generalizations. In some cases there may be a limited strength and range of generalizations. The reader is left to make the judgment about how the information might be applied to another individual or unit. Therefore, in these two methods of research as in other areas of qualitative study, the researcher must be specific concerning the methodology used and the resulting outcomes .

Unobtrusive and Nonreactive Methods

Unobtrusive or nonreactive methods refer to observing, recording, and analyzing human behavior in a situation where interaction with people generally does not occur and where people are unaware that their behavior is being observed. The methods do not require the cooperation of individuals. Unobtrusive measures are often used to provide supplementary data for research studies or they may, in some cases, be used on their own. As in other methods, varying degrees of quantification or qualification may be used.

In unobtrusive or nonreactive methods, the anonymity of people is almost certain. Usually some kind of activity, such as watching the behavior of individuals in a public park or tracing activity such as by counting the types of vandalism that occur in a park, is observed. The data generally consist of physical evidence, archives, or observation. The unobtrusive measures may be systematically developed and planned in a research study or they may be found accidentally when some other data for a research project are being collected. Examples of unobtrusive measures that may be used to obtain data about people's behavior include: observations of body language and other nonverbal behavior, short cuts or worn grass in a park indicating where people walk most frequently, what constitutes graffiti and where it is likely to be found, noting the stations that car radios are tuned to in a parking lot, the number of beer and soda cans in the household garbage, litter frequency and kind along a highway, and rental records for a business. Sometimes these unobtrusive methods require detective-like tactics. Most importantly, however, they offer clues as to what people are doing.

Some of the strengths of unobtrusive methods are the face validity, the simplicity and directness, the inconspicuous and noninterventional nature, nonreactivity, their use with other methods, the stability over time, and the independence from language (Guba and Lincoln, 1981). Webb et al. (1981) suggested that unobtrusive methods can provide a check and balance to confirm information found in more reactive techniques such as interviews and participant observation.

Problems exist in using the unobtrusive method because it is heavily inferential, information often comes in bits and pieces, and the situations can not be easily controlled. Since unobtrusive methods alone do not tell how people see and experience their activities, the methods are seldom used as a single source of material for a research study. Additionally, if subjects are aware in some way that they are being observed, their actions may be distorted and confounded. Hardware such as hidden cameras, gauges, and one-way mirrors may be used for data collection although some ethical problems may exist in using these devices if there are ways in which people can be identified and their privacy invaded. Further, unobtrusive studies may also have bias associated unless appropriate random sampling procedures are used.

Observation in public places is one type of unobtrusive method used in studying recreation, parks, and leisure. In this unobtrusive method, a researcher uses observation and personal introspection with the assistance of casual conversation. A participant observer in a public place may be less conspicuous than a complete observer. This observation in public places is sometimes hard to do but one can get a sense of such aspects as exterior physical signs (clothes, bumper stickers, license plates) expressive movement, physical location of types of activity, conversational sampling, and time sampling. The data could be recorded and analyzed similarly to other research techniques that might be used with either the qualitative or quantitative approach.

Content Analysis (Hermeneutics)

Another method that researchers may use qualitatively relates to the area of content analysis. Content analysis is the process used in analyzing documents, records, transcribed conversations, letters, or anything in a textual form. It is more an analytic strategy than a data collection strategy. Like unobtrusive techniques, this method may be used with a study that stands alone or may be used in triangulation with other qualitative methods. Field researchers frequently use document analysis as a form of content analysis to obtain historical information about a setting or situation that is being studied. Hermeneutics is the analysis of the meaning associated with a written text. Another way of thinking about hermeneutics is as textual analysis. The use of textual analysis, content analysis, and document analysis can be tied to philosophical as well as historical research. The fundamental aspects of the content analysis method are that it is nonreactive, unobtrusive, and uses words and/or numbers to describe particular phenomena. Content analysis and its many forms relate to a process of ascertaining meaning about a written phenomena being studied.

According to Marshall and Rossman (1989), content analysis is a process for making inferences by objectively and systematically identifying characteristics of messages. It is usually rule-guided, systematic, aims for generality, and deals with manifest and sometimes latent content (Guba and Lincoln, 1981). It can be applied to any form of communication (Babbie, 1986a). Content analysis may be done in words, phrases, sentences, paragraphs, sections, chapters, pictures, books, or any relevant context. It may be highly statistical but often a qualitative content analysis may be useful because frequency may not necessarily be associated with importance and meaning. Qualitative content analysis and hermeneutics have similar outcomes. The major point of content analysis, however, is that it allows researchers to analyze systematically some dimension that appears in written form.

Content analysis may be deductive or inductive. In the deductive form, there is usually an elaborate numerical coding system used which use either latent or manifest content of a unit of analysis. In the inductive form, the themes and patterns will emerge from analyzing the data rather than using a predetermined code. The inductive form is most often done qualitatively and utilizes the analysis techniques used for other qualitative methods. Gunter (1987) and Wyman (1985) also used content analysis to determine the meaning of leisure experience and nature experiences respectively. Both researchers used written personal accounts that were content analyzed for meaning. *See Exemplars 6.2 and 6.3*

Exemplar 6.2 Gunter, B.G. (1987). The leisure experience: Selected properties. *Journal of Leisure Research*, *19*(2), 115-130.

Gunter qualitatively analyzed leisure from a psycho-social perspective by examining 140 self-report essays concerning leisure experiences. Gunter was critical of the unclear, ambiguous conceptualizations of leisure that have been used in research. Because of the lack of agreement about leisure, he felt that the qualitative methodology would provide the best way to get a sense of what assumptions people made about leisure. Therefore, he attempted to combine research on theoretical properties and the technique of reconstructing leisure events from memory. He asked individuals to answer two questions: (a) the most memorable experience they had ever had, and (b) their most meaningful types of leisure. Gunter did not provide much information about his method or justification for using it, but he did find that the first question was the most useful in identifying properties or characteristics of leisure. He was able to uncover eight characteristics of leisure through a content analysis using these self-report essays. Gunter made use of quotations to exemplify what some of the characteristics meant.

Exemplar 6.3   Wyman, M. (1985).   Nature experiences and outdoor recreation planning. *Leisure Studies, 4*, 175-183.

Using the method of document analysis, Wyman analyzed fifty-five andscape architecture students' written descriptions of memorable places in their lives. Wyman was interested in examining the reference made in environmental autobiographies to nature experiences. The college students in this study were asked to be "co-researchers" in this project and write about their everyday involvement in the environment including childhood and present participation. She used a charting display system to organize the materials and descriptions of the writers, the places, and the feelings that were invoked. Through the development of ideas about what constitutes nature spaces, Wyman concluded that what people describe may be different than what recreation professionals think. Wyman concluded that this method and these descriptions provided valuable insights into what people think is important and may be used in recreation planning.

Document and records are often used to supply certain types of data for content analysis. Records are used to keep track of events and serve as official chronicles. They are generally used for trend analysis and integration. Examples of records might be sales records or minutes of a meeting. Documents are either personal or public and are often used to provide a historical context for a study. These documents may be letters and diaries, brochures, or newspaper articles. Archives is another word that might be used to describe certain kinds of records.

Textual analysis or hermeneutics is another method that is qualitative in nature. In a sense, all research using words rather than numbers represents hermeneutics. Hermeneutics refers to the interpreted meaning that results from a content analysis. Textual analysis or hermeneutics has as its focus looking for patterns and understanding within texts that have been written. It is a method grounded in experience and emphasizing meaning. As in the other methods, it utilizes similar qualitative techniques for data discovery and interpretation. Duncan (1985) used a hermeneutical method in her paper that analyzed thematic continuities in the literature which described the experience of play and the diverse collection of play theories. Leaman and Carrington (1985) used an ethnographic hermeneutical approach to examining athleticism and gender and ethnic marginality. *See Exemplar 6.4.* Textual analysis might be also be used by a researcher interested in analyzing how the philosophy and mission of an organization has emerged. In this case, the researcher would probably need to analyze the written materials of an organization over a period of time. The researcher could then employ content analysis to ascertain the meaning of the textual data.

Historical analysis is another type of textual qualitative analysis although it has its own disciplinary roots and set of rules. Historical research is much more than content analysis although it utilizes the techniques of content analysis as well as other techniques. It is beyond the scope of this book to discuss historical research but it is a method that has a direct relationship to hermeneutics and textual analysis.

Exemplar 6.4 Leaman, O. and Carrington, B. (1985). Athleticism and the reproduction of gender and ethnic marginality. *Leisure Studies*, *4*, 205-217.

Leaman and Carrington used an ethnographic hermeneutical approach for examining the construction of ethnic and gender identities through sport. They suggested that gender and ethnicity affect attitudes toward sport. Leaman and Carrington used the theoretical framework of marginality to explain and justify the status of women and minorities in society. They suggested that marginality is a matter of one's life being in some ways at the disposal of others and not under one's control. Existing research literature was the data that were used in developing their theses. They used examples to show how both women and minorities were defined marginally in sport but from two different extremes.

Both advantages and disadvantages exist in using the content analysis method. One may choose to use written materials, according to Guba and Lincoln (1981), and Webb et al. (1981), because they are stable, rich, easy to use, often legally attainable, a "natural" source of information, usually available at low-cost although they may be difficult to track down, nonreactive, and supplementary and contextual. One would not use written materials if they were unrepresentative samples, lacked objectivity, or were not valid. For researchers who like social interaction, the content analysis method of research may not be enjoyable because it involves working with written or transcribed materials and not directly with people. Content analysis may, however, be used in combination with other more reactive qualitative methods as well as with quantitative techniques. Cowin (1989), for example, used a personal journal that campers kept over the summer and combined this written journal with other quantitative measures to describe the self-concept of campers. *See Exemplar 6.5*

Exemplar 6.5 Cowin, L. (1989). Programming and self-concept: How does what you do affect how they feel about themselves? *Camping Magazine*, *61*(7), 46-49.

This short article is a summary of Cowin's master's thesis done at Dalhousie University in 1989. Cowin used a qualitative method of having campers write personal journals during "lights out" periods on a daily basis for a 54-day period at camp. Data were collected from 147 campers. Cowin provided a journal for each camper that had a series of open-ended questions that they were asked to answer each day. The campers wrote what they liked most and least during the day and how they felt about those experiences. A content analysis procedure was then used which identified eight categories related to self-concept and psychological well-being. She attempted to use quantitative measures as well as qualitative, but found the quantitative data were not nearly as helpful as the qualitative comments. In this write-up, Cowin identified some of the examples of the kinds of emic comments reflective of the experience of children at this particular camp.

Audio-Visual Analysis

Tapes, films, and photos are ethnographies of a culture. Audio-visual aids allow us to examine a phenomena a number of times. They may also be used as a technique to communicate data about a particular situation. Another form of content analysis that uses these ethnographies of the culture is audio-visual analysis. Audio-visual analysis can be divided into three categories. One category may refer to a content analysis of media such the Burrus-Bammel, Bammel, and Angotti's (1984) study of advertising in *Parks and Recreation* magazine where media was used as a source of data. A second category includes audio-visual analyses that may refer to using photos and media to collect data which can be analyzed or shown to others for analysis. For example, time lapse photography may give information about patterns of movement in a park. Another variation of this category is to make a tape or film and then show it to people to get their reactions. It is not possible to take everyone out into the wilderness, but one may be able to capture a sense of meaning by showing people a film, video, or slides and getting their reactions. A third category of audio-visual analysis is as a form of communication to present findings (Schwartz and Jacobs, 1979). For example, video tapes have been used to present the findings from focus group interviews.

The method of using audio-visual devices to collect and analyze data has pros and cons. Sometimes the use of audio or visual recordings presents a way to get better samples if a researcher cannot observe everything at one time. On the other hand, there is a problem with not being able to observe everything even when cameras or recording devices are being used. Most researchers have found that initially people may be bothered by a video-camera or tape recorder but they eventually forget the presence of these devices. It appears, in general, that the use of audio-visual equipment does not affect the qualitative data that may be collected. As in the other methods, data collection and analysis using audio-visual devices may be analyzed quantitatively or qualitatively depending on how the research study is designed.

Consensus Methods

The last set of methods that will be addressed in this section include those methods that may be used in research to develop consensus. The most often used is the Delphi technique. While the data in a Delphi study are often analyzed quantitatively, they are initiated using as a qualitative process. Other possible methods are the use of scenarios and the morphological technique. With the exception of the Delphi, none of these methods have been widely used in recreation, park, and leisure studies literature although they may offer some possibilities.

The Delphi technique is frequently used to establish goals, determine strategies, predict problems, access group preferences, and project needs. Weatherman and Swenson (1974) suggested that the critical characteristics of the Delphi technique are that it relies on the informed judgment of knowledgeable panels on a topic in which reliable objective data are hard to obtain. The technique is done anonymously with controlled feedback given in order to produce a group response. The first step involved in the technique is to select a panel of "experts" about a topic. The number of individuals is not as important as the quality of the panel. An open-ended questionnaire is then sent to the panel. The responses to that questionnaire are converged and tabulated and a second questionnaire is sent out generally asking people to rate the importance of the initial responses. The second questionnaire is tabulated and a final questionnaire is sent to try to see how much consensus can be obtained. The final product of the Delphi generally looks like a ranking of the most important issues that the panel addressed. Hunt and Brooks (1982) used the Delphi technique to identify the research needs surrounding people with disabilities. They were able to develop a list of important needs that could be addressed. *See Exemplar 6.6*

Exemplar 6.6 Hunt, S.L. and Brooks, K.W. (1982). A projection of research and development needs: Implications for disabled persons. *Leisurability*, *9*(3), 28-32.

Hunt and Brooks used the Delphi technique as a projective method to identify research needs concerning disabled persons. Their study used the typical steps of the Delphi process and consisted of twenty-seven panelists who were sent an initial open-ended questionnaire. In the second round of the Delphi, convergence of the topics were addressed, and in the last round each of the needs were rated quantitatively to obtain mean scores. Altogether, thirty-four needs were identified with the panel determining the most important need to be "determining the social rather than the activity deterrents of choice in leisure." This method was an effective way to develop ideas about needs and to reach some agreement about the importance of the research topics that were suggested.

Scenarios and morphological analysis are other consensus related methods that have been used by this author. In the scenario method, stories are written about some phenomena. Respondents are then asked to respond to how realistic those scenarios are in relation to the experience that the respondent has had. Henderson and Bialeschki (1984) used scenarios to examine what camp directors thought the future of camping might entail. General consensus was gained concerning what the camp directors believed were realistic expectations about the future of organized camping.

The morphological method was applied qualitatively to data to forecast the future of urban recreation (Henderson, Bialeschki and Berndt, 1982). The purpose of this method is to identify a range of possible options that might be considered about a phenomenon. In the study by Henderson et al. (1982), answers to questions about the future from a panel of experts were analyzed by not presenting specific conclusions but by presenting a broad range of possible alternatives. The purpose of morphological method is not necessarily to gain consensus but to present divergent views so that all possible conclusions can be set forth for consideration.

Summary

This chapter has provided an introduction to other qualitative methods beyond field research/participant observation and indepth interviewing. The methods described include case studies and single subject designs, unobtrusive and nonreactive measures, content analysis (hermeneutics), audio-visual analysis, and consensus methods. While none of these methods has been used extensively in recreation, park, and leisure research, they may be useful tools for addressing some types of research questions. Any of these methods may be used either in the qualitative or quantitative approach depending on how the research study is designed and how data are analyzed. Any of the methods might also be used in combination with one another or with field research and/or indepth interviewing.

The key concepts addressed in this chapter were: case studies, single subject designs, unobtrusive measures, content analysis, document analysis, hermeneutics, audio-visual analysis, consensus methods.

For Further Consideration

1. Discuss why the methods mentioned in this chapter have not been used more extensively in the study of recreation, parks, and leisure?

2. How might content analysis be tied to the major qualitative methods? Give an example of a research project that might use content analysis as a triangulated method.

3. Assume for a moment that you are interested in what goes on in a particular recreation or park setting. If you were to conduct a case study using that particular setting, what might be some of the sources of data that you would use?

4. Develop plans for an unobtrusive study that you might conduct to answer some question relative to recreation, parks, and leisure.

For Further Reading

If you are interested in more information about any of these methods, you might consult the following texts:

Webb, E.T., Campbell, D.T. Schwartz, R.D., Sechrest, L., and Grove, J.B. (1981). *Nonreactive measures in the social sciences.* **Boston, MA: Houghton Mifflin.**
This reference by Webb et al. provides the foundation for research done in the social sciences using unobtrusive or nonreactive measures. The authors present a number of examples of such research and provide the reader with ideas for conducting this type of research. While not all nonreactive measures are qualitative, the authors provide ways to set up research that may gather either or both qualitative and quantitative data.

Yin, R.K. (1984). *Case study research.* **Beverly Hills, CA: Sage Publications.**
Yin provides everything you would ever want to know about conducting case studies. He describes the procedure from beginning to end and offers a number of examples of data sources and well as of final reports. He particularly encourages researchers not to make final reports so boring that no one will be interested in reading them.

Part Three

Qualitative Techniques

Introduction

The preceding pages have provided a framework for the philosophy of science and the assumptions made about research that embodies the qualitative approach. The qualitative methods that may be used were also described. The dimensions of choice theme presented in this text suggests that the researcher can decide how to use particular methods. The positivist may choose any appropriate deductive method to answer a research question. A researcher operating from the interpretive paradigm will choose inductive qualitative methods. The interpretive social scientist will make assumptions about emergent designs, the use of words, the value of data discovery in the natural environment, and the use of grounded theory for theory generation and/or verification.

The purpose of this final part of the book is to describe the specific techniques that one may use in conducting a study based on the assumptions of interpretive research and the qualitative approach. Some variation exists in techniques among qualitative methods and these differences will be noted. Far more similarities than differences, however, are noted in the aspects of research planning, data discovery, data interpretation, data explanation and reporting, and other issues surrounding the qualitative approach. The researcher must understand these techniques and know what her/his options are because of the emergent nature of interpretive research using the qualitative approach.

Chapter 7

Research Planning and Designs

Introduction

Getting started on a research problem is sometimes difficult. Many researchers find they have more questions or "things they wonder about" than they could possibly research in a lifetime. Other researchers, particularly students who are only beginning to understand the nuances of research, may find the selection of a research topic very difficult and may feel overwhelmed with either the infinite possibilities, or their apparent lack of questions. Some researchers have a tendency to want to solve all the problems of the world with one big project and have a difficult time narrowing a problem down to a manageable size. Still other researchers have good ideas, but given their time and resource constraints, are not able to carry out a project for realistic practical reasons. Some researchers may have a brilliant idea but are not able to gain access to a setting which will allow them to research the problem. On the brighter side, some researchers have a specific problem in mind and need only to make decisions about the best way to approach it.

The purpose of this chapter is to describe how to get started. It will outline some of the choices to be made, the way that a research plan or proposal can be developed, the issues that may be considered in developing initial questions, the associations with organizations, getting started in the research, and a framework for conducting the project.

Making Research Choices

In developing research choices, one must initially proceed carefully to determine what is the best topic to choose. Unless the researcher has a specific problem in mind, it will be necessary to focus one's alternatives. The best place to start is with oneself.

Research inevitably involves personal interests. The topic is not necessarily personal, but one's personal interests can create a sense of motivation related to the research. In addition, one's personal preferences for method will generally emerge early in the planning phase. Since you are reading this book and have gotten this far, I assume that you have some sense of fascination with the qualitative approach. Ideally researchers choose a topic and then choose the best method to address it; the reality is that for many questions either quantitative or a qualitative methods could be applied. One's biases for methods will definitely affect the research chosen.

In making research choices, one must decide if the interpretive view with its focus on the emergent/contextual approach is better for a particular situation or for herself/himself than the predetermined/mechanistic aspects of positivist research (Ellis and Williams, 1987). Further, one may look at the limitations of each approach such as whether valid measurement instruments exist and whether one has enough time to complete a project. Related to these aspects are the major dimensions of subject/object relationships including the observer's interaction, the subjects' awareness of the research, and the situation (Guba and Lincoln, 1981). Does one want to be a participant or an observer, is the research to be overt or covert, is the situation to be natural or contrived? On a practical basis, one might want to consider how much time, money and other resources such as mechanical devices and computers are available. Table 3 provides a checklist of some of the major questions that one may ask in addressing the use of qualitative and quantitative approaches.

A specific topic is another choice that the researcher must obviously make. A group, setting, organization, concept, or some other unit of analysis that is personally meaningful and interesting may serve as the focus of the research. The role of experience may be extremely important in making research choices (Strauss, 1987). Personal investments, on one hand, can cause methodological and ethical difficulties. On the other hand, linkages between the personal/emotional and intellectual operations are an important dimension of the qualitative approach. Intuition is a part of analysis and it is important to be true to the approach in which one is emotionally engaged (Lofland and Lofland, 1984). All of this is to say that you must start where you are with an important question or a current issue that must be accompanied with your personal interest and concern. Several qualitative researchers in recreation, park, and leisure studies have described where they "were" and how this contributed to the development of a published social analysis. For example, Glancy (1986;1988) was interested in the play behavior of adults so chose to examine a softball team and auction sales that were available in her community in order to determine the adult play experience. Stebbins (1979) chose to interview amateurs active in theater,

| **Table 3** |
| Checklist for Considering Qualitative or Quantitative Approach* |

- Is the researcher interested in individualized outcomes?
- Is the researcher interested in examining the process of research and the context in which it occurs?
- Is detailed indepth information needed in order to understand the phenomena not under study?
- Is the focus on quality and the meaning of the experiences being studied?
- Does the researcher desire to get close to the data providers and immersed in their experiences?
- Do no measuring devices exist that will provide reliable and valid data for the topic being studied?
- Is the research question likely to change depending upon how the data emerge?
- Is it possible that the answer to the research question may yield unexpected results?
- Does it make more sense to use grounded theory than existing *a priori* theory in studying the particular phenomena?
- Does the researcher wish to get personally involved in the research?
- Does the researcher have a philosophical and methodological bias toward the interpretive paradigm and qualitative methods?

If the answer is *YES* to any of these questions, the researcher ought to at least consider qualitative methods as possible ways to approach the research question being addressed.

* adapted from Patton, 1980b, p. 88-89.

archaeology, and baseball because he got interested in the behavior of amateurs since he was an amateur musician. *See Exemplar 7.1.* I chose to examine the meaning of work and leisure among farm women (Henderson and Rannells, 1988) because I had grown up on a farm and had seen what the lives of my mother and other female relatives were like. I wanted to understand better how women in this life situation viewed their lives from a life span perspective.

> Exemplar 7.1 Stebbins, R.A. (1979). *Amateurs: On the margin between work and leisure.* Beverly Hills, CA: Sage.
>
> Although many full length books exist that describe the results of studies done using a qualitative approach, we have few works that pertain directly to the area of recreation, parks, and leisure studies. Stebbins's book provides a fascinating account of how amateurs pursue "serious leisure." He delineated the difference between popular leisure in which everyone participates and serious leisure which results in an often misunderstood commitment to particular activities. The issues raised in the book pertain to sociology and social psychology theory as well as to leisure

studies and the practice of providing better leisure opportunities. Stebbins used ethnographic interviews to obtain data about three areas where amateurs are active: theater, archaeology, and baseball. The nuances of "getting into" a site, the way that interview data were collected, the description of each type of amateur setting, and the perspective of the amateurs was addressed in all three areas. Stebbins tied these three examples together with a discussion of the sociological framework of marginality to leisure. This book is easy to read and portrays an illuminating picture of the lives of the amateurs and the settings that were researched. While the book contributes much to theory, it is also written in a style that makes the reader want to find out what conclusions can be drawn from the descriptions. The use of direct quotes and colorful descriptions seem to make this book not only interesting to researchers but also to persons who consider themselves amateurs in the areas studied of theater, archaeology, and baseball.

The perceived inferiority and lack of understanding about doing interpretive research and using the qualitative approach needs to be addressed. A researcher may be able to justify the use of the qualitative approach by using previous knowledge and the discussion presented in this book. One may, however, have to address feelings of marginality in choosing qualitative methods (Shaffir, Stebbins and Turowetz, 1980). These methods are sometimes scorned by positivists who do not understand the interpretive possibilities of science. While the public may better understand the results of qualitative reports, many believe that statistics are the "end all and be all of research." Further, participants (respondents) may feel that the research you are doing also has some marginality. The use of qualitative methods, while becoming more common in recreation, parks, and leisure research, is still far from predominant. Further, doing any type of research study may feel like a lonely experience. All of these attitudes and feelings may create humbling experiences for the researcher and she/he should be aware of the potential obstacles before the topic and method choices are made. Conducting research can be both an exciting and a frustrating experience; the researcher choosing to use qualitative methods will want to know as much as she/he possibly can about the approach and will benefit from finding others who are supportive of the interpretive process.

The researcher should also be aware that ambiguity is the nature of qualitative methods. Qualitative methods generally focus on "letting the data speak" and utilize a flexible design. The research questions are the product and not necessarily the antecedent of data collection (Bullock, 1983). The design is purposely kept loose. On the other hand, the emergent qualities of the research are rigorous in that one must have a research plan that is definitive but that can be changed as the data emerge. Ambiguity in interpretive research is evident in that while one wants to remain open and flexible, it is also important to have a design or plan for how one remains open and flexible. In other words, the qualitative approach relies on detailed descriptive and contextual information and the researcher must have a plan for guiding the work and a plan for being flexible.

Some qualitative studies will use tight, prestructured plans and others will be loose and highly emergent. Most research using the qualitative approach lies between these two extremes. For novice researchers, it may be well to develop a fairly structured initial design to serve as a road map. The researcher, however, must continually remind herself/himself of the inductivity of the research being conducted. Miles and Huberman (1984) recommended that when the researcher is interested in a better understood phenomena within a familiar culture or subculture, a tighter design may be necessary. For example, if I am choosing to examine the leisure experience for a particular group of individuals such as home-bound elderly, it may be necessary to establish a specific plan in order to get access to the sample. I also may have less flexibility in how I collect data than I might with another group. In conducting the research, however, I must remain as flexible as I can in order to let the most valid data from the research emerge.

A researcher could sit around for years pondering many of the questions posed and seeking to determine what would be the "perfect" research design. Most of us do not have that much time if we ever hope to graduate, to be tenured, to make a contribution to the body of knowledge, or to get an evaluation report to whomever desires the information. Probably the best advice is to make a decision about a topic and the methods and techniques that seem most appropriate and then "just do it." As a researcher, you may want to wade out in the water before totally immersing yourself, but it is important to get into the real world, begin to understand a phenomenon, and then decide how to proceed next.

Research can be a fearful undertaking. Even after almost 15 years of conducting a variety of research projects, I still feel trepidation each time I embark on something new. I always wonder whether it will work and whether the outcomes will be worth the time and effort. We must not let our fears, failures, and desire for perfection stop us from getting on with adding to the body of knowledge in recreation, parks, and leisure studies. Researchers do take risks and for many of us, that is what makes our research so exciting. Old adages such as "no pain, no gain" and "you have to spend money to make money" may be appropriate to contemplate as you set off on this research adventure.

Preparing the Research Plan

Researchers are generally required to write research proposals before embarking on their research. Many of us have found that writing the proposal is the hardest part of the entire research project. Once the proposal is done well, one usually has a picture of the road map and a sense of the departure point; the remainder of the project is a matter of choosing the roads to take in order to get somewhere in the end. In interpretive research using the qualitative approach, the destination may be fuzzy and it may not be the same at the end as was envisioned at the beginning, but an initial road map will at least get the researcher started. The research study will still take time and effort but a sense of direction will make the research a more delightful experience.

Most writers about qualitative methods offer a basic plan for how research should be conducted (cf. Denzin, 1978; Lofland and Lofland, 1984; Marshall and Rossman, 1989; Spradley, 1979; 1980). These procedures are fairly standard across all methods except there may be more variations in qualitative approaches particularly concerning data discovery and data interpretation which generally occur simultaneously.

The basic steps in conducting any research project include:
1. Problem formation/theoretical perspective development/methods choices
2. Exploration of possibilities/literature review
3. Planning/proposal development/guiding question development
4. Getting into a site or "in" with informants
5. Getting started and getting along
6. Data collection/discovery and logging
7. Data organization, reduction, and focusing
8. Data interpretation
9. Reporting/explaining/presenting data and findings

As has been noted, the researcher conducting any type of research will develop a plan using the above steps. In reality, however, as a study using the qualitative approach is begun, most of these steps will likely be occurring simultaneously. As the data discovery continues, the original research hypotheses may change as new information is added. As was stated in Chapter 3, the development of theory is not a linear process but one that is multilinear and dependent on past, present, and future data. In working with data, the researcher will generally use a series of techniques that may be tentative, emergent, propositional, rival, and alternative until the presentation of a final analysis is found (Denzin, 1978).

Regardless of the multilinear nature of the qualitative approach, the research is still dependent upon some type of initial "plan of action" or proposal. The researcher must know what she/he wants to learn as well as how she/he will know when the study is completed. An assumption of the interpretive paradigm is that one has a "blank" mind without the preconceived notions of what the outcomes of research will be. This assumption, however, does not mean that one charges into a situation and blindly begins to collect quantities of data (Fielding and Fielding, 1986). In qualitative studies, the details of the research design will emerge, but the researcher must have a plan or road map to describe what general questions and propositions are to be explored, what data units will be used, what methods are likely and practical, and a possible framework for interpretation. For example, the researcher may not define just exactly who and how many people will comprise a sample, but a starting point for the sample must be developed with parameters for how one knows when enough people have been sampled or how one will know when it is time to leave the field. The good research design will anticipate problems of entry, reciprocity, role maintenance, and receptivity as well as address ethical issues (Marshall and Rossman, 1989). Unfortunately, while it is easy to state that this is how qualitative studies are theoretically planned, it is not possible or necessary to give a formula for how actually to conduct a study. The most important advice to give the researcher is that she/he needs a plan for how to be flexible and how to continue to be open to whatever possibilities the research may present.

> Marshall and Rossman suggested that:
> The time, thought, and energy expended in writing a proposal that is theoretically sound, methodologically efficient, thorough, and that demonstrates the researcher's capacity to conduct the research, draw sound conclusions, and write the final report will reap rewards throughout the research endeavor (1989, p. 153).

In summary, the research proposal for a qualitative study should include the substantive focus, the design based on assumptions of interpretive research, sample selection logic, justification for design and data, issues of trustworthiness, and an acknowledgement of how hypotheses, data discovery, and data interpretation will evolve. In addition, a data management plan should be in place before data are collected (Werner and Schoepfle, 1987). With the volumes of data that are often generated with qualitative methods, a specific plan for organizing the data is an absolute must.

Marshall and Rossman (1989) also suggested that in the proposal the researcher may want to describe several other aspects that relate specifically to the qualitative approach. A researcher may address the competence she/he has to undertake a qualitative study. The ideal research setting is where the researcher obtains easy access, establishes immediate rapport, and gathers data related to the research interests. This ideal research situation, however, rarely occurs (Taylor and Bogdan, 1984) so the researcher must plan carefully for as many contingencies as possible in the proposal. The researcher may also want to address the interest that the she/he has and the style of working that may be used. A theoretical plan for the data discovery and a review of the literature that is comprehensive and shows that one is current with the field concerning similar studies that may be applied is necessary to include in the proposal. If the theory is to be grounded, the researcher needs to explain what this grounding may mean. Finally, information about human subject protection and ethics should be addressed in the proposal before any data collection takes place. The proposal should describe how the project will be explained to informants and participants. It is important that everyone involved in a qualitative study understands the boundaries and parameters of the study.

Developing Guiding Hypotheses

Even the researcher conducting the most inductive qualitative study should have a few broad research questions or guiding hypotheses in mind when she/he begins the project and, subsequently, the data collection. As has been stressed, however, the researcher must be willing to let those questions change as the study progresses. For example, in the study we conducted on the camping experience at Women's Week (Henderson and BIaleschki, 1987), our initial idea was to examine what this camping experience was like as a metaphor for women's lives. We found very quickly that this camping experience was in many ways antithetical to their lives and it became obvious that the research would be more fruitful to examine what the broader experience of the week meant to these women. The more specific aspects of the meaning of play and learning eventually emerged from the data discovery and concurrent interpretation that was done in this study.

The initial guiding questions or hypotheses do not have to be completely clear and the priorities for them do not have to be set. Miles and Huberman (1984) suggested that if one is foggy about the questions, then one should use foggy questions and attempt to defog them. The researcher may want to use major guiding questions and guiding subquestions, or she/he may develop a conceptual framework for guiding the study. As noted previously, the researcher may go back to the conceptual framework as the data are collected and rewrite the conceptual framework. This process is perfectly acceptable within the interpretive paradigm although sometimes positivists cringe at the thought. One of the values of writing the questions or the conceptual framework initially is that at least you can see if the hypotheses are researchable. The guiding questions should be continually examined as the researcher proceeds through the data discovery and interpretation.

Developing the guiding questions may take some time. The researcher may go through many revisions before the questions are appropriate for the proposal. As a suggestion, Lofland and Lofland (1984) offered a framework for asking questions about units of social life. They suggested the researcher may want to consider questions about what is the unit's type, structure, frequency, causes, processes, consequences, or people's strategies. Within a research setting the researcher may want to ask questions about meanings, social practices, episodes, encounters, roles, relationships, groups, communities or settlements, organizations, social worlds, and/or lifestyles. The questions may change as one begins to discover data, but they provide a way to begin to think about how the data might be organized and interpreted.

"Getting In"

The researcher may have the best plan in the world for conducting a qualitative study, but if data are impossible to collect, the plan is useless. Therefore, the researcher must carefully consider how to get into an organization, how to "get in" with a group of individuals, and/or how to locate written materials in order to begin the data discovery. Sometimes this "getting in" will require some sort of formal agreement with an organization while in other cases, it will be an individual choice made by respondents concerning their willingness to let you participate in data collection.

In recreation, park, and leisure research, we often look to groups of people as sources of data and we also look at places where recreation takes place. Therefore, it is common that permission needs to be granted from someone at some level. The researcher will need to determine who to talk to first and what type of permission is needed. Convincing people who are in power, often referred to as "gatekeepers," to let the researcher "in" is not always an easy task and the researcher will need to start early in this endeavor. "Getting in" may take a lot of time. It is often a catch-22 as well. One needs a plan before she/he can confidently go to an organization to ask permission, and yet, the plan may depend to some extent on the nature of the site chosen. This dilemma is another example where the qualitative approach does not necessarily follow a linear pattern. The researcher should keep in mind that "getting in" may be a part of the data discovery so it is important to keep field notes on every step of the procedure.

As the initial research proposal is developed, the researcher may want to explore possible research settings. The first step in "getting in" is to pick a possible setting or group of people and see if there is someone who might be a connection for you. Your credentials as a student or researcher may help you get your foot in the door, but you will also need to be concerned about developing rapport with the gatekeepers and/or respondents once you have made contact. It is easier to gain access if the researcher's interests coincide with the organization's goals and the participants see some clear benefit of their participation. The researcher must be prepared to address the question of "why should we let you in?" with ideas about the mutual benefits that may be possible. In some cases, there may be no payoff to the participants and the risks may be greater than the outcomes. Whatever the case, the researcher and the participants should understand what the advantages and risks are. Gaining access may depend on having an appropriate and relevant project that the agency or individuals see as having value. In some cases the gatekeeper(s) or individual(s) in charge may want to see a formal proposal such as one that you might present to your graduate committee or to a funding agency. In most cases, however, a one page summary of your research idea and procedures will be adequate to present upon your initial contact with the gatekeeper or participant.

In obtaining permission to enter a site, it also may be helpful if the researcher is familiar with the routines and the social setting that she/he wants to explore. Johnson (1975) suggested that the researcher may have to do "pre-research"

research. People will frequently want to be assured that their routines will not be disrupted by the research. In explaining the research to gatekeepers or participants, one must also decide how much information is to be given. It is generally best to be truthful but vague and imprecise (Taylor and Bogdan, 1984). It is generally best not to give too many details unless you are asked specifically for the details. A paradox in conducting qualitative studies is that the outcomes of the research may be different than the outcomes that were hypothesized initially because of the emergent nature of the qualitative approach. Therefore, the researcher must be careful in making promises about the outcomes of the research and is advised to keep the purposes of the study broad. The researcher should emphasize that she/he will try not to disrupt the setting but that being unobtrusive is not always possible. Confidentiality and anonymity should be assured and the researcher has an ethical obligation to make sure this confidentiality occurs. Once permission has been obtained, the researcher must maintain trust by keeping her/his bargain and by frequently keeping the gatekeeper(s) informed of the progress of the research.

In some organizations, a formal contract may be necessary in order to do research. This contractual agreement does not necessarily assure cooperation but it does describe the expectations of the researcher and the respondents. A formal contract may be written that includes an agreement concerning the researcher's overall purpose, the presumed contribution to knowledge, projected goals and emergent design, and the selected approach. Some of the following terms of agreement should also be included: the identification of the parties, the expectations, access to research resources and records, confidentiality and anonymity, researcher(s) autonomy, withdrawal agreement, products of research, reporting, management and scheduling, budgets if any resources are being shared, research protocols, and signatures (Chenery, 1988; Guba and Lincoln, 1981). A sample letter of agreement is included in Sample 2.

Sample 2
Example of Agreement Form

LETTER OF AGREEMENT
regarding

RESEARCH TO BE CONDUCTED AT TRAIL BLAZER CAMPS
Summer, 1986

for Trail Blazers, Inc.   for the Research Team:

Judith L. Myers   Mary Faeth Chenery
                                            Helen A. Finch

This letter of agreement outlines the intentions, obligations, and expectations of those involved in the research study to be described.

Sample 2 continued...

CONTENTS

TERMS OF AGREEMENT

   I. Personnel

   A. Identification

The sponsor for this research is Trail Blazer Camps, New York, NY.

Members of the camp community who will be actively involved in the project are Judith L. Myers and Jean Garvin. Purposefully selected camp staff and campers will be involved as necessary.

The research team is Mary Faeth Chenery, Assistant Professor of Recreation, Department of Recreation and Park Administration, Indiana University and Helen A. Finch, Doctoral Research Assistant, Department of Recreation and Park Administration, Indiana University. Others concerned about this project include Stephen C. Anderson, Associate Professor, Department of Recreation and Park Administration, and Egon Guba, Professor, School of Education, Indiana University, who may participate in the project's activities as members of Helen's doctoral dissertation committee.

   B. Expectations

The Camp expects the research team will:

   (1) present as little disruption as possible to the normal occurrence of events at camp;
   (2) support the Camp in its actions and decisions;
   (3) regularly inform the director of project progress;
   (4) immediately inform the director of any event, conditions, or circumstance which could, in the researchers' professional opinion, cause harm to the camp or endanger the health and safety of any person; and
   (5) maintain the anonymity and confidentiality of the persons participating as subjects in the study.

The Research Team expects the Camp will:

(1) provide background information and local expertise to the project;
(2) work collaboratively with the research team on the project activities;
(3) share problems and concerns about the project;
(4) provide the researchers with access to necessary records and files;
(5) provide the researcher with the opportunity to observe and record all aspects of the camp setting;
(6) allow the researchers to have access to campers and staff;
(7) respect anonymity and confidentiality of the data;
(8) inform staff of their support for and endorsement of the research project.

II. Access to Research Resource and Records

Access to the researchers' field notes and other data collection records shall remain solely with the research team, the dissertation committee members, and research consultants. The data collected for the research project are acknowledged to be the property of the researchers.

III. Confidentiality and Anonymity

The researcher(s) shall promise confidentiality and anonymity to camp community members who take part in the study. Field notes and data collection records will be kept private, and summaries of notes and records will be coded to avoid identification of individual contributions. The Camp will have the opportunity to decide whether it wishes to be identified in any publicly available reports.

IV. Researcher Autonomy

The research team will work in collaboration with the Camp at all times, allowing the director to be fully informed of all developments and study modifications. The Camp shall respect, however, the researchers' right and abilities to make professional decisions concerning the developing directions and emergent findings of the studies. At all times, either party shall respect the other's appeal for negotiation concerning perceived problems with the research.

V. Withdrawal from the Agreement

It is understood that either party, at any time, may withdraw from the research agreement, without fault, explanation, or obligation.

VI. Products

A variety of products are expected at or near the completion of this project. They include:

(1) an evaluation summary;
(2) complete documentation of the research;
(3) audio tapes and possibly photographs;
(4) a doctoral dissertation;
(5) a final report provided by the research team to the Camp;
(6) a summary report of the findings of the studies to be sent to the staff; and
(7) article(s) for publication.

Products which shall be provided to the Camp include copies of the final report, the summary report for staff, any articles for publication, and the doctoral dissertation. As well, copies of any photographs which the Camp desires to have will be made available to the Camp at no charge.

VII. Reporting

The Camp shall:

(1) be entitled to raise questions of factual accuracy, judgment, and interpretation in any report and to negotiate resolutions to these questions until joint satisfaction is reached; and

(2) be entitled to determine whether it wishes the camp name to be identified in any products made available to the public.

The researchers reserve the right to:

(1) make reports in whatever form(s) are deemed appropriate for the particular audiences involved ; and

(2) govern the content of all reports and the editing process.

VIII. Management and Scheduling

Planning and feedback meetings will be scheduled on a weekly basis between the directors and researchers. Of major emphasis will be decisions concerning emergent design, modifications of the methodology, project progress, perceived problems and/or concerns, and any project agreement changes. Such developments will be documented.

Our intention is to complete this study in a relatively short time period... The plans of work are indicated below:

June 14: Begin study; observe and document staff meetings.
July 02: Observe small groups during July session
July 31: Analyze data; complete member checks.
Sept. 15: Complete final report.
Oct. 15: Submit final report to the Camp.
Oct. 15: Submit copies of summary report of the finds of the study to staff of the Camp.

IX. ACA Standard regarding Research

In compliance with university policy and with the American Camping Association Standard with regard to research, this research project proposal has been reviewed and approved by the Indiana University Committee for the Protection of Human Subjects.

By our signatures, we agree to participate in the research project as described above.

For Trail Blazer Camps: For the Research Team:

_____   ____   _____   ____
Judith L. Myers   Date   Mary Faeth Chenery   Date

                                         _____   ____
                                         Helen A. Finch   Date

Getting Started

Qualitative data discovery consists of three stages: (a) entry and getting started or learning one's role, (b) data discovery/organization/analysis and maintaining relationships, and (c) leaving or finishing the project. One's role as a researcher may change throughout these stages. Getting started will be discussed briefly here and the latter two stages will be discussed in subsequent chapters.

Getting started with data collection ought to be a "piece of cake" after the initial planning is done and one has her/his "proverbial" foot in the door. Getting started will, however, be highly variable depending on the situation, the researcher's personality, and the group members' feelings. It is often an overwhelming experience to actually begin. The researcher may experience positive and/or negative feelings of being overpowered. On one hand, the researcher may feel exhilarated to finally be into the heart of the study. The first day in the field or the first interview or the first document analyzed may be, on the other hand, extremely confusing and one may wonder why in the world the research project was ever undertaken. The amount of time and energy the first encounter takes may also seem enormous and the researcher may really wonder if all of the effort is going to be worth the end results. One needs to persist and eventually patterns and familiarity will come. Several guidelines and strategies exist that the researcher may want to acknowledge.

Before collecting data, one must first learn the language of the respondents and individuals. Words and symbols may have different meanings in the real world of the informant or interviewee. One must learn how terms are defined and must be willing to define terms for people if words are causing confusion. It is essential that meanings of words not be imputed by either the researcher or the respondents. In doing field research, particularly, it may be useful to get acquainted with a couple potential key informants early on as they may be able to help in explaining language that the researcher will need to know.

Establishing rapport is a blend of external and internal ingredients of day to day involvement (Shaffir et al., 1980). It is necessary that the researcher establish trust in order to collect valid data. It is possible to do good research and also maintain warmth, interest, and trust. While the researcher may be the observer or the interviewer, she/he will also be observed and interviewed. Frequently first impressions are very important. The first few days in a research setting will generally set the stage for the researcher for the remainder of the project. The role of being a researcher may be an obstacle initially. Suspicion of and resistance to your role may exist. If you, as the researcher, become actively involved in the culture you are studying and if you show a genuine interest in the people with whom you are interacting, they may eventually forget that you are conducting research. As the researcher, you should continually ask and answer the question, "why should anyone in the group bother to talk to me?" (Johnson, 1975). Further, you should check your behavior as a researcher by asking and answering, "would I be willing to participate in this research project if I were on the other side of the fence?" The researcher will need to translate the answers to these questions in a way that will help her/him empathize with what the respondents and informants are experiencing. The researcher will want to keep in mind that the respondents and informants in a qualitative study are really "co-researchers."

The best advice in any kind of interactive situation is to try to be liked and to develop the bonds of trust by being friendly, sociable, open, sharing, easy going, and having a sense of humor (Douglas, 1976). This advice may be good for life in general.

Summary

This chapter has begun the exploration of techniques that can be applied to most interpretive research using the qualitative approach. All research is concerned with research design, data discovery, data organization, data interpretation, and data reporting. In the qualitative approach, these techniques will likely be occurring simultaneously. It is necessary, however, to begin somewhere by developing a research plan and gaining entry to a research setting. The focus of this chapter has been on making choices about research topics and the factors that enter into these decisions. The chapter also provided a framework for writing a research proposal and developing a design to guide the research. Considerations for "getting into" a site to conduct research and for getting started with empirical observations were also discussed.

The key concepts addressed in this chapter were: topic choices, methods choices, research proposal, guiding hypotheses, gatekeepers, and rapport building.

For Further Consideration

1. Make a list of your particular interests related to recreation, parks, and leisure. Are there any of these interests which might develop into a research project? What would be reasons for choosing a topic close to your interests? Why might you want to avoid a topic in which you have a strong personal interest?

2. Find out what the requirements are for a formal research proposal that you might submit to your university committee or that might be required for entry into an organization.

3. Talk with a professional whom you know in the recreation and parks field and ask her/him what she/he knows about the value of research. How would this individual feel about someone conducting research in her/his business, organization, or agency? What does this person see as the drawbacks to data collection? How might the chosen topic of the research affect how she/he feels?

4. Think about the research project that you would like to undertake. Try to remove yourself as the researcher and think of yourself as one of the informants. Explain whether you would be willing to be involved in your own research project?

5. From your own ethical framework, how much about a research project should be divulged to the gatekeepers and how much should be divulged to the informants. What factors would effect how much you tell others?

For Further Reading

Kirk, J., and Miller, M.L. (1986). *Reliability and validity in qualitative research.* **Beverly Hills, CA: Sage Publications.**
This short publication provides a wealth of information that the qualitative researcher will want to consider in designing a research project. Kirk and Miller provide ways that the researcher can provide reliability and validity in their research so that the qualitative methods will not appear to lack rigor or be sloppy. A researcher who is concerned about whether others will consider her/his methodology valid may want to consult this book.

Lofland, J., and Lofland, L. (1984). *Analyzing social settings.* **Belmont, CA: Wadsworth Inc.**
This text provides a number of approaches to be considered in designing qualitative studies. The rationale for analysis and the possible frameworks that can be used to ascertain meaning using qualitative methods are described in some detail. This text has application to all aspects of the qualitative process, but may be useful for the reader when she/he is getting started in developing possible guiding hypotheses that may be used in the qualitative approach.

Marshall, C., and Rossman, G.B. (1989). *Designing qualitative research.* **Beverly Hills, CA: Sage Publications.**
Marshall and Rossman provide a practical and current view of how qualitative projects should be designed and presented for approval. They offer concrete ways to provide a framework for the research without eliminating the opportunity for an emerging design to also occur. Anyone not familiar with writing research proposals, especially related to qualitative designs, could learn much from this succinct text.

Shaffir, W.B., Stebbins, R.A., and Turowetz, A. (Eds.) (1980). *Fieldwork experience: Qualitative approaches to social research.* **New York, NY: St. Martin's Press.**

This collection of chapters provides a variety of perspectives on how one gets a research project going. The chapters all focus on various methodological techniques used in establishing rapport and beginning the research. The novice researcher can learn much from the accounts given by these sociologists of the trials and tribulations, as well as the success stories, that they experienced.

Chapter 8

Data Discovery and Organization

Introduction

In the qualitative approach, the researcher is generally the instrument and is using the self as the measuring device for collecting data. Data refer to all information collected by the researcher in the situations in which they occur (Bullock, 1983). Data are discovered by translating observations and inquiries into written notation systems. In qualitative methods, this system is generally words. The data are the inventories of the real world (Schwartz and Jacobs, 1979). The amount of predetermined structure used for data collection will depend on the conceptual focus, the research questions, and the sampling criteria. Pure "raw" data really do not exist since the human being as the instrument is always involved in some form of interpretation, but the focus during data discovery is to try to collect as much raw data as possible.

Data discovery is only one part of what the qualitative researcher does. The data must be organized and managed so they can be effectively interpreted. Johnson (1976) suggested that a field researcher normally puts in a 16 hour day with 8 hours spent collecting data and 8 hours spent recording, organizing and coding data. Further, in using qualitative methods, enormous amounts of data are generally discovered. For example, on a two or three day field trip up to 40-80 pages of typed field notes might be collected and these will require several hours to organize for interpretation. The purpose of this chapter is to describe some techniques for data discovery and organization that will enable the researcher to do a better job in data interpretation and reporting.

Behavior Necessary for Data Discovery

In the previous chapter, getting started on the research project was discussed. The next stage in the research is to become immersed in the data discovery by deciding what to observe, record, and analyze. Data collection, according to Spradley (1980), will depend on how simple the phenomena is to observe, the accessibility of certain information, one's obtrusiveness, the frequency of certain occurrences, and the amount that one can participate. People in field studies can usually be observed more than once so the researcher will likely get a more complete picture of a phenomenon over a period of time.

How the researcher thinks and feels about a situation may impact upon the data that are discovered. The researcher must be in touch with her/his personal thoughts and feelings and should keep a record of those feelings along with detailed notes about the phenomena being observed. The researcher must continually access her/his reliability and validity as an information gatherer (Miles and Huberman, 1984). If data gatherers are being hired rather than the principal researcher collecting the data, they should also have a familiarity with the phenomena or setting, have strong interests in the project, and have good investigative skills such as doggedness, ability to draw people out, and the ability to ward off premature closure (Miles and Huberman, 1984). No matter how the data are collected, they should be reliable, factual, and confirmable.

Notetaking

The purpose of data discovery is to collect facts and information. As a researcher you can only trust your memory so far. As new data are discovered, it is easy to forget previous information. Therefore, it is necessary to take many notes. The notes are the data. Notes can take a variety of forms and may include different types of information. In notetaking, the researcher should be particularly careful to identify whether the idea is a fact, quote, or interpretation. One must indicate what she/he knew happened as well as what she/he thought happened. Just as you cannot observe everything, you cannot record everything so the researcher must practice recording the most important observations.

In discovering data, one should become proficient at the conscious task of remembering items of who, what, when, and where. In other words, the researcher must be able to take good mental notes. It may be possible in some field settings to make jotted notes but it is usually best, at least initially, to take notes in secret. If the researcher is unable to take extensive notes "on the spot," she/he will need to develop a good memory. The jotted notes will help to jog one's memory for later when the researcher actually writes the field notes in detail. Hunter (1987) told of his system of notetaking on a wilderness trip whereby he had little opportunity for extensive notetaking. He had to rely on taking mental notes, using a small notebook to record as much as possible generally late at night with the aid of a flashlight, making memos to himself, and planning further data collection for each day while on the trip.

Several types of field notes may be collected. According to Spradley (1979; 1980), these notes may be condensed accounts using phrases, expanded accounts which are highly descriptive, fieldwork journals that describe the processes of the research being conducted, and analytic provisional accounts that organize one's interpretation. These types of notes can be kept separate or can be combined in some fashion. Each individual will have her/his own best methods for notetaking, but several strategies may be useful to keep in mind:

- Record your notes as soon as possible after doing the observation or interview. This recording takes time and discipline but is an essential part of the rigor of qualitative methods. Lofland and Lofland (1984) suggested that forgetting has to do with acquisition of new experiences, not sleep. Thus, the researcher does not necessarily need to record detailed notes immediately after being in the field, but she/he should not collect more data until the previous data have been recorded. Interview tapes also should be transcribed as soon as possible after each interview.

- Write, type, or word process the notes in as much detail as possible. The notes should include a running description of events, people, things heard and overheard, conversations among people, conversations with people, and incidents that occur. Transcriptions of tapes should include detail such as long pauses, laughter, or any other information that relates to the interview. In today's computer age, the use of computer programs may make analysis much easier if notes are recorded initially in some kind of computerized filing system such as the Apple™ HYPERCARD© or the program THE ETHNOGRAPH©. If possible, especially for the novice researcher, it may be useful to have a trusted colleague read over your notes to make sure you are being descriptive enough.

- Make copies of the notes as soon as possible. If a computer is not used, get the copies photocopied so they can be coded, indexed, or cut and pasted. Even if a computer is used, make a back-up copy of the disk as well as a hard copy of the notes immediately.

- In the notes include a summary for each entry concerning who, what, when, and where. This may be put on a title page for each field site visit or interview or may be included on each note sheet.

- Indicate on the notes whose language was being used. Who exactly said what? Did you? Did someone else? Include verbatim quotes, if appropriate, and always use concrete description with specific detail. The written text is always either the researcher's or the interviewee's/ informant's words and this distinction should be noted. If a dialogue occurs, you should try to note such aspects as the gestures, nonverbal cues, tone of voice, and pace of speaking. In transcribing interview tapes these nuances also should be noted on the transcriptions. Keep your interpretations separate from the notes or record the information in such a way that you know clearly what notes are interpretations and what notes are descriptive facts. You may want to use a notation system for insights, interpretations, working hypotheses, and initial analyses. Meaning should be described separate from the behavior. For example, Kirk and Miller (1986) suggested using [" "] for direct quotes, [' '] for paraphrases, [( )] for interpretations, and [< >] for emic action or words.

- Record both the nature and the intensity of your feelings as a researcher as you proceed through the research process. Your feelings and hunches may be valuable information as the qualitative study progresses. Some people note "OC" in their notes which means "observer comments".
- Use pseudonyms for people's names to assure confidentiality but keep a master list of those names so you can refer back over time. The master list of names should be in safe keeping and should be destroyed as soon as the study is completed in order to assure confidentiality.
- Record as much data as possible with as much detail as possible, especially at the beginning of your study. You generally cannot be sure what is important and not important until sometime later. Everything is initially a source of data and "one never knows" what may be ultimately important. You will definitely not use all of your notes in data interpretation and reporting, but it is necessary to have as much data as possible. Be liberal in your recording of notes. You can always go back and disregard notes but it is difficult and unethical to invent notes.
- Leave wide margins on the note sheet so you can write ideas in or note additional interpretations if they occur to you. Start new paragraphs often so the note sheets can be easily read.
- The length of field notes will differ enormously. A rule of thumb might be a couple of single spaced pages for each hour of observation.
- It is possible to talk your field notes into a tape recorder and then have someone else transcribe them. If this seems appropriate, the researcher will need to review the transcriptions as soon as possible.
- Notes are not meant to be taken and then set aside until data discovery is over. The researcher should continually refer to notes made earlier as more data are discovered. This review of field notes will likely result in the emergence of patterns and themes.
- Do not be afraid to record notes about what you do not understand. Something may not make sense at one time, but it will possibly become clearer later. Record your notes at will and do not be afraid of making mistakes. Mistakes of omission rather than commission are the most problematic in qualitative data collection.

- Continually monitor yourself as a data gatherer. Your tiredness, reactions, relationship with others, consumption of alcohol, discrete observations, and technical problems may all affect the data discovery and these manifestations should be noted. The researcher as data collection instrument is a part of the factual reality of qualitative methods (Johnson, 1975).
- Realize that writing and rewriting field notes may not only be time consuming but also it may, at times, be boring. It is necessary, however, if the researcher is to collect the data reliably and validly.
- The length of time spent in notetaking will depend on the research question being asked. Projects with a singular focus will not require as much time spent notetaking as those with a broader focus (Patton, 1980b).
- And finally, remember "If it is not written down, it never happened" (Taylor and Bogdan, 1984, p. 52).

Sample 3 shows an example of notes that were constructed from a white water rafting outing.

Sample 3
Sample Notetaking
The following notes were the actual notes taken during participant observation from the study of a Women's Week conducted by Henderson and Bialeschki (1987):
Two women, B and L were talking about the experience of going rafting last year and about how it made you 'either be best friends with that person you were with or worst enemies.' They said you 'really had to learn to depend on that person and really trust what they were doing and it built somewhat of a bond between the two.' They said the river had several sets of rapids that would be quite challenging to anyone who had never gone rafting before...
(The ride to the river was quiet.) We got on the bus early in the morning and everyone had already chosen their partners. Most of the partners sat together on the bus. Most people were talking quietly to one another. The ride took about half a hour. The women were dressed in their riverwear–swimsuits, shorts, hats, and old tennis shoes. (No one seemed to be too concerned about their appearance except several people mentioned wanting to get suntans and wondering how bad the mosquitoes would be.)
continued...

Sample 3–continued

Once we got to the raft rental spot, the women filed off the bus quickly and were instructed by the camp leader to claim a suitable life jacket and paddle. The rental man had the rafts situated along the river so it was easy to get started. The leader gave a couple of instructions about the individuals who were carrying the first aid kits. (Most of the women were busy getting themselves and their gear organized into the rafts and did not seem to be concerned about the final instructions.) A contest seemed to be going on between S and G and A and C concerning who could get to floating down the river first.

The first hour was easy on the river. Most of the group of 12 rafts stayed within sight of each other. Most of the women were paddling along leisurely getting used to how the rafts reacted (or didn't react) to their paddling. (No one seemed to be in a hurry and there was no reason to be since we would not be picked up until 3:00 some 15 miles down the river.) I was enjoying the trip and trying to remember as much as I could to write down when we had a chance to stop for awhile.(OC)

At the first set of rapids it was really interesting to note how the pairs of rafters reacted. <When B and F came to the rapids, they just pulled in their paddles and let the water take them wherever it would. S and G were experimenting by trying to go on different routes in order to find the best white water. When D and P got hung up on a protruding rock they just sat there and laughed and laughed.> (They didn't seem to think it was any big deal and they would sit and rock and rock until they freed themselves from the boulders.) A and C did not like being hung up on the rocks and they were very intense about getting off the rocks and continuing the trip. J left her lifejacket on the entire trip even when we stopped on the shore for lunch. She remarked at lunch, "I was afraid. I have never done anything like this before and I really don't consider myself a very daring person."

Data Discovery Devices

Tape recorders can be used for interviews or for field notes. It is important that caution is taken not to become complacent as a researcher because these devices are being used. Always make sure the tape recorder is functioning properly and that the quality of the tape is what you had hoped. In addition to using a tape, the researcher ought to jot some notes in case there is a mechanical problem; these jottings will also help to supplement the transcription. The notes taken in conjunction with the tape recording can also help one to formulate new questions and will help to facilitate later analyses (Patton, 1980b). If a tape cannot be used in an interview, the interviewer must take thorough notes and must do extensive editing afterward to fill in the parts that could not be recorded on the spot. It is important that the meaning of responses are not imputed without data to back them up.

Some people have mixed feelings about tape recordings. Spradley (1979) recommended that the researcher always take a recorder along in conducting qualitative studies and use it as much as possible. The researcher may need to go slowly in getting people comfortable with the recorder. The researcher may want to let the individual know that the interviewer can be more attentive if a tape recorder is used. Some feel a tape recorder may keep people from talking honestly even though it may help the researcher to remember better. This concern is an issue that each researcher will have to resolve. Whatever is decided, the tape recorder should not be a substitute for concentration. The tape recorder is a useful device for collecting data but one must not rely completely on it for verbal interactions.

Along with taping comes the need to transcribe. If good taping equipment is used, the transcribing will be much easier. One must review the transcription compared to the tape to assure accuracy and to fill in areas where names or places may have been spelled incorrectly. Transcribing takes a lot of time. The ratio of transcribing a tape is about four hours of transcription for one hour of speaking (Patton, 1980b). A 45 minute interview is likely to result in 20-30 pages of double spaced transcriptions (Werner and Schoepfle, 1987). After a tape is transcribed, the researcher should spend as much time studying the transcriptions as was actually spent in collecting the data since the transcription process provides another way to further review the data.

Organizing the Data

After the data are written or transcribed, another written procedure may be used to summarize some of the "raw" data. This data management requires judgment calls and decision rules that each researcher will need to develop. It may be necessary to package and repackage and summarize and resummarize the data (Guba and Lincoln, 1981). Guba and Lincoln further suggested a number of ways for organizing the data such as chronologs or running accounts of groups' behavior, context maps that show the physical layout of activities, taxonomies or category systems that lay out possible hypotheses, sociometrics, the use of rating scales, checklists, and other techniques that provide additional ways to organize data short of making final interpretations.

The field notes can be converted into "write-ups" or "memos" which should be intelligible to anyone (Miles and Huberman, 1984). The write-up indicates the most important content of a study at a particular time. Memos can also be used which describe how the data are evolving, the possible patterns, marginal notes, and clarification of concepts. One also might want to include memos addressing personal emotional reactions as well as any methodological difficulties that might have occurred during the data collection. These memos may be "gut reactions" to what is going on, inferences about the quality of the data, new hypotheses, notes of what to address later, elaborations, or clarifications.

Memos or write-ups should be dated, titled, and anchored to particular places in the field notes. They are frequently the basis for "grounded theory" (Miles and Huberman, 1984). The memos require the researcher to continue to "think" rather than to just collect ideas. It helps one to address grounded theory by continuing to tie the information to the site and the conceptual underpinnings. A write-up should also be done for each interview conducted and attached to the verbatim transcript. This write-up should provide additional information and summarize the data collected. A copy of the write-up used in the oral history project (Henderson and Rannells, 1988) is included in Sample 4. Write-ups and memos will take a time to write but they are a link between the techniques of data discovery and data interpretation.

Sample 4
Memo Writing Example

Mrs. H
Background

Mrs. H was born in XYZ, IL on August 6, 1910. After her graduation from high school in Scales Mound, she worked outside the home when she could get work doing childcare, light housework, or restaurant work. She married Walter H in 1931. They worked for several farmers before settling into a long term (eventually 42 years) relationship farming on shares. Mrs. H helped with most of the field work and chores often being outside more than she was inside. The couple raised two foster girls and were interested and active in their 4-H, school, and church activities.

They left the farm and moved into town in 1976. Mrs. H continues to enjoy card playing with friends, her Homemakers group and the Senior Center. She volunteers several days a week helping to cook meals at the Center.

Interview

The interview with Mrs. H took place on Feb. 22, 1985 at her home in ABC, Wisconsin from 1:30 p.m. to 3:30 p.m. Her experiences with the foster child system are documented on the tape as well as her experiences as a woman working on a farm. Mr. H was in the room during the interview and answered the phone that rang several times. Gentle chimes are also in the background occasionally.

continued...

Sample 4–continued

Description of the Rural Women's Oral History Project
The oral history project entitled "A Historical Perspective on the Leisure and Recreation Related Involvement of Rural Women" is designed to view the "everyday" experiences of rural women over the years. These everyday experiences, the activities one does, the attitudes toward work and "free time," religious and community involvement, informal education, and relationships that women have with others all provided important content and linked rural women in a common history. Thus, oral histories are an articulation of the quality of life perceived by rural farm women in Wisconsin.

For this research twenty-seven rural women, over the age of sixty who were nominated by other community members, were interviewed in their homes in a one to three-hour interview. The qualitative nature of the study allows for the development of themes and perspectives relative to leisure and rural living for these Wisconsin women.

Jean S. Rannells, Project Assistant
Karla A. Henderson, Project Director

Coding and Indexing the Data

Despite the fear of becoming too positivistic, it is necessary for the researcher using the qualitative approach to consider how to organize data so that one can return to it quickly without having to read through reams of material. Coding may also be referred to as data reduction or the process of selecting, focusing, simplifying, abstracting, and transforming the "raw" data (Miles and Huberman, 1984). Strauss (1987) referred to data organization as the conceptualization of data.

Coding is probably one of the most difficult aspects of qualitative research for the inexperienced researcher to master (Strauss, 1987). An incredible amount of reading and re-reading of data is necessary for data interpretation. This reading is, however, necessary and is the best way to become completely familiar with the data. As a qualitative researcher with volumes of data, it is tempting to become mechanistic in organizing the data. One is cautioned, however, not to make the organization of the data too automatic. In other words, coding by reducing data to numbers is not appropriate in keeping with the tenets of interpretive research. Some coding by numbers does help one to reduce the data and may make it more accessible but the researcher must be careful not to replace the rich meaning of words with numbers.

Codes or indices for qualitative data may be descriptive, interpretive, or explanatory and these codes are likely to change over time. One way to start is to code the data descriptively according to the research questions or guiding hypotheses that were originally conceptualized. These indices can then be revised as new hypotheses emerge and are revised. If possible, it may be useful to have two researchers code the "raw" data to assure greater reliability. Coding may be done line by line but is usually initially done with "chunks" of qualitative data. Not all notes will necessarily need to be coded or indexed initially. The coding however, will help one to become familiar with the kinds of data that are being discovered and may help in focusing the interviews or observations in different directions for further data discovery.

One must be careful, as always, not to become prematurely locked into coding procedures that are "carved in stone." The initial descriptive coding should provide the springboard for further interpretive coding and indexing. The coding may be quite general at first and then more focused later. The researcher should be continually cautioned that while coding may be economical, one does not want to lose the rich dimensions of the qualitative data.

A filing system can also be developed for keeping track of the data. This system may be developed on the computer for coding chunks of data or actually physically cutting and pasting a copy of the field notes and putting these edited pages into file folders. This system is referred to as keeping fieldwork files. In addition to data files, one might also want to keep (a) bibliographic files, background or mundane files on people, places, and chronologies (Lofland and Lofland, 1984); and (b) analytical files which offer information to support the working hypotheses. These files may exist physically or they may be files kept on a computer system.

Data Displays

Data display is the process of making visual pictures of how the data are emerging in a qualitative study. A display means a format that can be systematically used. Using only narrative text and coding may be overwhelming and tedious. Therefore, a display of the data in the form of matrices, tables, maps, and checklists may facilitate the development of conclusions. Data displays are not required but they may be helpful. Like coding or indexing, data displays may occur as an aspect of data discovery, interpretation, and reporting.

A number of ways exist to display data as a means for organizing for data interpretation. Each researcher will find that certain display strategies work well and others do not depending on the research situation. In each case, no matter what kind of visual ways are used to help in organizing data, the researcher will have to make judgments about what data are important and what are not.

A typical display format that may be used after data are coded is the matrix (Miles and Huberman, 1984). A matrix may also be used as a framework for coding data. A matrix can be easily eyeballed, compared to other matrices, and may use words or phrases. Usually one will develop categories for the matrix and then fill the matrix in with the words or examples from the data that describe the categories. A matrix may be used to outline specific examples that fit particular themes or it may be used for enumerating the responses to particular categories. The data entered into the matrix may be emic or etic but this meaning should be specified. The researcher will probably want to code the data entered into the matrix back to the field notes so she/he can go back and find that information quickly within the context in which it occurred.

A researcher can develop a number of matrices for a set of data and can be as creative as she/he wants by making them description or explanatory, single site or multiple, time ordered or not, categorical according to roles and groups, and/or one-way, two-way, or no-way. Some people prefer to build a matrix on a huge sheet of paper with 15-20 variables (although five to six is usually more manageable). As in any form of qualitative analysis, one must stay open to new roles and other matrices that may emerge. One may also find a large sheet of paper useful when one is doing cross-site comparisons concerning particular components, patterns, domains, or themes. The matrix may be useful for developing further questions for data discovery or it can be easily scanned for the development of preliminary conclusions. These conclusions can then be checked with the field notes. The matrix may or may not be useful for the final report write-up. Sample 5 shows the framework for a matrix developed to display the concept of "containers for leisure" (Henderson, 1990).

The use of visual maps is another data display technique that is useful to some researchers. A context map or causal network may be used to show the interrelationships that make up a context of behavior. Boxes and circles can be used to describe members of a group and what is happening in terms of relationships (Miles and Huberman, 1984). Diagrams are often helpful in organizing ideas and themes as well as patterns and configurations of interaction. Cognitive mapping may be used to describe the thought patterns that one uses as one reaches conclusions about data. Conceptual maps, which may be likened to a flow chart, involve tying patterns together with arrows and directional lines. They may be useful in stimulating thinking and can also be tested through further data discovery.

Guba and Lincoln (1981) suggested a technique of using notecards to sort ideas into look-alike piles that can then assume a category set. As will be mentioned later in this chapter, computers can also do this category set sorting. The use of cards or computers allows one to visually display the grouped data and to visualize how data may be organized. Using this technique also allows one to reduce data to labeled categories.

A similar technique for data display suggested by Miles and Huberman (1984) is factoring. This technique is not done in the sense of numbers and eigenvalues, but in trying to list ideas that fit under particular headings so that patterns can be found. Events listings and critical incidence charts may also be useful in organizing data.

Sample 5 Data Organization Matrix		
Work/Leisure Typologies		
Code **Workhorse**	**Delayed Gratifiers**	**Busy Bees**
LR It seems as if my work was never done anyway so if something needed to be done in the evening I'd still do it (p. 10).		
LM	I've gotten to the point that for so many years I did what I had to do, what I was expected to do, and now I'm free. I can do what I want to do (p.22).	
AR When you get done with one thing you start something else (p. 15).		
GS		I suppose I had a little free time but not too much, though I used to read at times. I did a lot of fancy work, embroidery, crocheting when I had the time—evenings maybe (p. 17).
DH A lot of people feel they need a vacation but to me my work and my pleasure were so closely related that I never felt that I needed a vacation and I still feel that way. I'm enjoying what I'm doing (p. 30).		
AH	You know it's coming and you know you have to slow down...where did we ever get the energy to get it done beforehand? (p.28)	
HC		No, I think I belonged to everything. Didn't make much difference. I put the kids in the car and away we'd go (p. 15).

A final note about data display relates to what Spradley (1980) called a "cultural inventory." The inventory may include all of the lists of domains or themes, maps, examples to support themes or theory, emerging theories, indices, table of contents, and descriptive data that provide the preliminary framework for conclusions about the research undertaken. One of the best technical ways to display data, ultimately, is to actually begin writing. The cultural inventory as a cumulative display of data will provide the framework for initial drafts of the research report.

These suggestions for displaying data are tools to be used in interpreting data. Data display is not the end product but is a technique to assist the researcher. The display techniques are means to the ultimate end of developing grounded theory and providing a rich description and explanation of the meaning of the research results.

Using a Computer

Computers may be used throughout the research process. The computer can be an effective tool for data management and analysis of qualitative studies. Unfortunately (or perhaps fortunately) the computer cannot do the interpretation for us, but it can be a tool that can make data management much easier. It can save time, cut down on fatigue, cut down on the tedium of cutting, pasting, filing and other clerical tasks, and can allow the researcher to have more time to devote to actual thinking and interpretation (Conrad and Reinharz, 1979). By using a computer, attribute descriptors can be embedded in the context and the indexing or coding of words or phrases is easier.

Cautions in using a computer should be noted as well. For example, the software should not define the research. It should enhance but not control what the researcher does. Further, there may be a high startup cost associated with a computer but the pay-off may be great in the long-run. Most qualitative analyses in the future will likely be done with the computer.

The computer offers a way to keep track of text and to manipulate data. The computer will probably not be useful for data collection but it can be used for coding and reducing text into retrievable units. The coding and retrieving will allow the researcher to be more flexible and efficient. As has been emphasized, notes should be recorded into the computer as soon as the data are collected with the format for coding set up shortly thereafter. Once the data are entered, it is possible to recode and reorganize as one progresses with the study.

At the time of this writing, there appear to be several qualitative data analysis programs available. One is QUALOG© (Chenery, 1988) and the other is THE ETHNOGRAPH© (Seidel and Clark, 1984). In general these two work by preparing a data file through word processing, numbering the lines, identifying the meaningful segments with coding, and sorting out the coded segments. The programs are based on assumptions of grounded theory in that the researcher can sort the text on the basis of the coding which emerges subsequent to grounded theory. Chenery (1990), for example, used THE ETHNOGRAPH© for her national study of the impact of camping on young people. THE ETHNOGRAPH© is currently available for both mainframe and microcomputers.

By the time this book is published, many other text analysis possibilities may exist because of the rapid advances in technology that are being made, especially with personal computers. In 1988, for example, Apple™ Computers developed a HYPERCARD© system (Gerson, 1988). This program is NOT a qualitative analysis program but its usefulness for qualitative studies is being applauded and encouraged. The principle behind the program is a set of stacks which are analogous to 3x5 cards. Each card can contain a number of fields. While there are limitations, HYPERCARD© can handle the tasks of entering field notes, summarizing them, coding according to analytical categories, sorting, and retrieving passages by categories. HYPERCARD© appears to be a very flexible program which is readily available and has numerous other applications for researchers besides just qualitative data analysis.

Sampling in the Qualitative Approach

Sampling is an issue that has been alluded to but has not been addressed directly up to this point. One of the major differences between quantitative and qualitative methods is the sampling procedures. Sampling in interpretive research using the qualitative approach is not the same as quantitative sampling and is not subject to the same procedures. One of the biggest criticisms of qualitative research results from an apparent lack of understanding about how sampling is done. Often sampling procedures are not reported in qualitative studies because no clear canon exists for how sampling is to be done. It is essential, however, that the researcher using the qualitative approach is able to formulate the theoretical and conceptual framework of a study through the technique that is referred to as theoretical sampling.

Sampling means deciding what group of people you want to study. Further, it involves realizing that you cannot observe everything so you can only address certain aspects related to people, settings, events, and social processes. Sampling in the quantitative approach means following a set of rules concerning selection and adequate numbers of respondents. In theoretical sampling in the qualitative approach, the researcher puts herself/himself in a situation to record behaviors which have relevance to the concept or theory being studied (Denzin, 1978). In other words, the researcher using the qualitative approach is not concerned about adequate numbers or random selection, but in trying to present a working picture of the broader social structure from which the observations are drawn. Within qualitative methods, the researcher is interested in sampling so that the observations made or data collected are representative of the more general class of phenomena and whether the observations or interviews made are representative of all the possible observations or interviews that could have been conducted (Babbie, 1986b).

Qualitative researchers use flexible research designs. The exact number or type of informants is not specified ahead of time although one may have some sense of what those numbers might be. The researcher must realize that this proposed number may change over time as data are discovered and interpreted. The researcher cannot say exactly how many people will be studied at the beginning, but she/he can count how many were involved at the end. In some cases, the researcher may need to spend more time in the field or interview more people than was originally proposed in order to get data that are trustworthy. In other cases, the data may be grounded more easily and quickly than was hypothesized.

Generally because of the nature of the data, samples are smaller, more purposive than random, subject to change, and investigative in nature (Miles and Huberman, 1984). The qualitative strategy is concerned with theoretical sampling of constructs rather than the quantitative accrual of large, random sample sizes. In the qualitative approach, the researcher decides when to quit on the basis of the amount of theoretical saturation (Glaser and Strauss, 1967). Saturation is reached with simultaneous data gathering and analysis and it occurs when the researcher realizes that the data collected are repetitive and no additional new information is being found.

Theoretical sampling is a process of data collection for generating theory whereby the researcher collects, codes, and analyzes data and decides what data to collect next and where to find them in order for the theory to emerge. Theoretical sampling is a procedure where researchers consciously select additional cases to be studied according to the potential for developing new insights or for expanding the grounded theory that is emerging (Glaser and Strauss, 1967). In theoretical sampling, the number of cases is unimportant. After the first few cases, you may select the sample in order to gather data and get a number of perspectives. Toward the end of data discovery, the researcher will focus more on interpretation and verification of data. The more variability in responses or observations one uncovers, the more one investigates further. The researcher is continually cautioned to avoid premature closure.

In using theoretical sampling in qualitative studies, there are several ways to get samples. In quantitative studies we address random sampling whereas in the qualitative approach we use purposive sampling (Patton, 1980a). Purposive sampling is used to get the most comprehensive understanding of a phenomenon. It may consist of sampling extreme or deviant cases as well as typical cases. Maximum variation is explored. One might choose for particular reasons to sample critical cases or politically important or sensitive cases. For some part of the sampling, one might also choose convenient cases. One might get informants or interviewees by using the snowball approach. The researcher can get people she/he knows or becomes acquainted with to recommend others. The researcher may ask friends, go to an agency and ask for suggestions, or advertise for volunteers just to get the process started. All of those are possibilities if they fit the theoretical sampling framework. When possible, representative or quota sampling is useful but it may also create a bias. In any sampling done using the qualitative approach, one should consider how each individual is important. Generally it is impossible to sample everyone, so the researcher must determine how individuals can contribute to the emerging research design and grounded theory. Purposive sampling may also be used for not only deciding what people to observe and interview, but which activities to observe, what locations, and what time periods.

Theoretical sampling is multistage where one is continually seeking out new possibilities and discovering grounded theory. Sampling error can occur in qualitative studies but this potential error can be mitigated by sampling for as long as is necessary to develop theoretical constructs. While the sampling procedures for the qualitative approach do not follow the rules that are prescribed in statistical studies, they are no less rigorous and are much more labor intense.

Trustworthiness

Interpretive research and the qualitative approach are frequently criticized for lack of precise descriptions, their suggestive rather than definitive conclusions, the questionable reliability, and the lack of generalizability. These studies are sometimes criticized for lacking rigor because they fail to employ a methodology that is conceptually clear and consistent, that reduces and eliminates bias and subjective inferences, and that minimizes the way the data might be rationally interpreted (Smith, 1980). Guba and Lincoln (1981), on the other hand, contend that the qualitative approach does meet the tenets of rigor and that we can find trustworthiness in qualitative research by paying attention to the methodology.

A parallel exists between the terminology for the quantitative approach and the qualitative approach. These parallel terms are internal validity, external validity, reliability, and objectivity juxtaposed to credibility, transferability, dependability, and confirmability (Lincoln and Guba, 1985). Credibility or internal validity refers to how truthful particular findings are. Transferability or external validity refers to how applicable or generalizable the research findings are to another setting or group. Dependability or reliability refers to how we can be sure that our findings are consistent and reproducible. Confirmability or objectivity refers to how neutral the findings are in terms of whether they are reflective of the subjects and the inquiry and not a product of the researcher's biases and prejudices. These terms are referred to by Lincoln and Guba (1985) as the "truth value" or trustworthiness. Trustworthiness and rigor are equally meaningful to qualitative and quantitative researchers, respectively.

Credibility

Internal validity or credibility can be questioned in qualitative research because of the apparent "subjective" way that data are collected. The narrow and impressionistic stereotype of methods such as field research suggest a lack of internal validity. In essence, perfect validity is theoretical impossible given the nature of the qualitative approach (Kirk and Miller, 1986). Since initially the qualitative researcher may not know what she/he wants to measure, it is difficult to know if the measurement is appropriate. The credibility of the research is largely controlled by the researcher. According to Kirk and Miller, "In the best of worlds, a measuring instrument is so closely linked to the phenomena under observation it is 'obviously' providing valid data" (1986, p. 22). Valid data are the reason why qualitative methods are selected. Internal validity is also related to the theory which emerges. Findings will be credible if the grounded theory corresponds to the observations. Theoretical invalidity will lead to wrong conclusions (Kirk and Miller, 1986).

The effect of the observer or the researcher must be addressed in examining the credibility of qualitative studies. Reactive effects, selective perception, and limits on what the observer can see all affect validity (McCall and Simmons, 1969). People often do not understand their behavior and yet when asked, they come up with insights about themselves. People tend to find meaning very easily in their lives but the critical question is how valid and reliable is that meaning to the individual. Further, the effect of the observer's or interviewer's presence may also change the statements made by the participants. We would like to think that the development of trust would make the participants' responses more credible but if the interviewer or observer becomes too "native" the credibility may also be affected because of the researcher's bias. Validity related to qualitative studies probably should be considered more personal and interpersonal than methodological.

Several suggestions, however, can be offered to improve the credibility of qualitative methods. It is important the researcher has a sense of what she/he is researching. As has been emphasized, the guiding hypotheses may change over the course of the data collection, but some direction must be initially set. Since the qualitative researcher trives to explain perspectives rather than elicit a strict cause and effect, internal validity may be defined more broadly. It is important for the researcher to explain how certain conclusions were reached and to provide descriptions and quotes that support the conclusions in the final report. The use of extended contacts, repeated observations, continuous observations, corroboration, and triangulation of data sources and techniques will also increase the internal validity. The researcher can reduce the effects of her/his presence by prolonged engagement in the study. Data collection biases can be minimized by documenting all the data gathered with extensive field notes and the use of written records and memos. Validity will also be increased by using the data discovery–data interpretation–data discovery–data interpretation loop continually.

Using "member checks" or cross examination by going back to individuals and checking out conclusions will increase the credibility of the research. This checking should be done on an ongoing basis and not just at the end of data discovery. Key informants might be good individuals to use for the "member checks." One might also like to use surrogate audiences as well as the original members (Guba and Lincoln, 1981). If the members do not agree with the findings then one may want to get new information from them, see where biases have occurred, and analyze where the disagreement or misunderstanding occurred. Wyman (1985) suggested that another way of increasing the validity or credibility of a study was to work with informants or interviewees as "co-researchers."

Transferability

In addressing transferability or external validity, the researcher is concerned with how the individuals or units studied are representative of the units to which the results might be generalized. The researcher must know both the research setting and other literature and related settings if generalizations are to be possible. The way that research is useful and expanding is by being able to generalize beyond the immediate situations studied. The transferability may be a matter of degree and this degree needs to be acknowledged. Guiding hypotheses as well as thick descriptions of the data will make judgments about transferability easier. The researcher must keep in mind that external validity or transferability is not a function of the number of units or people studied but of the kinds of units or people that are examined.

Differing views exist about whether the qualitative researcher should attempt generalization or whether that should be left to the reader of the research. One of the most useful ways to view external validity is to consider the findings as working hypotheses that can be transferred to other situations depending upon the degree of fittingness between two contexts (Guba and Lincoln, 1981). Other research can then use the established working hypotheses as guiding hypotheses for further study. On the other hand, it may not be necessary to generalize at all to other situations but to use the theoretical framework as the test in and of itself. In Melamed's (1986) study of the experience of play in women's development, she provided a transferable framework of substantive theory about play that researchers or practitioners could use in addressing women's play in other settings. *See Exemplar 8.1*

> Exemplar 8.1 Melamed, L. (1986). The experience of play in women's development. *Recreation Research Review, 13*(1), 7-13.
>
> Melamed used the qualitative approach because she felt the area of women's play was uncharted and not easy to predict. Play was described as attitudinal, affective, and integrated within one's lifestyle. She indicated that she was interested in studying play among women because of the role it has in her own life. The article is written from a first and second person perspective to indicate the heuristics of play. She also felt that to study play using premature hypotheses, predictability, neatness, and numerical uniformity seemed incongruent to the meaning of play. Further, because the area of women's play had not been previ-

ously explored, a qualitative approach was the best to use and Melamed felt women's lives would be more accessible by using an interview and case history method. She used semi-structured and guided fantasy interviews with nine women to examine their perceptions of play. She found that women described playfulness as a way of seeing and being in the world. It was difficult for women to talk about play without talking about the rest of their lives. Melamed offered a clear summary of her research in the form of a model and used emic quotes effectively in telling the story of how women integrate play into the whole of their lives.

Dependability

One cannot overlook the value of reliability or dependability in qualitative research. Reliability or dependability in qualitative studies may be considered a fit between what researchers record as data and what actually occurs in the setting (Bullock, 1983). Differing views exist concerning reliability. Some researchers argue that a well designed and documented study automatically will be reliable. Others, such as Marshall and Rossman (1989), contend that the qualitative approach does not pretend to be replicable because one avoids controlling variables and further, the world changes continually so replicability of any study is impossible. As Taylor and Bogdan suggested, "It may not be possible to achieve perfect reliability if we are to produce valid studies of the real world" (1984, p. 7). Reliability or dependability, however, is an issue that the qualitative researcher should try to address whether it is possible to obtain complete dependability or not. Dependability has not been stressed as much as validity in qualitative studies, yet qualitative methods are not necessarily less reliable than any other research methods.

A number of ways exist to increase dependability in qualitative studies. Having a plan for the research and being able to be flexible with it, while documenting how the changes in the plan occurred, can greatly affect the dependability of the findings. Triangulating methods and replication or prolonged engagement within the study can also help. Using an "auditor" or a second opinion in data interpretation is useful (Guba and Lincoln, 1981). If the researcher has left an audit trail in terms of describing how she/he came to the conclusions that she/he made, another person ought to be able to follow that trail and obtain the same conclusions. Auditability allows one to test for consistency. In Glancy's 1986 study of play on a softball team, for example, she addressed reliability by careful documentation, repeated observation, and documentation of her role with the team.

Confirmability

Objectivity or confirmability is the essential foundation for all research. Objectivity suggests as much reliability and validity as possible. Data should be factual and confirmable. Qualitative studies lack confirmability if the research is not reported to give accessibility to others and if theoretically meaningful variables are not reported. To be objective means to see how the world would appear to an observer who has no prejudices about what she/he observes.

No researcher can be totally objective but the data collected can be objective (Guba and Lincoln, 1981). A researcher may give up some objectivity in order to be close to the data but this is not necessarily a problem. As Scriven suggested "distance does not guarantee objectivity; it merely guarantees distance" (1972, p. 337). One may be better being factual about observations rather than being distant. Some people would argue that there is no such thing as objectivity. Researchers should, however, strive to be objective not by controlling variables, but by looking for a variety of explanations for the behavior that is being studied. Further, qualitative reseachers should aim to explain one hundred percent of the variance in a study.

Credibility, transferability, dependability, and confirmability are hard to separate in qualitative studies. Several strategies can be summarized that can serve as guidelines to help the researcher to assess the trustworthiness and methodological rigor of a qualitative study: make data collection explicit, use analytic constructs, account for negative information as well as contrasts and comparisons, acknowledge known researcher biases and be aware of these biases, document analytic decisions and leave an audit trail, use specific examples from the data, assess the participant's truthfulness, make the theoretical significance explicit, check for representativeness, triangulate data sources and methods, go back and forth between data discovery and data interpretation, get feedback from informants, be open to changes, and share methodological learnings (Guba and Lincoln, 1981; Marshall and Rossman, 1989; Miles and Huberman, 1984; Patton, 1980b).

Summary

Data discovery is the heading that includes data collection, data organization, sampling techniques, and trustworthiness. In qualitative methods there are no precise rules that one must follow for data discovery, however, this chapter has provided a number of strategies that the researcher might consider. The ever present aspect of behavior necessary to collect data was discussed and a number of pointers were given for effective notetaking. The organization of reams of data must be carefully considered by the researcher or she/he will be completely overloaded with data. The use of coding, indexing, data displays, and the computer were described. Theoretical sampling as a uniqueness of the qualitative approach was detailed. Lastly, issues of reliability and validity as they relate to the concept of trustworthiness were discussed with suggestions given for how data discovery in qualitative studies should be undertaken to lead to optimal credibility, transferability, dependability, and confirmability.

The key concepts discussed in this chapter are: notetaking, data collection, coding, indexing, data reduction, data displays, theoretical sampling, reliability, validity, objectivity, trustworthiness.

For Further Consideration

1. Find out what kind of computer software might be available to you that could be used for qualitative data organization.

2. Observe a recreational activity for half an hour and take as many notes as you can. Go back through the notes and indicate what data collected are facts and what are interpretations that you have made. Practice taking only descriptive facts.

3. Using the set of notes done in Question 2, go back and begin to make interpretations of what you saw. Indicate some particular behaviors that would be well to further investigate in a future observational session.

4. Describe the precautions a qualitative researcher might take to be sure data are trustworthy and that ultimately the research project findings are trustworthy.

For Further Reading

In addition to some of the literature that has already been described, the researcher may want to consult the following literature for further information about data discovery.

Miles, M.B., and Huberman, A.M. (1984). *Qualitative data analysis.* **Beverly Hills, CA: Sage Publications.**

Miles and Huberman provide the most comprehensive examination of data analysis and how one precedes this with data organization and data reduction. Although some of the techniques suggested are quantitative in nature, the reader will get a good sense of how one can begin to examine raw qualitative data and put them into some framework for further interpretation.

Chapter 9

Data Interpretation

Introduction

My hope is that you are not reading this chapter after having, in your perception, gathered all your data. Once again, I would like to reinforce that the nature of the qualitative approach is such that the design for data discovery and interpretation emerges as one works in the setting, with the interviewees, or with a particular context or text. Therefore, it is really antithetical to have a separate chapter on techniques of data interpretation but this chapter seems necessary simply from the standpoint of describing how all these data can be brought together. I would like to emphasize further that data analysis does not just happen, but that there are some strategies that the researcher might use to make the study more credible.

This chapter is divided into several parts that interface with one another. The main purpose of this chapter is to help the researcher understand how to simultaneously take data as they exist or are being discovered, display them, and find meaning within them. Ultimately the purpose of research interpretation is to develop grounded theory and more practically, perhaps, to know when to quit collecting data. Another purpose of this chapter is to dispel the notion that data interpretation is private, mysterious, idiosyncratic, or simplistic. Interpreting data by generating categories, themes, and patterns is difficult, complex, ambiguous, and fun (Marshall and Rossman, 1989). One needs, however, to be open to discovering the meaning that data hold.

The Process and Strategies

The complete data analysis process includes the simultaneous techniques of discovery, coding and displaying data, and interpreting data in its context (Taylor and Bogdan, 1984). Interpretation involves attaching meaning and significance to the data. Interpretation occurs during data discovery and throughout the entire research process. There are several reasons why this simultaneous process occurs in the qualitative approach. Data can be collected that will help one fill in the gaps that may become evident when data interpretation is undertaken or when new guiding hypotheses emerge. With the voluminous amount of data collected in qualitative studies, analyzing during collection helps to organize the data and make it less overwhelming. Interpretation also forces the researcher to think during the data discovery phase (Miles and Huberman, 1984). Data interpretation should, therefore, begin as soon as possible after data discovery.

Interpretation is time consuming although, since it occurs simultaneously with data discovery and data organization, it is difficult to separate interpretation into a specific time frame. Nevertheless, the researcher will spend hours going over notes, organizing the data, looking for patterns, checking emergent patterns with the data, cross-validating data sources and findings, and making linkages (Patton, 1980b). The initial guiding hypotheses and the insights that emerge are continually kept in mind.

The first cardinal strategy concerning data interpretation is, therefore, not to stop the interpretation process too soon. While the researcher may be focusing on the end product, one must make sure that one does not reach the end too soon or become locked too quickly into a pattern and miss other possible meanings. The emergent nature of qualitative research is foremost and these emerging patterns must be allowed to happen. No magic formula exists for when it is time to conclude a study, but the researcher must explore all possible explanations before closure is drawn.

A way to avoid premature closure is to employ the second strategy of interpretation which is to be "playful" with the data and look at data in as many different ways as possible. Using rival hypotheses and checking for biases may not sound like playful procedures but they are a way to cross check the data from a number of different perspectives to assure trustworthiness.

Thirdly, interpretation is a process that involves a strategy for thinking. It is systematic although very few rules exist for how one ought to interpret data to lead to systematic generalizations. As you will see in this chapter, there is no one path for making meaning out of facts. The qualitative approach requires introspection and examining one's thoughts and feelings as well as taking on the verstehen of the people being studied.

Another key strategy to keep in mind is that interpretations in qualitative studies come from being intimately familiar with the data. Therefore, one of the important tasks the researcher does is to read, read, read. The interpretation of meaning is not a task that can be assigned to someone else like one might hire someone to enter data into a computer or to run the statistics and give the researcher the print-out. Only through the researcher's interaction with the data will she/he become familiar enough to see the emerging patterns and themes.

Meaning is the most important outcome of any strategy related to data interpretation. During data interpretation, one must keep in mind that both the emic (the categories of meaning that people give) as well as the etic (the researcher's application of the concepts) are important. This is referred to as a "thick description" (Geertz, 1983) whereby the context and the meaning are closely associated. The goal of the interpretation is to group the meanings of a context by examining the relationships among the groups studied and focusing on the emergent ideas. The findings from a qualitative study are more than the recording of facts; these facts must be presented, analyzed and shaped into an explanatory scheme (Denzin, 1978). In some cases the researcher may be examining broad nomothetic meaning about a phenomena and in other cases it may be idiographic meaning related to finding the specific meaning that fits within a larger theoretical framework.

A final strategy relates to how much data are needed for adequate interpretation. This judgment call has no hard and fast rules. More data should be collected than will likely be needed. On the other hand, one of the problems that the novice researchers may encounter is collecting too much data that are difficult to manage. The concomitant process of data discovery and data interpretation along with theoretical sampling and striving for grounded theory should alleviate the problem of collecting too much data. The researcher should also keep in mind that some data will be used only for descriptive purposes and not for specific theory generation or confirmation.

Content Areas to Consider

As was described in Chapter 8, one has to have a way to organize the voluminous amount of data in the form of words into more manageable units. A coding system will be useful if there is a relationship between data coding and interpretation. The researcher may use some numbers for coding but she/he must be careful not to lose the richness of the data for the sake of efficient data management. Codes can be made and added at any time. Pattern codings may be thought of as "hunches" and can also be used to get data into categories that can then be subanalyzed. From these codings, the next interviews or observations can be developed and memos can be written. Always, however, the researcher should keep her/his mind open and not eliminate any possibilities too soon.

A number of categories for interpretation are possible, but initially one might think of several specific ways of summarizing data: categories and domains, themes, causes/explanations, relationships among people, and theoretical constructs (Miles and Huberman, 1984; Spradley, 1980). While the exact areas that you wish to explore may already be delineated in your guiding hypotheses, additional content areas are likely to emerge during interpretation. The researcher may be focusing on a holistic analysis of a phenomena or she/he may be studying a few selected domains. The exact content that will be the focus of the study will depend on one's personal interests, the informants one used, the theoretical underpinnings, and the organizing domain (Spradley, 1980).

Cultural domains evolve from categories of meaning. The most fundamental and ubiquitous analysis is meaning (Lofland and Lofland, 1984). A domain, according to Spradley (1979), includes categories that have a relationship to one another. All the members of a domain share at least one feature of meaning. Some of the categories for analysis might be particular settings or locales, objects, processes (stages, periods, phases, cycles, spirals, temporal sequences and other sequences), actors, activities (events), practices, episodes, encounters, roles (ascribed, learned, formal, informal, and how one performs a role), relationships (and intimacy), groups, conversations (language, interactions, nonverbal, frequency), organizations, interactions (intentions, functions, rules, consensus), and communities. The informants know much about the domains but it is up to the researcher to identify what the informants say, look for how they identify the categories, and then seek to confirm that these domains are credible for the group studied.

One may choose to examine causal accounts which may be single causes, a list of causes, or cumulating causes (Lofland and Lofland, 1984). Related to causes one may want to know under what conditions and circumstances they exist, and upon what variation depends. For example, Fryer and Payne (1984) used a qualitative study to identify the manifest and latent consequences of unemployment in order to develop a conceptual framework for successful unemployment.

Spradley listed a number of relationships that might be explored in looking at the content of data. Some examples include: strict inclusion (X is a kind of Y), spatial (X is a part of Y), cause-effect (X is a result of Y), rationale (X is a reason for doing Y), function (X is used for Y), sequence (X is a step in Y), and attribution (X is a characteristic of Y) (1979, p. 111). In a project I was working on recently, I was having problems finding a way to organize data about the leisure of women. After trying several approaches, I realized that "Y" was the container for leisure and that there were a number of "X's" that fit that container notion. The framework for interpretation as strict inclusion (X is a kind of Y) became clear as a way to examine the relationship between activities and the containers women have for leisure (Henderson, 1990).

Themes and theoretical constructs are larger units of thought that are used to create a higher degree of generality. They include frameworks for categories, domains, cause-effect, and relationships. As has been stressed, it is important to avoid imposing categories from the outside that create order and pattern rather than discovering it and seeking the conceptualizations of the informants (Spradley, 1979). If during the latter part of the data discovery-data interpretation process it appears that the data collected may fit already existing theory, then it may be appropriate to link the grounded theory to formal theory. Therefore, themes are generally used to describe substantive theory and theoretical constructs are used to explain the interpretations of data within existing formal theory.

The possibilities of content areas for data interpretation are numerous and the plethora of options may be overwhelming to the researcher at first. One is encouraged to remain patient and to try a variety of interpretations to see what might be best. The researcher is encouraged to arrive at the final conclusions several times before the data are actually reported.

Data Interpretation Techniques

In the interpretation of data the researcher is identifying categories, domains, and subsequently themes, that will lead to grounded theory. During the discovery and interpretation process, the researcher is encouraged to record memos about the data. She/he is encouraged to keep track of possible themes, hunches, and ideas. The researcher is also continually encouraged to look for categories and develop concepts and theoretical propositions based on the initial descriptions and the guiding hypotheses. By at least the midpoint of the research process, it may be useful for the researcher to go back into the literature of the content area to see if any formal theory might be confirmed in the study. The literature may help in illuminating the data that are being discovered. At this time, the researcher may also want to begin to develop a story line that may be useful in guiding the grounded theory (Taylor and Bogdan, 1984). From this point, a framework is developing for conducting the remainder of the data discovery and interpretation. The researcher, however, must continue to remain flexible until the possibility for new emerging hypotheses has been exhausted. The researcher should also continually evaluate the data for adequacy, credibility, usefulness, and other dimensions of trustworthiness (Marshall and Rossman, 1989). All data should be evaluated concerning the relationship it has to the unfolding story.

Most qualitative researchers have their own unique strategies for interpreting data. LeCompte (1984) has, however, delimited five major data analysis techniques which will be used as the framework for explaining data. These techniques are neither exhaustive nor mutually inclusive but they do provide processes for data interpretation and explanation.

The five major data analysis techniques and their proponents are: standardized observation (Goetz and LeCompte, 1981), enumeration (Denzin, 1978), typological analysis (Lofland, 1971), constant comparison (Glaser and Strauss, 1967), and analytic induction (Znaniecki, 1934). These techniques range from purely deductive to purely inductive, from a focus on verification to a focus on the generation of theory, from enumeration to abstract construction, and from objective to subjective. The technique for analysis that one will choose to use will depend upon the appropriateness, clarity, comprehensiveness, credibility, significance, and creativity desired by the researcher. In essence, these five techniques build on one another to reach analytic induction which is the most inductive, generative, constructive, and subjective technique. In a research study, one might also use more than one technique for analysis

In all data interpretation, the uncovering of patterns, categories, domains, themes, and grounded theory requires judgment. Making sense of data requires developing an indepth understanding of the content of the data as well as the techniques that can be used in data interpretation. Meaning can be found in many different ways.

Quantitative Modes

The first two areas that LeCompte (1984) discussed, standardized observation and enumeration, have a major relationship to positivism and quantitative approaches because generally one assumes some type of *a priori* theory in standardized observational protocols and enumeration. In the standardized protocol, the researcher uses a predeveloped instrument or develops an instrument for helping to organize the data. The technique is highly deductive and is used to verify hypotheses.

Enumerative strategies are often used to supplement descriptive data. In this technique the researcher codes data and counts it. One may be interested in the number of times certain behaviors occur or the duration of behaviors. Numbers are used in this case to show the intensity and amount of interaction. Numbers are useful in helping one to see easily and rapidly what the general results of the data may be. These numbers may also help the researcher to be analytically honest. In a qualitative study, the researcher may do some analysis with enumeration but generally a qualitative researcher will rely primarily on words and use numbers only as supplementary material.

Typological Analysis

One can do analysis on the basis of either verification of existing theoretical frameworks or the generation of substantive theory. Typologies refer to classification systems that describe categories of a phenomena which may result in verification or generation of theory. Typologies help to divide a phenomena into parts. The term is used quite broadly to refer to any number of possible categorical judgments which might include patterns, themes, or theories. In a typology, each case should fit into only one category and each case should be able to be classified into a category.

The researcher examines the completeness of category systems or typologies in terms of internal and external plausibility, inclusiveness of data, reducibility, and credibility (Patton, 1980b). In developing typologies, the researcher examines convergence and recurring regularities. The typologies developed may be emic or etic. The participants may have words or labels that describe their views. In other cases, the researcher may construct the typologies based on grounded or formal theory. As in any data interpretation, however, one must be careful not to force the data into typologies where the data will not fit.

In developing typologies, the researcher may select a type of relationship such as X is a kind of Y. She/he then examines the data and selects possible terms and subsets that will fit in order to develop possible categories or domains. These typologies can then be compared back to the data where new questions can be asked of interviewees or participants in order to construct a completed typological framework. For example, Shank (1986) did an exemplary job of using cases and thematic categories to allow typologies of dual career women to emerge. *See Exemplar 9.1*

> Exemplar 9.1 Shank, J. W. (1986). An exploration of leisure in the lives of dual career women. *Journal of Leisure Research, 18*(4), 300-319.
>
> Shank used indepth interviews with twelve women to explore the consequences of limited discretionary time on the role, function, and meaning of leisure in the lives of dual career women. He referred to his study as a preliminary investigation using multiple case studies. He specifically stated that he wanted to raise issues about the women's perceptions of time without limiting subjects to preconceived ideas. He felt the phenomenological approach was the best way to preserve the integrity of the subjects' sense of reality and to understand the meaning of leisure from their experience and perspective. The technique of using guided conversation interviewing was described in some detail. Shank also described the simultaneous process of collecting data and coding for interpretation. Using typological and inductive analysis, he developed typologies to describe the women's use of discretionary time and identified the prevalent themes of superwoman, guilt, leisure as directed at the self, and the lack of role models. Shank also suggested areas where further research is needed as well as the implications of this research to leisure education.

Constant Comparison

Glaser and Strauss (1967) have been the proponents of the constant comparison technique. Constant comparison is a systematic method for recording, coding and analyzing data. The goal of this technique is to maximize credibility through comparison of groups and data. It involves comparisons among data, data sets, literature, and different groups sampled. Different "slices of data" can also be compared. For example, one might use survey, observations, and anecdotal records, and see how the results obtained compare to one another (Glaser and Strauss, 1967).

Three stages comprise the constant comparison technique. First the researcher fits incidents to categories by identifying and coding categories and seeing how incidents fit. This proceedureis similar to what is done in typological analysis. The second stage is to integrate the categories and their properties by comparing them to one another and checking them with the data. In the third stage, the categories are delimited and reduced, if necessary, to gain parsimony and scope as well as to see if the data are theoretically saturated. Theoretical saturation means making sure that there are no other themes or categories that might be included. If new themes are discovered, then the researcher must go back through the data and compare them to the new categories.

The constant comparison method causes one to look continually for diversity. It allows the assurance of accurate evidence, establishes generality of a fact, specifies concepts, verifies theory, or generates theory. According to Glaser and Strauss (1967), constant comparison does not generate a perfect theory but rather a theory that is relevant to the behavior and the context in which it is observed.

Analytic Induction

The most inductive, generative, constructive, and subjective technique for analysis is analytic induction. It is the purest of the qualitative interpretation techniques. The technique involves the uncovering of categories of phenomena and relationships that can be applied to theory. One looks directly at the relationship between data and explanations and the interaction of method and substance (Znaniecki, 1934). The focus in on creating universals.

Analytic induction may be a procedural technique for generating or testing theory. The researcher is trying to arrive at a perfect fit between the data and explanations. According to Denzin (1978), there are both advantages and disadvantages in analytic induction. It allows the researcher to disprove theories while testing other theories. Old theories can be revised and incorporated into new theories. It shows the relationship between facts, observations, concepts, sampling, and theory and it leads to grounded theory. The disadvantages are that it is causal and not definitional and there are economic-temporal drawbacks to its use.

Analytic induction represents an approximation of the experimental model to the extent that comparisons are made. The steps of analytic induction include developing a definition of a phenomena, formulating a hypotheses, studying a case to see how the hypotheses fit, reforming hypotheses, searching for negative cases, reforming hypotheses, and so on until the hypothesis is adequately tested and a universal definition emerges (Denzin, 1978; Katz, 1983; Taylor and Bogdan, 1984). The inductive analysis ends when no more new patterns or theories emerge. The focus in on theory development and not on sampling (Denzin, 1978).

In using analytic induction, Bruyn (1966) suggested there are four levels of analysis: the original expression and meanings, themes, organizational themes, and theoretical linkages. Glancy (1988) used these levels of analysis in her study of the auction culture. In the first level she observed the patterns of activity and customs, formulated participant typologies, documented the detail, and reviewed the data with informants. On the second level, she let the perceived themes emerge and identified the social systems through a structural analysis. In the third level, she created a total configuration of the culture investigated and compared it to the real world, to other studies, and philosophical works. Lastly, she developed the linkage between the data and the theory and made logical theoretical associations. These procedures provide a definitive way to organize analytic induction as a data interpretation technique.

Alternative and Rival Hypotheses

One of the uniquenesses of the qualitative approach is the intent to describe not only the convergence of data but the divergence. Thus, in developing grounded theory, the researcher must continually be aware of rival and alternative explanations. When data diverge from grounded theory, the researcher must explain the divergence or collect more data to assure that the grounded theory is appropriate. Sometimes divergent data will be a result of the situation or the characteristics of the researcher or the interaction, but the researcher must not ignore these alternative findings. As was stated previously, the reseacher strives to explain one hundred percent of the variance.

By checking the data that does not seem to fit, one's basic interpretation of the findings can be strengthened. Those informants who have extreme views may be quite useful in understanding a phenomena. An examination of rival hypotheses also helps to rule out spurious relationships. By addressing rival hypotheses one assures that the ideas will not be lost, that the hypothesis is given a chance, and that grounded theory can be improved. A researcher using the qualitative approach should always be looking for negative evidence. She/he should not ignore divergent evidence but should try to explain what it means related to the emerging grounded theory. Disconfirming evidence is useful if the researcher is to remain open to all the perspectives possible in interpretive research. Cross-checks on distortions and exaggerations, rather than ignoring the data, will also improve the internal validity or credibility of the study and will give the researcher greater perspective on the data. Looking for rival hypotheses should prevent the researcher from forcing the data to fit a substantive or formal theoretical framework that may not be appropriate. The search for alternative explanations is the critical act of challenging the emerging patterns and acknowledging that in interpretive research, alternative explanations always exist (Marshall and Rossman, 1989).

Eliminating Bias in Data Interpretation

If the preceding techniques and strategies have not helped you to see how researchers try to eliminate bias in the qualitative approach, I am not sure what will convince you. Several additional strategies may be useful to emphasize. As researchers, we want to avoid Type I errors (believing a principle is true when it is not), Type II errors (rejecting a principle when it is true), or Type III errors (asking the wrong questions) (Kirk and Miller, 1986). We want to make sure that the data we discover are adequate and that we have efficient ways of interpreting them (Zelditch, 1962). Further, the system of classification of data and the techniques used for data interpretation should rise from the nature of the data.

The researcher should also be realistic about the data and realize that some informants are better than others, some circumstances of data collection may have been better (i.e., repeated contact, specific settings), and some systems of validation may be more fruitful (Miles and Huberman, 1984). It is helpful for the researcher to be continually evaluate the data quality. Some data may need to be discounted because of the observer's influence on the setting, who was there, the source of data, or the assumptions and presuppositions that may have been operating (Taylor and Bogdan, 1984). In general, the researcher may need to continually play the role of devil's advocate and carefully monitor the entire process of data discovery, display, interpretation, and reporting. Notetaking should be as value free as possible, the data should be applied to testing, and an audit of data collection and analytic strategies should be kept to assure appropriate interpretation (Marshall and Rossman, 1989).

Ending the Data Discovery/Interpretation Process

The last stage of the qualitative approach after getting started and gathering data is leaving the project. The researcher should be getting feedback from the informants and interviewees all during the research process, but she/he should not leave a project without conducting member checks. A member check is the discussion of the researcher's interpretation of the data or grounded theory with key informants or selected interviewees. These opportunities for feedback with "members" in the study should be planned, data displays should be used if they make the data more understandable, and informants should not be overburdened with theory. The meanings found in the research ought to be discussed with someone and informants are frequently the best sources.

The researcher should stop collecting data when no new situations exist from which to collect data, when redundancy is reached, and/or when she/he feels the data can be integrated and interpreted adequately. Determining the end of a project is subjective, but a high degree of generalizability should indicate it is time to quit. A general recommendation is that a researcher should remain at a site or with a project long enough to witness the full cycle of routines. Each study, however, will vary greatly concerning what the cycle of routines mean. As a researcher, you want to be assured that you have tentative hypotheses and not just "noise." After you think all the data are collected, you need to spend a little more time in contemplation and provisional writing and then make the decision about when to stop the data gathering.

When one has confidence in the descriptive and interpretive meanings applied to the data, then it is time to write the final draft of the results. The departure from people, particularly in field research, should be carefully planned particularly if one has spent a lot of time with individuals. The researcher should first of all make sure that she/he has upheld the bargain and the contract that was originally set with the organization or with individuals. One may then want to ease out or set an appropriate ending point for data collection. Roadburg (1980) described one of the problems of leaving the field as being related to the intense interpersonal friendships made and the experiences shared. The participants may feel they are being abandoned and the researcher may feel guilt and isolation upon leaving. Therefore, leaving the field should be acknowledged as an important stage in the research process.

After completing data gathering, one may want to return to the library to do final theoretical analysis, although it is better if much of this literature review is done during the course of data discovery and interpretation. If one decides to leave and then discovers insufficient data, it may be possible to return for more data but that is not the best situation once the researcher has already said her/his farewells. One may have to admit the limitations of what one did as a researcher in the written report rather than return to the setting or to the interviewees. If data are well collected, one should not feel the need to return to further data gathering.

Summary

Data interpretation and data discovery are ongoing throughout the research process. Specific techniques, however, may be used when one begins to interpret what the data mean. This interpretation occurs in order to collect more data as well as a way to find meaning in the data. In this chapter the steps used in data interpretation were described. The specific techniques of quantitative modes, typological analysis, constant comparison, and analytic induction were described along with the use of guiding hypotheses and alternative hypotheses. How one leaves the project and ends the data discovery/data interpretation loop was also discussed.

The key concepts addressed in this chapter were: data analysis, interpretation, guiding hypotheses, meaning, patterns, themes, enumeration, typologies, constant comparison, analytic induction, and rival hypotheses.

For Further Consideration

1. How do you know when you are ready to terminate a qualitative study?

2. Why should a researcher be suspicious if the early interpretation of a phenomenon seems to be so obvious?

3. Select an article from a leading leisure research journal and try to develop some rival hypotheses that you might use if you were to conduct the research with a qualitative approach.

4. Using the constant comparison technique, take any three textbooks related to recreation (introductory, programming, or administrative) and determine what seem to be the major themes common to the textbooks.

For Further Reading

A number of the annotated references already noted address data interpretation, and you may wish to consult those further as well as any of the following:

Fielding, N.B., and Fielding, J.L. (1986). *Linking data*. Beverly Hills, CA: Sage Publications.
    While the focus of this book is on linking qualitative and quantitative data, it provides a system for making qualitative interpretation that must be understood if data are to be linked. The book is also useful in showing the differences between the types of data that may be collected using the qualitative and the quantitative approaches.

LeCompte, M.D (1984). *Ethnography and qualitative design in educational research*. Orlando, FL: Academic Press.
    This book provides a thorough discussion of the techniques that can be used for data analysis. The ideas provide guidance but do not impose hard and fast rules for making data interpretations.

Strauss, A. (1987). *Qualitative analysis*. New York, NY: Cambridge University Press.
    This is a very useful handbook for helping one to analyze and interpret social phenomena. The purpose is to instruct anyone who is interested in learning and improving the way that they qualitatively analyze data. The book assumes that data are being collected appropriately and further provides a framework for the effective and efficient analysis of data. The book is straight forward and offers many valuable insights.

Chapter 10

Data Explanation by Writing the Report

Introduction

According to Miles and Huberman (1984), a researcher using qualitative methods has four recurring nightmares: that the data are not good, that systematic measurement error exists, that conclusions are trivial or trite, and that data resist analysis. If any of these occur, then the researcher does not have to worry about explaining the data and writing the final report. It is assumed, however, that the data are good and the researcher has something to say, so it is critical that the data are explained through writing in a way that the reader becomes immersed in the data just as the researcher did.

Writing qualitative study reports, articles, or books is not easy to do largely because the written work is the integrative explanation for the research (Strauss, 1987). Writing can be made easier, however, in two ways. One way is to read qualitative studies to see how other researchers captured their topics. Spradley (1979) suggested that if you read well-written ethnographies during the process of writing, your own writing will improve unconsciously. Another way to make writing easier is "simply" to write a report or article and use that as the basic foundation for further expansion and elaboration.

It is not easy to translate the explanation of the meaning of a phenomena to readers who may not know anything about the particular culture or topic that you have studied or who may know about the topic but do not understand the qualitative approach. Further, in the case of writing for publication in journals, it is difficult to take pages and pages of data and reduce them to a 10-page journal article that will capture the general meaning as well as the details of a study. A further problem identified by Mason (1988) who wrote about older women and leisure, was the difficulty of forcing data from a qualitative study into generalized findings for a short article when one has the sense that the data are constantly speaking against crude generalizations and classifications.

The researcher will find that frequently the real meaning of a study will become interesting, central, and important only after the researcher begins writing (Schwartz and Jacobs, 1979). Writing forces one to do soul searching and intensive thinking. The written report reflects the reading and analytic logic of the data interpretation. The time used for explanation through writing is just as important as data discovery in the field, although this writing time is often taken for granted. Therefore, writing like all the other aspects of the qualitative approach, should be going on simultaneously with data discovery and interpretation. When the researcher begins to actually write, she/he is able to organize the text and begin to see how an intended outline fits. At this point, as well as throughout the research process, the researcher must be open to novelty and excitement (Lofland and Lofland, 1984).

As Spindler (1982) and Locke (1986) suggested, writing is making the familiar seem strange or exotic and making the strange seem familiar. The interpretation will only be interesting if it departs from the "obvious." The report is written so the reader will feel like she/he was there and knows what it was like to be in that situation. In the writing phase, one specifically addresses the existing literature and one's own reflections and intuitions. Fielding and Fielding (1986) suggested that a dualist view in writing is needed to describe the detail of the foreground against the design of the background. Newly developed insights need to be presented. Therefore, the written product of qualitative study is science, art, and journalism. It is an interpretation and explanation of the world that constitutes meaning.

Both approaches and audiences should be considered when explaining the data by writing the report. Different approaches attract different audiences. The common aspects, however, of all writing are the meanings presented that are associated with behavior within a culture, the experiences of the researcher, and the role of the reader. The culture of a group or the meaning of a text is made visible by the writing that is done. The researcher as a writer wants to develop meaningful information without great distortion. She/he decides what to tell and how to tell it with the focus on a particular audience. The researcher must understand the characteristics of the audience for whom the particular written materials are designated. For example, the writing would most likely be different for a thesis committee than for your family.

Van Maanen (1988) has identified three major types of readers. Colleagial readers are those in your field who will probably be interested in techniques, language and text, coverage and scope, generalizations, and analytic approaches. The social science audience will be concerned with how well the research was done and what the facts represent. The general audience will be looking for a story that is entertaining, interesting, free of jargon, and simplified. The researcher may be writing more than one report or article depending on the various audiences that she/he wishes to address. The researcher should keep in mind that while journalistic style may be important, the interpretive nature of the report will be most useful for building the body of knowledge.

Organizing the Report

In writing the results of a qualitative study, the researcher will need to consider conveying credibility of the discovered theory by using both emic and etic descriptions, presenting the evolving theoretical framework, and describing the subjects studied and the strategies for data collection so the reader can identify with them. It is highly unlikely that all of these considerations will be perfectly addressed in the first draft. Most initial descriptions likely will be partial, incomplete, and in need of revision. First drafts are often inadequate but informants can often help the researcher to clarify thoughts. Therefore, the researcher is encouraged to begin writing before leaving the data discovery phase of the field (Daniels, 1983; Johnson, 1976).

Werner and Schoepfle (1987) suggested that the writer should plan on making at least five drafts with a different focus on each revision. The first draft should focus on making sure all the information is included that one wants to communicate. The second draft will seek to see if the text is clear and well organized. The third draft should address the style of writing. The fourth focuses on writing succinctly and concisely, while the fifth draft is used to polish the style. During each subsequent draft, one can rearrange information and give further thought to the grounded theory. It is usually best to allow plenty of time to write as distance from the data and the passage of time will often help to solidify thoughts. It is impossible, and ill-advised, to include all data in one's writing, so the researcher must make judgments what to include and what to omit.

Qualitative reports and articles may follow the general frameworks that are used in traditional research reports or they may vary a great deal depending on the data and experiences that emerge. The traditional approach to technical research writing as related to what the researcher using the qualitative approach would do includes: posing a general question (describing the context), introducing the data and how it was obtained (the researcher's role), giving a review of previous work, presenting the main report (including topics and themes and how they relate), developing conclusions and implications (using comparative studies and grounded theory), and adding any footnotes or appendices that are needed. The emphasis given to these various parts may differ from study to study. The researcher writing about qualitative studies may start at different places but generally all of these aspects are included in most written reports. For example, the research on wilderness programs for adjudicated youth by Hunter (1987) followed a traditional research writing format. *See Exemplar 10.1.* On the other hand, Smith (1985) described working-class pubs in a narrative, story-like style. *See Exemplar 10.2.*

Exemplar 10.1 Hunter, R.I. (1987). The impact of an outdoor rehabilitation program for adjudicated juveniles. *Therapeutic Recreation Journal, 21*(3), 30-43.

Hunter used the participation observation method with ten adjudicated males participating in an outdoor experience. He rationalized the use of qualitative methods by suggesting that they "offer sensitivity to a broad range of variables" (1987, p. 30). The purpose of the study was to determine how and why participants in an outdoor rehabilitation program changed during the program. The techniques used in the study are described thoroughly. For example, constant comparison was used as the data interpretation technique. Hunter described how he used the technique to progress from incidents to categories, to integrate categories, and to delineate categories. Excellent descriptions of the program and the participants were made. Hunter also identified stimuli affecting the boys in the program and was able to explore the behavior change and the internal processes that were responsible for them. Hunter concluded that only a small number of participants were affected by the outdoor experience but those effects were profound. The explanations of the results helped to understand the reasons why the program was effective for some of the boys and was not effective for others. Hunter suggested that one of the strengths of a qualitative approach may be its use in studying changes in isolated cases.

Exemplar 10.2 Smith, A.A. (1985). A participant observer study of a "rough" working-class pub. *Leisure Studies, 4*, 293-306.

Smith did a three month participant observation of a "rough" working class pub in England. This pub was different from a respectable working class or middle class pub and presented some unique problems for the observation. The intent of the study was to raise sociological issues about the patterns of usage and the role of pubs in class-cultural patterning. Specifically, Smith was interested in the relationship among alcohol, leisure, and social contexts. The study is well written with the objectives clearly addressed and a brief explanation of how the data were obtained. The style of writing is narrative with only minimal attention paid to methodology. Smith appeared to be examining the data with the guiding question of "What kinds of relationships exist in this bar?" His description of the characteristics of the bar were particularly interesting. The findings of his research are woven into a story using primarily an etic perspective. He underlined his need to be "sociologically reflexive" in his efforts and in his description of a new perspective on understanding bars.

A few words on how to write about methods may be useful. One of the major criticisms of qualitative methods is that the data collection procedures are rarely explained. Thus, it is sometimes difficult to judge the trustworthiness of the data. The attitude that qualitative methods are esoteric and intuitive has not helped interpretive research's credibility. The researcher cannot assume that the reader naturally believes the findings are valid. Therefore, the researcher ought to explain the choice of a particular topic, the groups studied, the time and length of study, the nature and number of settings and informants, the research design and sampling, the frame of mind and the private feelings of the researcher, the relationship with informants, how data were checked, and the retrospective processes used in conducting the study (Lofland and Lofland, 1984; Taylor and Bogdan, 1984). Research techniques or strategies that failed are seldom reported and yet, this information may be very helpful for strengthening other's abilities to apply qualitative methods more effectively in the future.

The writing of the report should give the reader enough information to make decisions about the importance of the data. Thus, adequate information also must be provided about how decisions were made concerning data interpretation. The reader is going through a discounting process and it is a joint responsibility between the reader and researcher to find understanding and meaning in the writing.

Content of the Report

Writing the report involves more than thumbing through your notes. By the time you are ready to write, you should have a number of memos, written summaries, and visual displays to use. In fact, depending on your audience and the nature of the publication, the researcher should be able to go any number of directions based on the "inventory" of data, the frameworks developed from the interpretation techniques, and the working hypotheses that have emerged.

A difference exists between purely descriptive and theoretical/conceptual studies. The qualitative writing may be a variation along the continuum of these two ends. Directly related to this issue is emic and etic interpretation. The researcher as writer must decide whether to use the informants' words or the researcher's. She/he must also decide whether to allow the writing to speak for itself so the reader can draw conclusions or whether the researcher should draw the conclusions. The researcher must also determine whether the purpose of the research is to provide a transcendent perspective for the audience or to present more pragmatic outcomes (Lofland and Lofland, 1984). Any of these writing approaches are possible but the researcher must establish which will be pursued. On any aspect of the continuum, the use of "thick" description is necessary with the focus on a literal description of the entity, the circumstances under which the study was done, the characteristics of the people involved, and the nature of the context (Geertz, 1983). The use of exact quotes often adds much to the reader's understanding of and interest in the data.

Van Maanen (1988) described three types of ethnographic accounts that may be useful: realist, confessional, and impressionist. The realist account is written in a dispassionate, third person voice with the researcher seen as the expert or the scientist. It is descriptive and explanatory. It is usually done in a documentary style with a no nonsense way of presenting the interpretation as "short and sweet." The realist writer focuses on her/his subject matter without focusing on how she/he came to know this information. This realist account is the way that researchers are generally taught to write and this style is commonly found in the leisure literature (e.g., Henderson and Rannells, 1988; Shank, 1986).

The confessional "tale" is highly personal and focuses on the researcher's experience in infiltrating, building rapport, and includes the melodrama of the activity. It is autobiographical with an attempt to establish intimacy with the reader concerning what happened in the field and to show how the researcher had empathy and involvement with the informants. The researcher is very clear about her/his feelings and the surprises and shocks associated with discovering and interpreting data. The writer focuses on how data and interpretation came to be. Glancy (1986) effectively used this method in her study of using participant observation with an adult softball team.

The impressionistic writer sets out to describe a phenomena within a particular setting and time. Words, phrases, imagery, and recall of experience are used. The writer tries to write an evocative story that seeks to enable the reader to relive the lives of the people described and to feel like "you were there." Textual identity, characterizations, and drama are frequently used. The goal of this writing is to get the reader and the researcher together in a common empathy for the topic. Writing this type of account is a continual learning experience for the researcher.

Learning to write interpretively, according to Van Maanen, is "like learning to play an instrument rather than solve a problem" (1988, p. 118). Writing is a matter of practice and improving upon your previous accomplishments. You will have succeeded in learning how to write well when you can communicate what your respondents believe to be true about themselves in a way that researchers can also appreciate (Sanday, 1979).

Pointers for Writing

Many useful resources exist for writing research. Because of the nature of the qualitative approach, writing may be considered the frosting on the cake if the researcher has systematically and thoroughly discovered, displayed, and interpreted the data in the ongoing process of the research. I will, however, summarize and highlight a few ideas that the researcher can use to make the writing process a little easier.

- Jot notes about what might be included in a formal written report throughout the process of data discovery and interpretation. Your intuition will be most helpful throughout the research process. A "writing block" at the end of the project may be due to the fact that the data have not been adequately interpreted before the cumulative writing begins.

- You cannot include everything in the write-up but you must be careful to include enough so the reader feels as if she/he gets the "full picture" of the phenomena studied.
- Decide on the audience that you want to address. I have found that it is useful to think of a particular individual to whom I would like to explain the study in written form. It may be a thesis committee member, a supportive colleague, or a person who is likely to be very critical.
- Do not overestimate the technical knowledge that the audience may have. Many people are not familiar with the qualitative approach so it will be necessary to define the terms you are using and be as clear as possible about the techniques used. Let the reader know what you are doing and what they should expect.
- Be concise and direct. Because the primary means for communicating results in qualitative studies are words, the words must be precisely chosen.
- The data are the examples and the quotes that you have discovered. Link your interpretation to those examples. You have heard the phrase that a picture is worth a thousand words; in qualitative writing a quote or a colorful description or example may be worth a thousand words of elaborate explanation. It is usually best if the examples are short and used only once in the written report.
- Metaphors are often a useful way to make the data more understandable. Comparing methods or describing ideas in relation to other ideas may make the meaning of the study more easily perceived.
- The methods and data in qualitative writing should always be described within the context in which they occurred. An interpretation of data and analysis will help to achieve integration of the context in the writing. West (1984), for example, did an extraordinary job of describing the attitudes that people with disabilities expressed concerning the social stigma barriers they faced in community recreation participation. *See Exemplar 10.3.*

Exemplar 10.3 West, P.C. (1984). Social stigma and community recreation participation by the mentally and physically handicapped. *Therapeutic Recreation Journal, 18*(1), 40-49.

In this study and others that West reported (e.g., West 1982; 1986), indepth interviews were used as the method for data discovery. This particular study examined the social stigma barriers to community recreation participation experienced by people with mental and physical disabilities. He conducted one hundred and eighty interviews that were both quantitatively and qualitatively analyzed. He was interested in the interviewees' perceptions of negative stigmatizing attitudes and the degree that these attitudes restricted participation. West described the interview procedure in some detail in terms of how he got the people with disabilities to talk about issues that were quite sensitive to them. West explained how he tried to accomodate people with disabilities but also how he tried to push them to their limits in order to get information. He detailed the rapport building that was used and how it took several contacts to develop the trust needed for the respondents to provide useful interviews. He indicated that at times he had to use many follow-up probes in order to get the information that he desired. The quotes used in reporting the findings helped to reinforce the implications of the study that were offered for recreation professionals.

- If you are not sure how to begin the formal writing, it is best just to begin. Writing helps you think and when you are not sure what to do, writing anything can often get you started. It is not necessary to start with the introduction to your paper. You can start in the middle with a particular theme that you find interesting and easy to describe. Once you begin, the writing is likely to flow. If you are really having a problem, you may want to begin writing as if you were writing to a friend about your research. From the very act of writing, you may be enlightened about how to write the research for professional colleagues. As was mentioned before, the first draft usually differs quite markedly from your finished product so do not expect any kind of perfection the first time. Similarly, if you hit a "writing block," try to continue writing anyway. In using qualitative data, you may be able to return to the field for additional data or return to the data for further analysis. Be sure to start writing again as soon as possible.
- Develop your own style of writing. Some people are steady plodders while others are grand sweepers (Lofland and Lofland, 1984). Do what works best for you. I am the type of person who likes to sit down and concentrate completely on getting as many ideas as possible written down. These drafts usually take major revisions before I am done. I have a colleague who usually does not write anything until the ideas are well formulated in her mind and then she writes with little need for major revisions.
- Keep in mind the consequences of the research as you write. Consider such questions as: How is this research affecting me, what will be the reaction of colleagues, what will be the reaction to this research report from the people studied, what will foes of the study say, what impact

will the research have on social knowledge, and what will be the consequences of this research to the larger world? (Lofland and Lofland, 1984). The researcher must also keep in mind the bargains made during the "getting in" phase as well as the ethical agreements concerning confidentiality and anonymity in the course of writing.

- It is often useful for a colleague, a fellow student, a staff member, or perhaps an informant to read your draft paper and comment on it. After months of working with data, it is sometimes easy to lose some perspective. Therefore, other readers may help you to see where "holes" exist in your logic, and they can give you feedback about what is important and not so important to include.

- The writing should reflect an intimate familiarity with the data. The writing can be more interesting by being creative with the examples and interpretation but this process is only possible when you know the data inside and out.

- The writer should ask herself/himself whether her/his values are being made clear, whether the results are reproducible, and to what extent the results may be generalized and legitimately fed back into theory. In other words, the interpretive rationale must be made clear in the writing (Fielding and Fielding, 1986).

- Other good literary styles pertain to qualitative report writing. For example, one should write in an active rather than a passive voice, use examples rather than abstractions, use adjectives, use personal pronouns, vary the length of sentences, use connecting words between ideas, and avoid negative sentences. The researcher writing a report to explain a qualitative study must employ the best writing that she/he would use in any type of publication.

Getting Published

Some qualitative studies are done for the sole purpose of getting a degree or for getting information for some type of applied evaluation. While the goal of the research may not be publication in a research journal, this possibility should always be considered because publication is the way that we share our recreation, parks, and leisure research findings and build upon our knowledge base. Further, more examples of qualitative research are needed in the journals that address issues of interest to park, recreation, and leisure researchers and practitioners. The visibility of these studies will likely provide the impetus for other researchers to try the qualitative approach for other appropriate research questions.

Research that uses qualitative methods and techniques is frequently misunderstood. For example, in a research article that I wrote about the farm women that I studied, an initial reviewer for one of the field's major journals was very concerned about the sample size and selection process because it was not done randomly. I had explained the rationale for what I did, but I made assumptions that the reviewer knew about theoretical sampling which she/he obviously did not. Therefore, as has been noted before, it is important when trying to get published in traditional journals that have typically accepted manuscripts using quantitative methodologies, that the writer is clear about why particular techniques were chosen and used.

The researcher must be aware of other common criticisms that are leveled against the use of qualitative methods and techniques by individuals who do not understand the approach. Researchers must be careful that their work does not appear to be sloppy, without rigor, or unfocused. The researcher must try to present the research in a way that provides a framework, but indicates how the design was allowed to emerge and how it in fact, did emerge. Therefore, the procedures must be made clear. The researcher must help the journal reviewers and readers see that the qualitative approach results in more than just a good story. The researcher may also want to show how a qualitative study is not just exploratory for future quantitative studies, but has value for the generalizations and grounded theory that can be developed. With the traditional positivistic focus on correct method, a interpretive researcher often has her/his hands full in meeting publication expectations. Regardless of the assumptions made about the research world, studies reported that are rigorous, insightful, and theory framed (either *a priori* or as grounded) are likely to get considered for publication in today's recreation, parks, and leisure journals.

When writing for a journal as opposed to writing a book, the writing will be much different. Spradley (1979) suggested when writing a book one will want to address universal statements, comparative descriptions, general statements about the society and the specific cultural group, specific statements about the culture, and specific incident statements. Stebbin's (1979) book on amateurs addressed the framework that Spradley suggested. A professional journal article may focus more on the first two aspects than the others given the limitations in space.

The writing of a book, journal article, or evaluation report is the way that the researcher explains the meaning of the data and the techniques used for data discovery, organization, and interpretation. It signifies the end of the research as described by Glaser and Strauss:

> When the researcher is convinced that his (sic) conceptual framework forms a systematic theory, that it is a reasonably accurate statement of the matters studied, that it is couched in a form possible for others to use in studying a similar area, and that he can publish his results with confidence, then he is near the end of his research (1967, p. 224-225).

Now it's time to move on to the next great project!

Summary

Anyone who does not like to write will not enjoy using the qualitative approach to research. For some people the formal writing of the qualitative reports symbolizes the end of the project. For others who find writing difficult or have not included elements of writing as part of the data interpretation, the writing may be very time consuming and frustrating. While the actual finished product is the explanation of the data as embodied in the written report, this chapter suggested that writing is also an ongoing part of the research and not just something that is done at the end of the project. It is helpful if the author has a sense of how to organize a report, what content to include, how to write technically well, and where to look for publication outlets. This chapter described these aspects as ways to motivate the researcher to get the qualitative study published and available to interested readers.

The key concepts covered in this chapter were: data explanation, meaning, publishing.

For Further Consideration

1. Examine a published qualitative study and a published quantitative study from a leading leisure research journal. How do the two differ in the ways that the methodology is presented and the data are explained?

2. Why are qualitative research studies more likely to be written in the first person?

3. If writing is difficult for you, how might you learn to be a better writer?

For Further Reading

Most books do not spend a lot of time talking about how to write qualitative research. One can learn a great deal from reading studies that have been written. Two of the best, most recent sources that address how to write qualitative reports are:

Van Maanen, J. (1988). *Tales of the field.* **Chicago, IL: The University of Chicago Press.**
This is a delightful book that describes everything you would want to know about ethnographic writing. Van Maanen uses many examples of ways to write accounts of qualitative research. One gains a number of perspectives about writing and can see, after reading the book, how one's data and one's personality can fit together to write an interesting and trustworthy account.

Werner, O., and Schoepfle, G.M. (1987). *Systematic fieldwork, Vol I and II.*
Newbury Park, CA: Sage Publications.
    The two volume texts from Werner and Schoepfle offer a great deal of
information about doing field research. The sections about writing provide a
comprehensive approach to data explanation in light of how the data are discovered,
organized, and interpreted.

Chapter 11

Issues and Challenges

Introduction

This final chapter will examine briefly several other aspects of the qualitative approach that have been alluded to throughout the earlier parts of the book. As with other sections, one cannot look at these "odds and ends" without considering the "whole" context of the research process in which they are functioning. The issues raised in this chapter are preliminary issues that should be addressed prior to beginning a research study and should be continually acknowledged throughout the research process. Some of the responses to the questions raised by these issues may mean that research is never undertaken. Other responses will simply mean that the research is more rigorous and useful than it might have been if these issues had not been considered. The issues and challenges in this chapter are offered as additional food for thought. The issues to be addressed are: ethics, characteristics of the researcher, politics and funding, linking quantitative and qualitative data, the practitioner's use of qualitative data, and a summary of the challenges in using interpretive research and qualitative methods.

Ethics

Ethics include the "oughts" of living. The researcher must have principled sensitivity to the rights of others which she/he acknowledges may tend to limit her/his own choices (Bulmer, 1982). Little agreement exists on just what the ethical bottom lines of the qualitative approach are. Since ethics deals with right/wrong and morality, ethical dilemmas are sometimes taken for granted because of the values that we maintain in living our daily lives. Some researchers are "relativists" and argue that many practices in research can be justified in the name of scientific goals and knowledge advancement. Other researchers would suggest that any exploitation of others for research purposes should be avoided. These "purists" or "absolutists" believe that research is a sacred undertaking and the researcher should always avoid any implications of wrongdoing. The purists would suggest that "harm" cannot be justified no matter what the benefits. Some nonresearchers may even believe that to use people in any way to gain information or to get entree to others' lives in any way might be considered unethical. As a researcher, one needs to make decisions about how she/he can be a personal moral exemplar as well as a researcher who obtains valuable information.

I tend to be a "purist" and believe that researchers have important ethical obligations to participants in research; therefore, the perspective presented here is rather conservative. Since I suspect a number of students will be reading this book, I further believe that a novice researcher should try to avoid ethical dilemmas. Save those problems for the days when you become old and wise. Some considerations will be offered to the researcher, however, in terms of aspects to consider in the treatment of participants and use of methods, moral and legal conduct, and the writing (publication) of research reports.

A number of ethical alternatives exist in conducting research. I believe, as does Bulmer (1982) all social researchers should be concerned about the ethics of research because we care about people and what happens to them, because many institutions require that research be approved by an Institutional Review Board, and because we want to make sure that research has a good image so we can continue with the areas of study that need to be addressed.

No one is absolved from moral and ethical responsibility when doing research. Since there are few hard and fast rules, each researcher will need to determine her or his own ethics. For each research project, the researcher should ask three things: (a) to whom is one accountable?, (b) what are the ethical consequences or in other words, is what I am doing right?, and (c) what are the implications of this research, or is it right for me to be doing this research? (Denzin, 1978; Lofland and Lofland, 1984).

Above all, the researcher should be able to identify the ethical dilemmas that may be apparent in any given study regardless of whether the qualitative or quantitative approach is being used. According to Babbie (1986a), the researcher should know the technical shortcomings of the research, be willing to report negative findings, describe what findings arrive unexpectedly, and be honest and open. Ethical dilemmas can be resolved in one's conscience, through political realities (such as Review Boards), by the assistance of colleagues, and through the development of ethical sensitivities and professional codes of ethics. One of the safeguards that exists in most educational institutions today is a Human Subjects Committee or Institutional Review Board. The researcher, whether a student, educator, or practitioner will have to carefully follow the procedures of that committee in developing the research. Involvement in this process will allow the researcher to determine if specific ethical questions should be addressed. A sample form from the University of North Carolina-Chapel Hill is included in Sample 6.

An added problem with ethical behavior in qualitative studies is that frequently the researcher does not know everything that might happen in the "field." For example, one may not anticipate stumbling across illegal or immoral behavior in a group being studied. Further, one never knows what may be found in the process of data discovery that could be incriminatory or negative when analyzed as a part of the final report.

In thinking about the ethical dilemmas of any research situation, it is possible that the researcher will conclude that a particular research question should not be studied on the basis of ethical grounds. The rights of individuals may take precedence over research and guarantees of confidentiality and anonymity may not be enough to protect subjects. A number of dimensions must be addressed in the treatment of subjects.

Treatment of Participants

Researchers are frequently delving into personal aspects of people's lives when the qualitative approach is used. Researchers may be making public some of the feelings and behaviors that people prefer to keep private. The question must be considered concerning under what conditions the researcher might be exploiting respondents and informants. Further, what one person may believe is public information, another participant may perceive as her/his private business.

In treatment of the participants, there are several interrelated issues of ethics that must be addressed: harm to the individual, informed consent, privacy, and effects of deception. To avoid problems with these issues, the researcher may ask the respondents to sign an informed consent. An example of an informed consent is included in Sample 7. The purpose of these forms is to stipulate the purpose of the project and to describe the rights of the respondent. They specify voluntary participation, no physical or psychological harm, the assurance of anonymity and confidentiality, and the identity of the researcher. With informed consent in a written form, there is little chance of the respondent feeling she/he has been deceived.

Sample 6
Institutional Review Board Form Sample

ACADEMIC AFFAIRS INSTITUTIONAL REVIEW BOARD
Request for Review of Research Using Human Subjects
Proposal Form (from University of North Carolina-Chapel Hill)

Department/School/Unit_____Date Submitted_____
Review Request #_____Date Approved_____
Principal investigator or faculty advisor:_____
Other investigators_____

Status   _____Faculty   _____Staff   _____Graduate Student
(Check all   _____Undergraduate Student   _____Student project, thesis, or
that apply)   dissertation

Project Title_____

Grant proposal to_____ _____Specific project

Please TYPE responses to the items below, using as many sheets as necessary. Instructions and elaborations of the questions are on the instruction pages in the AA-IRB Manual. Please precede each questions with question number and heading. Staple this page to the answer sheets.

Attach questionnaires, nonstandard tests, consent forms, and other supporting documents.

All investigators must sign the Investigators' Assurance at the bottom of this page.

1. Brief project description
   a. Purpose, hypotheses, or research questions
   b. Procedure
2. Subjects
   a. Age, sex, and approximate number
   b. Inclusion/exclusion criteria, if any
   c. Method of recruiting
   d. Inducement for participation
3. Are subjects at risk?
4. Steps taken to minimize risk (if #3 is answered "yes".)
5. Are illegal activities involved? (Describe, if "yes".)
6. Is deception involved? (Describe, if "yes".)
7. Anticipated benefit to subjects and/or society. (Optional unless #3 is answered "yes".)
8. How will prior informed consent be obtained? (Attach copies of consent forms if they are to be used.)
9. Security procedures for privacy and confidentiality.

I have read the Principles for Research with Human Participants, adapted from the American Psychological Association, plus other principles that may be adopted by my Department/School/ Research Unit, concerning the use of human subjects in research and agree to abide by them. I also agree to report any significant and relevant changes in the procedures or instrument to the Committee for additional review.

Signature(s)

Sample 7
Informed Consent for Research

Letter of Informed Consent
Project: Entitlement to and Constraints on Leisure for Women

A research project is being conducted by Professors Karla A. Henderson and M. Deborah Bialeschki from the University of North Carolina-Chapel Hill to determine the experience that women have concerning leisure in their lives. You are being invited to participate in this exploratory study. The initial interview will last about an hour and will be tape recorded. You are free to withdraw from the interview at any time. Your name will be kept confidential and will not be connected with any of the study results. The data will be used by the researchers as a part of a larger study examining women and leisure. The tape recordings will become the property of the University of North Carolina. If you understand the objectives of this project and would like to participate, please sign below. If you have any questions at any time you may contact one of the researchers at 919-962-1222. We appreciate your cooperation.

Name_____

Date_____

Deception involved in field research, in particular, is an area that requires further discussion. There are two ways that respondents may be unable to give informed consent. One of these situations involves the observation of public open settings through unobtrusive studies and the other circumstance involves not telling the informants the purpose of the study or misrepresenting yourself or the purpose of the research study to them.

The ethics of unobtrusive studies relate to rights of privacy, informed consent, and protection of personal dignity. It may be unadvisable to conduct a study if these issues cannot be resolved. The question is whether researchers have a right to observe people for scientific purposes when these people do not realize they are being observed. We should not be casual about observing people but should decide what is appropriate for the situation and how much the information collected may incriminate people. The research must have some societal value and contribute to the total understanding of a phenomena. Therefore, the research must be necessary and justifiable if any deception is to be involved.

A second issue of deception relates to the researcher's role ranging on a continuum from being totally "undercover" (covert) to being completely honest (overt). A range exists concerning how much of the research details should be revealed. The continuum also relates to how the researcher might pretend to play a different role than what she/he is actually doing. In any case, in covert research, the respondents have no knowledge of the research. In covert research, the identity of an individual might be misrepresented as might the character of the research. In overt situations, the participants, respondents, and interviewees are fully aware of the purpose of the research. It is sometimes difficult to differentiate where the cut-off point is between overt and covert research. The question is how does the researcher decide how much to disclose or not disclose and where is the point when something might be considered unethical. Is total secrecy worse than partial secrecy? The question is also raised about how many people should know the nature of the research. If the research is completely revealed to the gatekeepers but the individuals who are being interviewed or observed do not know the exact research purpose, is the researcher being unethical?

Several justifications might be offered for covert research. Some people would argue that almost all research using the qualitative approach is secret in some way because the researcher often does not know what she/he is looking for, people's behaviors change because of the research, and subjects do not ever understand all aspects of the research. It is also possible that certain areas could not be studied without using covert techniques because subjects might behave differently if they knew about the research. Sometimes role playing may be the only way to get information. A disadvantage from the researcher's view is that being covert may limit the kinds of probes that one might use. One should keep in mind, however, that the covert researcher does not allow informed consent, may invade the privacy of others, must determine if benefits outweigh the possible damages, must assess the betrayal of trust and know what that means, must address the reaction to such research in the future if she/he is found out, and must determine whether covert research is one's only way to discover the data.

In thinking about ethics, problems can often be avoided by decision oriented research planning and the use of convincing explanations (LaPage, 1981). Sensitive issues may be important to study and this need for scientific information may be a justification for covert research. The researcher should ask herself/himself, "If the respondent did know the purpose and was assured anonymity, would she/he still be inclined to participate?" Few issues would be really sensitive if people understood exactly why the issues were being researched.

Moral and Legal Concerns

Another ethical dilemma relates to how moral and legal issues may relate to what one can observe or learn. One issue relates to the moral obligation that a researcher has to help human beings who may be in need of help. What if giving that help might affect the results of the study? What is the social responsibility of the researcher? For example, when Bialeschki (1984) was interviewing women about their leisure, she met a woman who was very distraught about her inability to function effectively at leisure or most anything else in her life. She had many questions to ask and was unable to respond to the semi-structured interview questions. What was the responsibility of the researcher in this situation? Was it to terminate the interview and leave or to terminate the interview and help the woman? The types of wrangles, loyalties, affections, perplexities, amusements, safety issues, and vanities in which one gets involved may raise ethical questions about the researcher and the research as well as issues of developing trust.

A second dimension relates to how much illegal activity one is able to observe before feeling a moral obligation to report this activity to the authorities. This situation can be very difficult as one tries to tell informants that they will be treated anonymously and with confidentiality. In some cases it may be important to get information concerning law-breaking. The researcher must decide the extent to which illegal and immoral activity will be allowed. For example, I suspect that Campbell (1970) was faced with some of these questions when he conducted a participant observation of depreciative behavior in parks. *See Exemplar 11.1.* Further a researcher may collect data that someone else may want to subpoena. The researcher should make all attempts to keep the informants anonymous if this has been promised. Anonymity is assured if the researcher uses codes for particular people and then destroys the code sheet after all data have been recorded.

Exemplar 11.1 Campbell, F.L. (1970). Participant observation in outdoor recreation. *Journal of Leisure Research, 2*(4), 226-236.

This rather "old" study is an excellent example of the use of participant observation to assess depreciative behaviors in campgrounds. The author acknowledged the need for different methods to collect data and suggested that participant observation may be a useful technique for gathering data and for developing useful hypotheses. He also raised the questions of how the field researcher can collect reliable and valid data. The sampling techniques used were both objective and subjective measures taken at assigned periods of time. Campbell also described the use of informants and document records about previous depreciative acts as part of the triangulated data set used. Issues were raised concerning the ethical responsibility the researcher has when depreciative behavior occurs. The study does not effectively use theory but describes how this initial observation led to the further development of hypotheses that could be tested in other ways. Most of the techniques Campbell described 20 years ago are now common among researchers using participant observation, but the study offers an interesting approach to a parks management problem that continues to exist today.

Writing the Results

Ethics are also evident in writing and using information from qualitative reports. Besides anonymity and confidentiality the researcher also has an obligation not to hurt informants in other ways such as by making derogatory statements that reflect on the respondents. Further, the ethics of data collection must be considered in writing. The ways that variations in questions asked, nonrandom sampling, and interviewer recall might affect what has been learned should be described. For example, what should one do with information collected from a dishonest or questionable informant? How do the researcher's own biases affect the writing of results? How does one's personal relationships with respondents affect the results? Hopefully through the process of systematic data discovery and interpretation, most of these types of ethical questions will be addressed.

The results of a study should be written as honestly and accurately as possible. The researcher is put in a dilemma if the valid findings are negative and potentially hurtful to those who were studied. How much does the researcher write if the data add to a stereotype about the group being studied? The procedures for data collection and interpretation should be included in the written report but if something illegal or immoral was done justifiably to collect data, then the researcher is faced with another dilemma about what to say (Johnson, 1975). The bargains and promises made to an agency in order to "get in" should also be considered in the write-up. Finally, the researcher must address what responsibility she/he has for social change when results are reported? Should the researcher imply the need or advocate for particular changes as a result of the research? These issues, as well as others that have not been addressed, are ethical issues that do not have any definitive answers but must be considered by the researcher before, after, and during the research process.

Code of Ethics

Ethical guidelines are not simply prohibitions, but help support the positive responsibilities of researchers (Diener and Crandall, 1978). Codes of ethics have been developed by many research associations. While recreation, park, and leisure researchers have not developed an explicit set of guidelines, the general guidelines that other disciplines have noted can be summarized to reflect our responsibilities as well. First, the researcher is obligated to consider all the possible ethical dilemmas that might be associated with research. Further, the informants should be considered first and their rights, dignity, safety, interests, sensitivities, cooperation, and privacy should be foremost. The objectives of the research should be communicated unless there are justifiable reasons to forego that courtesy. The value of deception should be carefully analyzed. The effects of publication should be considered along with the kind of interpretation or reports that will be generated. The use to be made of the research information should be made clear to informants and participants in the research. A review by other researchers and possibly informants should be done to assure that no harm exists in the research that is reported. The researcher is obligated to uphold the promises that were made at the onset of the research. And finally, the researcher should possess the competence and objectivity to undertake a study appropriately.

Characteristics of Researchers

The characteristics of researchers doing interpretive research using qualitative methods have probably become apparent as you have read this book. I would, however, like to reiterate a few considerations that one might want to keep in mind. Any method of research may create psychological anxiety. People who are able to use qualitative methods and techniques easily, however, may be successful because of their personalities. But, almost anyone can learn to use qualitative methods effectively if that is their desire.

The most important characteristic of a researcher using the qualitative approach is to have a good attitude. One must look at qualitative methods and techniques as an adventure with the opportunity for intellectual playfulness (Lofland and Lofland, 1984). In addition, however, these methods are often hard, boring, disciplined, and tedious. The researcher is the instrument for data collection. Some people are not good instruments because they rely on partial beliefs, biased judgments, and overemphasis on certain facts. The shortcomings of humans as instruments, however, can be overcome by acknowledging the strengths that an individual can develop. This section of the chapter examines the characteristics needed by the researcher to get along with others, the characteristics needed for self-discovery, and the ways that one can become or train others to become better researchers.

Getting Along with Others

Empathy is essential for the researcher employing the qualitative approach. One must believe that people are infinitely interesting. One must be able to listen and be responsive to what people have to say. Wilson (1977) suggested that the researcher should be able to transcend her/his perceptions and get into the lives of others. The researcher should be looking for ways to establish trust and to keep trust flowing. Trying to be nonthreatening, always open to others, and accepting of one's own incompetence will often be most useful.

The researcher using qualitative methods must be adaptable and flexible. By the nature of the emergent design of interpretive research this flexibility is necessary. People are not predictable so the researcher must be willing to "go with the flow" especially in the initial stages of the project. Patience and perseverance are characteristics that will be useful in research that tends to be time-consuming and wearying. A tolerance for ambiguity is another dimension which the researcher should possess. Sometimes data come quickly and sometimes they come very slowly.

It helps to be an extrovert but an introvert can also be effective in using the qualitative approach. The researcher must be able to talk well with heads of organizations and gatekeepers concerning research objectives as well as talk with a variety of other people from all backgrounds, educations, and other demographic characteristics concerning routine situations of daily life and work. Some people the researcher talks to will be good, honorable, and open while others will be suspicious, fearful, and closed.

The researcher using the qualitative approach needs chameleon like qualities and must be able to view her/his activities from a variety of perspectives. Creativity is a byword of the researcher's personality. Further, the researcher must be holistic rather than single focused. While the researcher wants to get close to the situation, she/he must also be able to step back and reflect on the whole of what is occurring. While facts, theoretical frameworks, and statements are important, the researcher should also be open to insights, apprehensions, symbols, hunches, impressions, and feelings. All of these perspectives may contribute to the process of data discovery and interpretation.

The researcher must be able to work intensely and for long periods of time in the research setting as well as for long periods of time in organizing and interpreting data. Although the length of time spent interviewing, immersed in the field, or immersed in texts may vary, interpretive research is usually a labor intensive and time-consuming process. Thus, the researcher will need to have energy and determination. Being in the field can be lonely and isolating work and the researcher must be willing to live with that knowledge and seek support from mentors, colleagues, family, and friends in sustaining the intensity that is often needed.

A somewhat minor characteristic but one that can make a difference in data discovery is the dress of the researcher. Generally it is best to dress as much like those people being studied as possible. This conformity puts people at ease and does not suggest a difference in power based upon the dress.

A final dimension that the researcher must avoid is what has been referred to as "going native" or becoming so involved with the people or the situation to the extent that one loses the ability to do research. While the focus of the qualitative approach is on subjectivity, one must be objective to a certain extent and must avoid biasing questions to get socially desirable responses or become too caught up with social injustice. An internal conflict may exist if one believes very strongly about an issue that is being studied and feels that it is difficult to continue in her/his role as a researcher. It may be frustrating to be marginal as a researcher yet some marginality is always maintained by virtue of the research role even when using the qualitative approach.

Getting Along with Yourself

This topic may seem strange to include in this book, but it is evident that in the process of doing qualitative studies, one is likely to learn a lot about the self. This learning possibility can be rather disconcerting so the researcher needs to be prepared for self changes. The researcher must have an interest in self-discovery since the researcher using qualitative methods needs to be able to immerse her/his identity into an interpretation of the data. The things we learn about ourselves are not always pleasant but these things can help us to grow and to become better researchers.

The researcher needs to discover the passions and curiosities that contribute to one's purposes for doing the research. Within this exuberance, the researcher may sometimes appear to be a fool (Wax, 1971). This apparent foolishness needs to be accepted and learned from rather than rejected and ignored. The researcher is likely to go through many feelings while discovering data including self-doubt, uncertainty, frustration, pain, embarrassment, agonies, ambiguities, and triumphs (Lofland and Lofland, 1984). It is fearful to "pry" into other people's lives because there is the risk of being rejected or feeling self-conscious. Depending upon the level of covertness of the research, one may be fearful about the role being played. It is easy for all these feelings to escalate. Unfortunately, these aspects are seldom mentioned in most of the literature, particularly the recreation, park, and leisure studies literature. The researcher needs to know that it is natural to have these feelings; these emotions are not necessarily a result of one's faulty research or inexperience. Even the best researchers feel inadequate about their work from time to time. Researchers need to acknowledge their feelings, record them as part of one's personal data, and see how they are resolved as time passes and one becomes less of a stranger to the situation, the people, and the data.

Therefore, one of the values of the qualitative approach for the researcher beyond the completion of a degree, the solving of an evaluation problem, the contribution to knowledge, or the publication of an article, lies in the potential for personal growth. All research that seeks to study human behavior in the natural setting will likely elicit personal feelings. Researchers may need to be willing to face their own self-discovery in order to understand other's experience. Douglas (1985) suggested that through self-exploration, it is possible to find a mutual understanding of life with others.

Improving Your Qualitative Research Skills

Researchers are not born, they are made. Thus, almost any of us can educate (socialize), or reeducate (resocialize) ourselves to be effective qualitative researchers. For some people, qualitative methods will be easier to use than for others, but nevertheless it is usually possible to learn to be a better interviewer, more careful observer, more rigorous analyst, and more sensitive to a variety of clues (Guba and Lincoln, 1981).

To be good at using qualitative methods and techniques, one needs to have basic cognitive abilities. It is highly desirable to have education in positivist research methods and quantitative techniques. Because of that education, one can understand the advantages in some situations of using the qualitative approach, and can then learn the methods and techniques needed. The resources needed to be an effective qualitative researcher will require adequate time, money, space, contact with other qualitative researchers through literature or personal contact, guidance from a mentor or from the literature, libraries, technical equipment, instruction in methods and techniques, interpersonal skills training, and opportunities to be a data gatherer (Reinharz, 1981).

The best way to become a better researcher is to practice. One can practice various components of being a researcher such as observing, notetaking, listening, and getting people to talk. One can begin to focus on how one filters, selectively perceives, misinterprets, oversimplifies, and reacts to communication in everyday life. The researcher can also train her/himself to pay attention and to listen in a way that information can be recalled more easily. Many of us spend a lot of time in distraction when we think we are paying attention. One can also practice self-reflection. The researcher can learn to pay attention to her/his emotions and see how those feelings are affecting what is done, thought, and said. Further, the more actual research studies that are done, the more one will learn about the self and the techniques needed to be an effective researcher.

Some researchers may be using research assistants throughout a study. This teamwork approach may be essential for particular projects. The principal researcher must be careful to hire individuals who are willing to work hard to become competent observers and/or interviewers. They will need instruction as well as a number of opportunities to practice before going into the field. As the supervisor of such individuals, the principal researcher will need to provide feedback and will need to find many ways to become familiar with the data if the research is to be successful. Training individuals for the qualitative approach is more complicated than training them to administer a structured closed-ended interview schedule or to code data into a computer. Practice and training, however, are necessary if one is to become good at getting along with others, challenging oneself, and becoming a successful researcher.

The Related Issues of Politics and Getting Support/Funding

Politics have a direct impact on the research that one conducts. One would be naive to believe that no problems will exist in justifying the use of a qualitative method or explaining the outcomes of the research study. The qualitative approach is sometimes criticized because of its focus on individualized outcomes, detailed in-depth information, focus on diversity, process orientation, social change focus, focus on quality which is difficult to "measure," lack of standardized instruments, lack of theory testing in favor of grounded theory, uncertain or unexpected outcomes, and flexible design (Patton, 1980a). Whether the researcher is a student getting the research approved by a thesis committee or a staff member trying to convince an organization to let research be conducted, one will need to confront the above concerns that may be connoted as political issues.

Within a research setting there will also be politics related to subjects, respondents, informants, gatekeepers, and granting agencies. Research cannot be value free. Outside the research settings will be politics related to colleagues, scientific and professional societies, and political communities. Science is surrounded by politics. The most important aspect for the researcher in any of these cases is to provide as much information as possible and to be ethical in the research. Education is still necessary for people to understand the qualitative approach and its methods and techniques, but if the possible problems are considered and the framework is properly presented, much political bias can be eliminated.

Cautions in Linking Qualitative and Quantitative Methods

Another issue that may be important to address is the linking of qualitative and quantitative data. Many opinions exist concerning the value of this linking and the assumptions that are made. As was stated early on, it is not possible to link paradigms because each represents a distinct world view, but it may be possible and desirable (particularly in evaluation research) to triangulate quantitative and qualitative methods (Reichardt and Cook, 1979). The purist of either paradigm would not agree that it is possible to link methods, but I would like to present some justification for it. In order to link methods, however, one would generally have to assume a positivist paradigm.

To combine methods the researcher must be able to describe the phenomena being studied. Ingersoll (1983) presented an interesting model for the relationship between qualitative and quantitative methods. He suggested that one can use qualitative and then quantitative methods as an approach to exploring the parameters of a phenomena. One can use qualitative and quantitative methods simultaneously in order to get differing perspectives on two data sets to answer research questions. One can use quantitative and then qualitative to suggest interpretations for quantitative results. For example, Kreppner (1986) used the latter in his study of development of families. The quantitative data were collected and then patterns were set to use in the qualitative case studies. The two methods can also be used for cross-validating or for getting the widest possible theoretical use of a set of observations (Fielding and Fielding, 1986). In combining methods, researchers can reveal aspects of the problem that the strongest method might overlook. The triangulation might occur "within method" by asking questions in different ways (open-ended and closed) or "between methods" by having each method serve as a check and balance of the other (Denzin, 1978).

The greatest drawbacks to linking qualitative and quantitative data are that researchers may lack the expertise in both methods and collecting both types of data may be time-consuming. Further, little guidance exists as to how this linkage is actually accomplished. Some of the sloppy research that has been done has been because a researcher has used incorrect assumptions about qualitative and quantitative methods and put data together inappropriately. The purists would argue that qualitative and quantitative methods can not be linked so that is why no one knows how to do it. Further, it is important to note that it is not a combination of methods if data are collected through an open-ended questionnaire and then are reduced to numbers for statistical quantification.

One should keep in mind that the use of different methods does not ensure the validity or reliability of findings. The researcher must be ready to address what to do if the data from two methods are in conflict. To compare data, they must be at the same level and this similarity is not always the case when linking the two distinct approaches. At any rate, the justification for using quantitative methods after qualitative methods should never be to get greater rigor because a qualitative study ought to be done rigorously. One approach should NOT be considered better than another.

A Special Note to "Nonresearchers"

If your normal role in life is not as a full-time researcher or student, but instead you have a "real" job, you may still find from time to time that you could benefit from the use of the qualitative approach through evaluation. As stated at the outset, the same procedures apply to evaluation as to research except that instead of seeking truth, universal theory, and generalizations as is done in research, evaluation research is looking for perspective, empirical accounts, and context-based information (Patton, 1980b). The same issues of ethics, politics, and project design occur except perhaps on a scale that relates to the specific aspects of a particular project. The linking of data is also possible in qualitative evaluation. Hopefully this book has gotten you thinking about some ways to use the qualitative approach for any number of problems to be solved.

A Summary of the Challenges in Using the Qualitative Approach

This final issue will be a summative look at how the researcher can address particular challenges that exist in interpretive research using the qualitative approach. If a researcher is comfortable with emerging designs, words, natural environments, and the meaning of experience then interpretive research will probably be exciting. A number of problems, however have been raised with qualitative research that can be rectified by a systematic, rigorous process which is just as much a part of the qualitative approach as of the quantitative approach. The researcher must keep in mind the labor intensity and the data overload possibilities of the qualitative approach.   Further issues of transferability, credibility, reproducibility, and confirmability must be kept in mind as well. Theoretical sampling is different in the qualitative approach and this difference with quantitative sampling must be noted. Further, data interpretation and writing in qualitative studies should focus on explaining the "commonplace" in such a way that new information is gained. Any method of research requires interest, knowledge, and skills. The interpretive paradigm and the qualitative approach is an important choice to have for increasing the body of knowledge about recreation, parks, and leisure. Viva la choice!

Summary

This final chapter has provided a delineation of some of the issues that have been implicit throughout the book but have not been directly addressed. Ethics is a critical concern in any type of research but the qualitative approach offers some unique concerns to address. The characteristics of the qualitative researcher have been addressed because of the emphasis and importance of the researcher as the data collection instrument. Many challenges confront the qualitative researcher. It is hoped that this text has provided information for researchers who intend to use these methods and techniques as well as those researchers who merely want to gain familiarity and appreciation for the qualitative approach. In the study of recreation, parks, and leisure, it appears that the qualitative approach may have much to offer as a means for better understanding the contexts, behaviors, and attitudes of people during leisure as well as to better understand how leisure services can be delivered.

The key concepts addressed in this chapter are: ethics, human subjects, politics, and linking data.

For Further Consideration

1. What would you do if you found something illegal was going on while you were conducting your qualitative study?

2. How will you convince your thesis committee or your funding agency that a qualitative approach would be the best to use given your particular research problem?

3. What cautions would a researcher have to use in linking qualitative and quantitative data?

4. How might a practitioner use this textbook? Is it of any value to someone who is not actively involved in research?

For Further Reading

Most of the books already mentioned address some of the above issues to some extent so the qualitative researcher may want to consult the other broad texts that have already been described. For the most complete discussion of ethics, the reader is referred to:

Diener, E. and Crandall, R. (1978). *Ethics in social and behavioral research.* **Chicago, IL: University of Chicago Press.**
This book provides a summary of many of the issues faced by researchers related to overt and covert research, using human subjects, moral and legal concerns, and writing results. Many opinions differ on how research should be ethically conducted. The reader is encouraged to use the perspectives presented in this book as a basis for asking questions about ethics issues.

Selected References

Adler, P., and Adler, P. (1987). *Membership roles in field research*. Newbury Park, CA: Sage Publications.

Allen, L.R. (1987, September). *Management and evaluation of leisure programs and services: Past, present and future research*. Paper presented to the NRPA Leisure Research Symposium, New Orleans, LA.

Allison, M.T., and Duncan, M.C. (1987). Women, work, and leisure: The days of our lives. *Leisure Sciences, 9,* 143-162.

Anderson, S.C., and Hultsman, J.T. (1988, October). *Epistemological problems with the positivistic study of leisure perceptions: The need for grounded theory*. Paper presented to the NRPA Leisure Research Symposium, Indianapolis, IN.

Askew, J. (1983, March). *Some thoughts on the value of grounded theory for the study and practice of higher education*. Paper presented at the Annual Meeting of the Association for the Study of Higher Education, Washington, DC.

Avedon, E. (1984). *Therapeutic recreation services: An applied behavioral approach*. Englewood Cliffs, NJ: Prentice Hall.

Avery, R.K., and McCain, T.A. (1984, May). *Evaluating qualitative research: Recognizing our personal judgments*. Paper presented at the Annual Meeting of the International Communication Association, San Francisco, CA.

Babbie, E. (1986a). *The practice of social research*. (4th Ed.). Belmont, CA: Wadsworth Publishing Co.

Babbie, E. (1986b). *Observing ourselves: Essays in social research*. Belmont, CA: Wadsworth Publishing Co.

Babbie, E. (1989). *The practice of social research*. (5th ed.). Belmont, CA: Wadsworth Publishing Co.

Beck, L. (1987, September). *The phenomenology of optional experiences attained by white water river recreationists in Canyonlands National Park, Utah*. Paper presented to the NRPA Leisure Research Symposium, New Orleans, LA.

Becker, H. S. (1970). *Sociological works: Method and substance*. Chicago, IL: Aldine.

Becker, H.S., Gordon, A.C., and LeBailly, R.K. (1984). Field work with the computer: Criteria for assessing systems. *Qualitative Sociology, 7*(1/2), 16-33.

Berger, P.L., and Luckman, T. (1967). *The social construction of reality.* New York, NY: Anchor Books.

Bernstein, R.J. (1983). *Beyond objectivism and relativism: Science, hermeneutics, and praxis.* Philadelphia, PA: University of Pennsylvania Press.

Bialeschki, M.D. (1984). *An analysis of leisure attitudes and activity patterns of women related to locus of control and perceived choice.* Unpublished doctoral dissertation, University of Wisconsin, Madison, WS.

Bialeschki, M.D., and Henderson, K.A. (1984). The personal and professional spheres: Complement or conflict for women leisure service professionals. *Journal of Park and Recreation Administration, 2*(4), 45-54.

Blumer, H. (1969). *Symbolic Interactionism: Perspective and method.* Englewood Cliffs, NJ: Prentice-Hall.

Boothby, J., Tungatt, M.F., and Townsend, A.R. (1981). Ceasing participation in sports activity: Reported reasons and their implications. *Journal of Leisure Research, 13*(1), 1-14.

Borman, K., LeCompte, M., and Goetz, J.P. (1986). Ethnographic and qualitative research designs and why it doesn't work. *American Behavioral Scientist, 30*(1), 43-57.

Brandenburg, J., Greiner, W., Hamilton-Smith, E., Scholten, H, Senior, R., and Webb, J. (1982). A conceptual model of how people adopt recreation activities. *Leisure Studies, 1,* 263-276.

Brandmeyer, G.A., and Alexander, L.K. (1986). "I caught the dream": The adult baseball camp as fantasy leisure. *Journal of Leisure Research, 18*(1), 26-39.

Brent, R.S. (1982). Community and institutional pubic social spaces. *Therapeutic Recreation Journal, 16*(1), 41-48.

Bridge, N.J. (1983). Important guidelines for improving community recreation opportunities for public housing tenants. *Leisurability, 10*(4), 36-42.

Brown, M.M. (1984, November). *The plague of analyzing qualitative data.* Paper presented at the Annual Meeting of the National Council for the Social Studies. Washington, DC.

Bruyn, S. (1966). *The human perspective in sociology.* Englewood Cliff, NJ: Prentice-Hall.

Bullock, C.C. (1982). Interactionist evaluators look for "what is" not "what should be." *Parks and Recreation, 17*(2), 37-39.

Bullock, C.C. (1983). Qualitative research in therapeutic recreation. *Therapeutic Recreation Journal, 17*(4), 36-43.

Bullock, C.C. (1985a). *Understanding the essence of the experience of being mainstreamed.* Paper presented at the NRPA Leisure Research Symposium, Dallas, TX.

Bullock, C.C. (1985b). *Proving self: The problematic imperative.* Unpublished doctoral dissertation. University of Illinois, Champaign-Urbana, IL.

Bullock, C.C. (1988). Interpretive lines of action of mentally retarded children in mainstreamed play settings. *Symbolic Interaction, 9*, 145-172.

Bullock, C.C., and Coffey, F. (1979, October). *Multimethod evaluation.* Paper presented at the NRPA Leisure Research Symposium, New Orleans, LA.

Buhyoff, G.J, and Wellman, J.D. (1979). Environmental preference: An initial analysis of a critical analysis. *Journal of Leisure Research, 11*(3), 215-218.

Bulmer, M. (1982). The merits and demerits of covert participant observation. In Bulmer, M. (Ed.), *Social Research Ethics* (pp 217-251). New York, NY: Holmer and Meier Publishing Inc.

Bultena, G.L., and Field, D.R. (1983, October). *Social systems: A new agenda for leisure research.* Paper presented at the meeting of the National Recreation and Park Association Leisure Research Symposium, Kansas City, MO.

Bundt, B.K. (1981, October). *The adult hangout: A key factor in leisure voluntary organization membership purchase.* Paper presented at the NRPA Leisure Research Symposium, Minneapolis, MN.

Burdge, R. (1983). Making leisure and recreation research a scholarly topic: Views of a Journal Editor 1972-1978. *Leisure Sciences, 6*, 99-126.

Burgess, R. G. (Ed.). (1982). *Field research: A sourcebook and field manual.* London, England: George Allen & Unwin.

Burrus-Bammel, L., Bammel, G., and Angotti, L. (1984, October). *Photographic gender content analysis of Park and Recreation journals, 1977-1982.* Paper presented at the NRPA Leisure Research Symposium, Orlando, FL.

Butler, D.E. (1984, November). *Ethnographic/qualitative research: Theoretical perspective and methodological strategies.* Paper presented at the Mid-South Educational Research Association, New Orleans, LA.

Campbell, F.L., Hendee, J.C., and Clark, R. (1968). Law and order in public parks. *Parks and Recreation, 3*(12), 28-31, 51-55.

Campbell, F.L. (1970). Participant observation in outdoor recreation. *Journal of Leisure Research, 2*(4), 226-236.

Campbell, D.T. (1979). "Degrees of freedom" and the case study. In T.D. Cook and C.S. Reichardt (Eds.), *Qualitative and quantitative methods in evaluation research* (pp 49-67). Beverly Hills, CA: Sage Publications.

Cartwright, C.A., and Cartwright, G.P. (1974). *Developing observation skills.* New York, NY: McGraw-Hill Book Company.

Chenery, M.F. (1988, March). *Techniques for conducting participant observation research.* Paper presented to the SPRE Teaching and Research Institute, Saratoga Springs, NY.

Chenery, M.F. (1990). *I am somebody: The messages and methods of organized camping for youth development.* Seattle, WA: Human Development Reasearch Associates, Inc.

Chenery, M.F., and Russell, R.V. (1987). Responsive evaluation: An application of naturalistic inquiry to recreation evaluation. *Journal of Park and Recreation Administration, 5*(4), 30-38.

Cherry, G.E. (1979). British observations on leisure research in Canada. *Society and Leisure, 2*(1), 239-254.

Chick, G. (1985, October). *Anthropology and the study of leisure: Searching for the missing link.* Paper presented at the NRPA Leisure Research Symposium, Dallas, TX.

Chilcott, J.H. (1987). Where are you coming from and where are you going? The reporting of ethnographic research. *American Educational Research Journal, 24*(2), 199-218.

Christensen, J.E. (1980). A second look at the informal interview as a technique for recreation research. *Journal of Leisure Research, 12*(2), 183-186.

Churchman, D. (1987). *Visitor behavior at the Melbourne Zoo.* Paper presented at Annual meeting of the American Association of Zoological Parks and Aquariums, Portland, OR.

Cicourel, A. V. (1974). *Cognitive sociology.* New York, NY: Free Press.

Clark, R.N., Hendee, J.C., and Campbell, F.L. (1971). Values, behaviors, and conflict in modern camping culture. *Journal of Leisure Research, 3*(3), 143-159.

Clifford, J., and Marcus, G.E. (1986). *Writing culture: The poetics and politics of ethnography.* Berkeley, CA: University of California Press.

Clonts, H.A. (1987, September). *Application of a Delphi technique for recreational planning in opinion based managerial decisions.* Paper presented at the NRPA Leisure Research Symposium, New Orleans, LA.

Coalter, F. (1985). Crowd behaviors at football matches: A study in Scotland. *Leisure Studies, 4,* 111-117.

Colaizzi, P.F. (1978). Psychological research as the phenomenologist views it. In R.S. Valle and M. King (Eds.), *Existential-phenomenological alternatives for psychology.* New York, NY: Oxford University Press.

Conrad, G. E. (1982). Grounded theory: An alternative approach to research in higher education. *Review of Higher Education, 5*(4), 239-249.

Conrad, P., and Reinharz, S. (1984). Computers and qualitative data. *Qualitative Sociology, 7,* 1-2.

Cook, T.D., and Reichardt, C.S. (Eds.). (1979). *Qualitative and quantitative methods in education research.* Beverly Hills, CA: Sage Publications.

Cowin, L. (1989). Programming and self-concept: How does what you do affect how they feel about themselves? *Camping Magazine, 61*(7), 46-49.

Cowin, L. (1989). *Factors affecting self-concept and psychological well-being in a summer camp setting.* Unpublished master's thesis, Dalhousie University, Halifax, NS.

Crandall, R., and Lewko, J. (1976). Leisure research, present and past: Who, what, where. *Journal of Leisure Research, 8*(3), 150-159.

Crawford, D.W., Godbey, G., and Crouter, A.C. (1986). The stability of leisure preferences. *Journal of Leisure Research, 18*(2), 96-115.

Csikszentmihalyi, M., Larson, R., and Prescott, S. (1977). The ecology of adolescent activity and experience. *Journal of Youth and Adolescence, 6,* 281-294.

Csikszentmihalyi, M. (1975). *Beyond boredom and anxiety.* San Francisco, CA: Jossey-Bass Publications.

Cunneen, C., and Lynch, R. (1988). The social meaning of conflict in riots at the Australian Grand Prix motorcycle races. *Leisure Studies, 7,* 1-19.

Daniels, A.K. (1983). Self-deception and self-discovery in fieldwork. *Qualitative Sociology, 6,* 195-214.

Dattilo, J. (1985). An alternative method to studying individuals with disabilities: Single subject research. *Leisure Information Quarterly, 12*(1), 11.

Dattilo, J. (1986a). Single subject research in therapeutic recreation: Application to individuals with disabilities. *Therapeutic Recreation Journal, 20*(1), 76-87.

Dattilo, J. (1986b, October). *Implications of single subject methodology on leisure research.* Paper presented to the NRPA Leisure Research Symposium, Anaheim, CA.

Dattilo, J., and Camarata, S. (1988, October). *Facilitating leisure involvement through self-initiated augmentative communication training.* Paper presented to the NRPA Leisure Research Symposium, Indianapolis, IN.

Dawson, D. (1984). Phenomenological approaches to leisure research. *Recreation Research Review, 11*(1), 18-23.

Dean, A. (1988). Researching leisure. *Leisure Studies, 7*, 195-199.

Deem, R. (1986). *All work and no play? The sociology of women and leisure.* Milton Keynes, England: Open University Press.

Denzin, N.K. (1978). *The research act.* New York, NY: McGraw Hill Book Company.

Dewey, J. (1925). *Experience and nature.* Chicago, IL: Open Court Publishing Co.

Dexter, L.A. (1970). *Elite and specialized interviewing.* Evanston, IL: Northwestern University Press.

Diener, E., and Crandall, R. (1978). *Ethics in social and behavioral research.* Chicago, IL: University of Chicago Press.

Dixey, R. (1987). It's a great feeling when you win: Women and bingo. *Leisure Studies, 6*, 199-214.

Douglas, J. D. (1985). *Creative interviewing.* Beverly Hills, CA: Sage Publications.

Douglas, J. D. (1976). *Investigative social research.* Beverly Hills, CA: Sage Publications.

Downing, K. (1983, October). *Qualitative naturalistic methodology in recreation research.* Paper presented at the NRPA Leisure Research Symposium, Kansas City, MO.

Duncan, M.C. (1985). *A hermeneutic analysis of play and leisure.* Paper presented to the NRPA Leisure Research Symposium, Dallas, TX.

Dustin, D. (1986, October). *Dance of the dispossessed.* Paper presented at the NRPA Leisure Research Symposium, Anaheim, CA.

Dustin, D. (1988, October). *The wilderness within: Reflections on a 100 mile run.* Paper presented at the NRPA Congress, Indianapolis, IN.

Ehrlich, C. (1976). *The conditions of feminist research.* Baltimore, MD: Research Group One Report No. 21.

Eisner, E.W. (1981). On the difference between scientific and artistic approaches to qualitative research. *Educational Researcher, 10*(4), 5-9.

Ellen, R.F. (1984). *Ethnographic research: A guide to general conduct.* New York, NY: Academic Press.

Ellis, G.D., and Williams, D.R. (1987). The impending renaissance in leisure service evaluation. *Journal of Park and Recreation Administration, 5*(4), 17-29.

Emerson, R.M. (Ed.). (1983). *Contemporary field research: A collection of readings.* Boston, MA: Little, Brown, and Co.

Erickson, K. (1967). A comment on disguised observation in sociology. *Social Problems, 14*, 366-373.

Ferguson, M. (1980). *The Aquarian conspiracy.* Los Angeles, CA: J.P. Tarcher, Inc.

Fielding, N.G., and Fielding, J.L. (1986). *Linking data.* Beverly Hills, CA: Sage Publications.

Filstead, W. J. (Ed.). (1970). *Qualitative methodology: Firsthand involvement with a social world.* Chicago, IL: Markham Publishing Co.

Filstead, W.J. (1981). Using qualitative methods in evaluation research: An Illustrative Bibliography. *Evaluation Review, 5*(2), 259-268.

Filstead. W.J. (1979). Qualitative methods. In T.D. Cook and C.S. Reichardt (Eds.), *Qualitative and quantitative methods in evaluation research* (pp 33-46). Beverly Hills, CA: Sage Publications.

Fine, G. A. (1980). Cracking diamonds: Observer roles in little league baseball settings and the acquisition of social competence. In W.B. Shaffir, R.R. Stebbins, and A. Turowetz (Eds.), *Fieldwork experience.* New York, NY: St. Martin's Press.

Fine, G.A., and Kleinman, S. (1979). Rethinking subculture: An interactionist analysis. *American Journal of Sociology, 85*, 1-20.

Fryer, D., and Payne, R. (1984). Proactive behavior in unemployment: Findings and implications. *Leisure Studies, 3*, 273-295.

Garfinkel, H. (1967). *Studies in ethnomethodology.* Englewood Cliffs, NJ: Prentice-Hall.

Gattas, J. (1980, October). *Anthropological approaches to leisure research.* Paper presented at the NRPA Leisure Research Symposium, Phoenix, AZ.

Gattas, J.T., Roberts, K., Schmitz-Scherzer, R., Tokarski, W., and Vitanyi, Y. (1986). Leisure and lifestyles: Towards a research agenda. *Society and Leisure, 9*(2), 529-539.

Geertz, C. (1983). Thick description: Toward an interpretive theory of culture. In R. M. Emerson (Ed.), *Contemporary Field research.* (pp. 37-59). Boston, MA: Little, Brown.

Gephart, W. J. (1978). On truth. *CEDR Quarterly, 11*, 2-6.

Gerson, E.M. (1988). A cautious hurrah. *Qualitative Sociology, 11*(3), 252-256.

Gibson, P.M. (1979). Therapeutic aspects of wilderness programs: A comprehensive literature review. *Therapeutic Recreation Journal, 13*(2), 21-33.

Glancy, M. (1985, October). *Participant observation: Investigating a recreation experience.* Paper presented at the NRPA Leisure Research Symposium, Dallas, TX.

Glancy, M. (1986). Participant observation in the recreation setting. *Journal of Leisure Research, 18*(2), 59-80.

Glancy, M. (1988). The play-world setting of the auction. *Journal of Leisure Research, 20*(2), 135-153.

Glancy, M. (1988, March). *Qualitative data analysis.* Paper presented at the SPRE Research Institute, Sarasota Springs, NY.

Glaser, B.G., and Strauss, A.L. (1965). The discovery of substantive theory. A basic strategy underlying qualitative research. *The American Behavioral Scientist, 8*(6), 5-12.

Glaser, B. G., and Strauss, A. (1967). *The discovery of grounded theory: Strategies for qualitative research.* Chicago, IL: Aldine Publishing, Co.

Glazer, M. (1972). *The research adventure: Promises and problems of fieldwork.* New York, NY: Random House.

Gluck, S. (1979). What's so special about women? Women's oral history. *Frontiers, 2*(2), 3-11.

Glyptis, S. (1985). Women as a target group: The views of the staff of Action Sport–West Midlands. *Leisure Studies, 4*, 347-362.

Godbey, G. (1982, October). *Problems in the sociology of leisure.* Paper presented to the NRPA Leisure Research Symposium, Louisville, KY.

Godbey, G. (1984). Letter to the editor. *Journal of Park and Recreation Administration, 2*(4), vii-ix.

Goetz, J.P., and LeCompte, M.D. (1981). Ethnographic research and the problems of data reduction. *Anthropology and Education Quarterly, 12*, 51-70.

Goffman, E. (1974). *Frame Analysis.* Cambridge, MA: Harvard University Press.

Gold, R.L. (1970). Participant observation. In N.L. Denzin, (Ed.), *Sociological methods* (pp. 370-380). New York, NY: McGraw-Hill Book Co.

Gorden, R.L. (1975). *Interviewing: Strategy, techniques, and tactics* (Rev. ed). Homewood, IL: Dorsey Press.

Guba, E.G. (1981). Criteria for assessing the trustworthiness of naturalistic inquiries. *Educational Communication and Technology Journal, 29*, 75-92.

Guba, E.G. (1985). The context of emergent paradigm research. In Y. Lincoln (Ed.), *Organizational theory and inquiry.* Beverly Hills, CA: Sage Publications.

Guba, E. (1987). What we have learned about naturalistic evaluation. *Evaluation Practice, 8*(1), 23-43.

Guba, E. G., and Lincoln, Y. S. (1981). *Effective evaluation.* San Francisco, CA: Jossey-Bass.

Gunn, S.L. (1982). Value of relationships in leisure. *Leisurability, 9*(2), 18-23.

Gunter, B.G. (1987). The leisure experience: Selected properties. *Journal of Leisure Research, 19* (2), 115-130.

Gunter, B.G., and Gunter, N.C. (1980). Leisure styles: A conceptual framework of modern leisure. *Sociological Quarterly, 21*, 361-374.

Habermas, J. (1979). *Communication and the evolution of society.* Boston, MA: Beacon Press.

Harper, W. (1981). The experience of leisure. *Leisure Sciences, 4*(2), 113-126.

Harper, W. (1983, October). *Phenomenology and the leisure sciences.* Paper presented to the National Recreation and Park Association Leisure Research Symposium, Kansas City, MO.

Haworth, J.T. (1978). Leisure and the individual. *Society and Leisure, 1*(1), 53-61.

Henderson, K.A. (1981). *A morphological study of the future of urban recreation.* Paper presented at the NRPA Leisure Research Symposium, Minneapolis, MN.

Henderson, K.A. (1990). Containers for women's leisure: A life history perspective. *Leisure Studies 9*, 121-133.

Henderson, K.A., and Bialeschki, M.D. (1982). *Recreation programming in urban areas in the the future.* Paper presented at the NRPA Leisure Research Symposium, Louisville, KY.

Henderson, K.A., and Bialeschki, M.D. (1984). Organized camping and the future: Research on major trends (FAC Occasional Paper). *Camping Magazine, 56*(3), 19-26

Henderson, K.A., and Bialeschki, M.D. (1987). A qualitative evaluation of a women's week experience. *The Journal of Experiential Education, 10*(2), 25-28.

Henderson, K.A., Bialeschki, M.D., and Berndt, D.D. (1982). *Futures forecasting: An analysis of the Delphi and morphological techniques.* Paper presented at the NRPA Leisure Research Symposium, Louisville, KY.

Henderson, K.A., and Rannells, J.S. (1988). Farm women and the meaning of work and leisure: An oral history perspective. *Leisure Sciences, 10*(1), 41-50.

Hendry, L.B., Raymond, M., and Stewart, C. (1984). Unemployment, school, and leisure: An adolescent study. *Leisure Studies, 3*, 175-187.

Hood, R., Allen, L., and Long, P. (1988, October). *An investigation of residents' perception of factors contributing to community satisfaction in a rural town in Colorado using an ethnomethodological approach.* Paper presented at the NRPA Leisure Research Symposium, Indianapolis, IN.

Horna, J.L.A. (1980). Leisure re-socialization among immigrants in Canada. *Society and Leisure, 3*(1), 97-110.

Howe, C.Z. (1980, October). *The use of ethnographic research techniques: A case study of a continuing education program.* Paper presented at the NRPA Leisure Research Symposium, Phoenix, AZ.

Howe, C.Z. (1981, October). *Triangulating research techniques: The evaluation of a regional therapeutic recreation symposium.* Paper presented at the NRPA Leisure Research Symposium, Minneapolis, MN.

Howe, C.Z. (1985). Possibilities for using a qualitative research approach in the sociological study of leisure. *Journal of Leisure Research, 17*(3), 212-224.

Howe, C.Z. (1988). Using qualitative structured interviews in leisure research: Illustrations from one case study. *Journal of Leisure Research, 20*(4), 305-323.

Howe, C.Z., and Keller, M.J. (1988). The use of triangulation as an evaluation technique: Illustrations from regional symposia in therapeutic recreation. *Therapeutic Recreation Journal, 22*(1), 36-45.

Howe-Murphy, R. (1988). Shifting paradigms: Implications for leisure studies curricula. *SPRE Annual on Education (Vol III).* Alexandria, VA: National Recreation and Park Association.

Howe-Murphy, R., and Murphy, J. F. (1988). An exploration of the new age consciousness paradigm in therapeutic recreation. In C. Sylvester, et al. (Eds.) *Philosophy of therapeutic recreation.* Washington, DC: National Recreation and Park Association.

Hunnicutt, B.J. (1985, October). *Playing and knowing.* Paper presented at the NRPA Leisure Research Symposium, Dallas, TX.

Hunnicutt, B. J. (1986, October). *Problems raised by the empirical study of play and some humanistic alternatives.* Paper presented to the National Recreation and Park Association Leisure Research Symposium, Anaheim, CA.

Humphreys, L. (1975). *Tearoom trade.* Chicago, IL: Aldine Publishing, Co.

Hunt, S.L., and Brooks, K.W. (1982). A projection of research and development needs: Implications for disabled persons. *Leisurability, 9*(3), 28-32.

Hunter, R.I. (1983). Methodological issues in therapeutic recreation research. *Therapeutic Recreation Journal, 17*(2), 23-32.

Hunter, R.I. (1987). The impact of an outdoor rehabilitation program for adjudicated juveniles. *Therapeutic Recreation Journal, 21*(3), 30-43.

Husserl, E. (1970). *Cartesian meditations.* The Hague, Netherlands: Martinus Nijhoff.

Hutchinson, R. (1981, October). *Ethnicity and urban recreation: Mexican-Americans in Chicago's public parks.* Paper presented at the NRPA Leisure Research Symposium, Minneapolis, MN.

Hutchinson, R. (1987). Ethnicity and urban recreation: Whites, blacks, and Hispanics in Chicago's public parks. *Journal of Leisure Research, 19*(3), 205-222.

Ianni, F.A.J., and Orr, M.T. (1979). Toward a rapprochement of quantitative and qualitative methodologies. In T.D. Cook and C.S. Reichardt (Eds.), *Qualitative and quantitative methods* (pp. 87-98). Beverly Hills, CA: Sage Publications.

Ingersoll, B. (1983, August). *Approaches to combining quantitative and qualitative social support research.* Paper presented at the Annual Convention of the American Psychological Association, Anaheim, CA.

Iso-Ahola, S. (1980). *The social psychology of leisure and recreation.* Dubuque, IA: Wm. C. Brown Company Publishers.

Iso-Ahola, S. (1986). Concerns and thoughts about leisure research. *Journal of Leisure Research, 18*(3), pp. iv-x.

Jacob, E. (1988). Clarifying qualitative research: A focus on tradition. *Educational Researcher*, 17(1), 16-24.

Jansen-Verbeke, M. (1987). Women, shopping, and leisure. *Leisure Studies, 6*, 71-86.

Johnson, J. M. (1975). *Doing field research.* Beverly Hills, CA: Sage Publications.

Kahane, H. (1980). *Logic and contemporary rhetoric.* Belmont, CA: Wadsworth.

Kamphorst, T.J., Tibori, T.T., and Gilgam, M.J. (1984, September). *Quantitative and qualitative research: Shall the twain ever meet?* Paper presented at the WLRA Leisure Research Meeting, Marli-le-Roi, France.

Katz, J. (1983). A theory of qualitative methodology: The social system of analytic fieldwork. In R. M. Emerson (Ed.), *Contemporary field research* (pp. 127-148). Boston, MA: Little, Brown and Co.

Kelly, J. (1980). Leisure and quality: Beyond the quantitative barriers to research. In T. Goodale and P. Witt (Eds.), *Recreation and leisure: Issues in a era of change.* State College, PA: Venture Publishing.

Kennedy, M.M. (1979). Generalizing from single case studies. *Evaluation Quarterly, 3*(4), 661-678.

Kirk, J., and Miller, M. L. (1986). *Reliability and validity in qualitative research.* Beverly Hills, CA: Sage Publications.

Kraus, R., and Allen, L. (1987). *Research and evaluation in recreation, parks, and leisure studies.* Columbus, OH: Publishing Horizons, Inc.

Kreppner, K. (1986, September). *A dual methodological approach in studying child and family development: Task description and quantification of family interaction episodes.* Paper presented at the International Society for the Study of Behavioral Development Conference, Rome, Italy.

Krippendorff, K. (1980). *Content analysis.* Beverly Hills, CA: Sage Publications.

Krueger, R.A. (1988). *Focus groups.* Beverly Hills, CA: Sage Publications.

Kuhn, T.S. (1970). *The structure of scientific revolutions* (2nd Ed.). Chicago, IL: The University of Chicago Press.

LaPage, W.F. (1981). A further look at the informal interview as a technique for recreation research. *Journal of Leisure Research, 13*(3), 174-176.

Lasley, K. (1987). Ethnography as a recreational needs assessment tool in rural settings. *Journal of Park and Recreation Administration, 5*(3), 60-64.

Lather, P. (1982, June). *Notes toward an adequate methodology in doing feminist research.* Paper presented at the National Women's Studies Association Conference, Arcata, CA.

Leaman, O., and Carrington, B. (1985). Athleticism and the reproduction of gender and ethnic marginality. *Leisure Studies, 4*, 205-217.

LeCompte, M.D. (1984). *Ethnography and qualitative design in educational research.* Orlando, FL: Academic Press.

Levy, J. (1982). Behavioral observation techniques in assessing change in therapeutic recreation/play settings. *Therapeutic Recreation Journal, 16*(1), 25-32.

Lewko, J.H., Bullock, C., and Austin, D.R. (1978). Communication patterns of counselors working with handicapped children. *Therapeutic Recreation Journal, 12*(4), 36-42.

Lidz, C., and Lidz, V. (1988). Editors's note: What's in a name?. *Qualitative Sociology, 11*(1&2), 5-7.

Lincoln, Y.S. (1985). The substance of the emergent paradigm: Implications for research. In Y. Lincoln (Ed.), *Organizational theory and inquiry* (pp. 137-157). Beverly Hills, CA: Sage Publications.

Lincoln, Y.S., and Guba, E.G. (1982, March). *The nature of naturalistic inquiry or...what's it all about Alfie?* Paper presented at the American Educational Research Association, New York, NY.

Lincoln, Y., and Guba, E. (1985). *Naturalistic inquiry.* Beverly Hills, CA: Sage Publications.

Little, S.L. (1985, October). *Conflict resolution processes which contribute to successful leisure program development.* Paper presented at the NRPA Leisure Research Symposium, Dallas, TX.

Little, S.L. (1988). A recreation programming model for linking individual level recreation behavior to actions of social groups. *Journal of Park and Recreation Administration, 6*(4), 90-102.

Locke, L.F. (1986, October). *The question of quality in qualitative research.* Paper presented at the Measurement and Evaluation Symposium, Baton Rouge, LA.

Lofland, J. (1971). *Analyzing social settings.* Belmont, CA: Wadsworth Inc.

Lofland, J. (1974). Editorial Introduction–Analyzing qualitative data: First person accounts. *Urban Life and Culture, 3*, 307-309.

Lofland, J., and Lofland, L. (1984). *Analyzing social settings.* Belmont, CA: Wadsworth Inc.

Lundsteen, S.W. (1986). *Ethnographic perspective: From beginning to final product.* Paper presented at the Midwinter Institute of the National Association for Gifted Children, Dallas, TX.

Malkin, M., and Del Rey, P. (1987, September). *Leisure attitudes of female suicidal psychiatric clients: A feminist sociological perspective.* Paper presented at the NRPA Leisure Research Symposium, New Orleans, LA.

Mannell, R. (1983). Research methodology in therapeutic recreation. *Therapeutic Recreation Journal, 17*(4), 9-16.

Mannell, R.C. (1985). Qualitative data for the psychological study of leisure: Perceptions of a "quantifier." *Leisure Information Quarterly, 12*(1), 5-6.

Manning, P. K. (1987). *Semiotics and fieldwork*. Newbury Park, CA: Sage Publications.

Marshall, C., and Rossman, G.B. (1989). *Designing qualitative research*. Beverly Hills, CA: Sage Publications.

Massarik, F. (1981). The interviewing process reexamined. In P. Reason and J. Rowan (Eds.), *Human inquiry: A sourcebook of new paradigm research* (pp. 201-206). New York, NY: John Wiley and Sons.

Mason, J. (1988). "No peace for the wicked": Older married women and leisure. In E. Wimbush and M. Talbot (Eds.), *Relative freedoms* (pp. 75-86). Milton Keynes, England: Open University Press.

Maurice, C. (1983, April). *Systematic investigation or methodological fragmentation: Toward a unified method of inquiry*. Paper presented at American Educational Research Association, New Orleans, LA.

McCall, C.J. and Simmons, J.L. (Eds.). (1969). *Issues in participant observation*. Reading, MA: Addison-Wesley.

McCormack, T. (1981). Good theory or just theory? Toward a feminist philosophy of social science. *Women's Studies International Quarterly, 4*(1), 1-12.

McDowell, C.F. (1984). An evolving theory of leisure consciousness. *Society and Leisure, 7*(1), 53-87.

McGeown, M. (1982). The concept of families in planning. *Leisurability, 9*(4), 24-29.

McMillan, J.H. and Schumacher, S.I. (1984). *Research in education*. Boston, MA: Little, Brown, and Company.

Mead, G. H. (1934). *Mind, self, and society*. Chicago, IL: University of Chicago Press.

Melamed, L. (1986). The experience of play in women's development. *Recreation Research Review, 13*(1), 7-13.

Mercer, D. (1971). The role of perception in the recreation experience: A review and discussion. *Journal of Leisure Research, 3*(4), 261-276.

Miles, M. B., and Huberman, A. M. (1984). *Qualitative data analysis*. Beverly Hills, CA: Sage Publications.

Mobily, K. (1985). *Thoughts on a reconstruction of leisure research*. Paper presented to the NRPA Leisure Research Symposium, Dallas, TX.

Mobily, K. (1989). Meanings of recreation and leisure among adolescents. *Leisure Studies, 8*, 11-23.

Moeller, G.H., Mescher, M.A., Moore, T.A., and Shafer, E.L. (1980). The informal interview as a technique for recreation research. *Journal of Leisure Research, 12*(2), 174-182.

Morgan, G. (1983). *Beyond method: Strategies for social research.* Beverly Hills, CA: Sage Publications.

Mzorek, D.J. (1983, October). *Mentality and behavior in the study of leisure: Can we know why we did what we did?* Paper presented to the NRPA Leisure Research Symposium, Kansas City, MO.

National Recreation and Park Association Leisure Research Symposium. (1987). *Point/counterpoint...the opening debates* (Cassette Recording No. NRPA-099). Alexandria, VA: National Recreation and Park Association.

Neulinger, J. (1981). *The psychology of leisure* (2nd. ed.). Springfield, IL: Charles Thomas Publishers.

Ng. D. (1988). Forecasting leisure futures: Methodological issues. *Recreation Research Review, 13*(4), 32-38.

Nisbett, R. E., and Ross, L. (1980). *Human influence: Strategies and shortcomings of social judgment.* Englewood Cliffs, NJ: Prentice-Hall.

Oakley, A. (1981). Interviewing women: A contradiction in terms. In A. Roberts (Ed.), *Doing feminist research* (pp. 30-60). London, England: Routledge and Kegan Paul Ltd.

O'Leary, J.T. (1976). Land use redefinition and the rural community: Disruption of community leisure space. *Journal of Leisure Research, 8*(4), 263-274.

Parry, N.C.A. (1983). Sociological contributions to the study of leisure. *Leisure Studies, 2*, 57-81.

Parry, N., and Coalter, F. (1982). Sociology and leisure: A question of root or branch. *Sociology, 16*(2), 220-231.

Patton, M.Q. (1980a) Making methods choices. *Evaluation and Program Planning, 3*, 219-228.

Patton, M. Q. (1980b). *Qualitative evaluation methods.* Beverly Hills, CA: Sage Publications.

Pelegrino, D.A. (1979). *Research methods for recreation and leisure.* Dubuque, IA: Wm. C. Brown Publishers.

Plourde, R.M. (1979). *Personal outcomes of physically disabled and able bodied individuals who participated in wilderness experience.* Paper presented at the NRPA Leisure Research Symposium, New Orleans, LA.

Pozzi, D. (1981). *Urban recreation case studies.* Paper presented at the NRPA Leisure Research Symposium, Minneapolis, MN.

Rabinow, P., and Sullivan, W.M. (Eds.). (1987). *Interpretive social science: A second look.* Berkeley, CA: University of California Press.

Rancourt, A.M. (1987). Undergraduate professional preparation: Curricular competencies in evaluation. *Journal of Park and Recreation Administration, 5*(4), 10-16.

Rapoport, R., and Rapoport, R.N. (1974). Four themes in the sociology of leisure. *British Journal of Sociology, 25,* 215-229.

Rawhouser, D., Harris, C.C., Grussing,L., Krumpe, E.E., and McLaughlin, W.J. (1989). Cooperative research for monitoring recreation use of the Lower Salmon River. *Journal of Park and Recreation Administration, 7*(1), 41-57.

Reason, J. (1981). Methodological approaches to social science. In P. Reason and J. Rowan (Eds.), *Human inquiry: A sourcebook of new paradigm research* (pp. 43-51). New York, NY: John Wiley and Sons.

Reason, P., and Rowan, J. (Eds.). (1981). *Human inquiry: A sourcebook of new paradigm research.* New York, NY: John Wiley and Sons.

Reichardt, C.S., and Cook, T.D. (1979). Beyond qualitative versus quantitative methods. In T.D. Cook, and C.S. Reichardt (Eds.), *Qualitative and quantitative methods in evaluation research.* Beverly Hills, CA: Sage Publications.

Reinharz, S. (1979). *On becoming a social scientists: From survey research and participant observation to experiential analysis.* San Francisco, CA: Jossey-Bass.

Reinharz, S. (1981). Implementing new paradigm research: A model for training and practice. In P. Reason, and J. Rowan (Eds.), *Human inquiry: A sourcebook of new paradigm research* (pp. 415-435). New York, NY: John Wiley and Sons.

Reynolds, R.P. (1976). The case study technique and in-service training. *Leisurability, 3*(2), 8-14.

Richardson, S.L., Long, P.T., and Perdue, R.R. (1988). The importance of economic impact to municipal recreation programming. *Journal of Park and Recreation Administration, 6*(4), 65-78.

Riddick, C.C., DeSchriver, M., and Weissinger, E. (1984). A methodological review of research in *Journal of Leisure Research* from 1978 to 1982. *Journal of Leisure Research, 16*(4), 311-321.

Rist, R.C. (1975). On the application of ethnographic methods to the study of an urban school. *Urban Education, 10*(1), 86-108.

Rist, R. C. (1980a). Blitzkrieg ethnography: On the transformation of a method into a movement. *Educational Researcher, 9*(2), 8-10.

Rist, R.C. (1980b). *On qualitative research: A bibliography.* Unpublished 3rd edition. Cornell University, Cornell, NY: College of Human Ecology.

Roadburg, A. (1976). Is professional football a profession? *International Review of Sport Sociology, 3*, 27-37.

Roadburg, A. (1980). Breaking relationships with research subjects: Some problems and suggestions. In Shaffir, W. B. , Stebbins, R. A., and Turowetz, A. (Eds.), *Fieldwork Experience.* New York, NY: St. Martin's Press.

Roadburg, A. (1983). Freedom and enjoyment: Disentangling perceived leisure. *Journal of Leisure Research, 15*(1), 15-26.

Roberts, J.M. (1983). Playing at work. *Leisure Studies, 3*, 217-229.

Roberts, J.M., and Cosper, R.L. (1987). Variation in strategic involvement in games for three blue collar occupations. *Journal of Leisure Research, 19*(2), 131-148.

Roberts, J.M., Koening, F., and Stark, R.B. (1969). Judged display: A consideration of a craft show. *Journal of Leisure Research, 1*(2), 163-179.

Robertson, R. D. (1983, October). *Leisure research and education or trading awareness for things of lesser worth?* Paper presented at the NRPA Leisure Research Symposium, Kansas City, MO.

Rowan, J. (1981). A dialectical paradigm for research. In P. Reason, and J. Rowan (Eds.), *Human inquiry: A sourcebook of new paradigm research* (pp. 93-112). New York, NY: John Wiley and Sons.

Samdahl, D. (1988). A symbolic interactionist model of leisure: Theory and empirical support. *Leisure Sciences, 10*(1), 27-39.

Sanday, P.R. (1979). The ethnographic paradigm(s). *Administrative Science Quarterly, 42*(4), 527-538.

Saunders, D.M., and Turner, D.E. (1987). Gambling and leisure: The case of racing. *Leisure Studies, 6*, 281-299.

Schwartz, H., and Jacobs, J. (1979). *Qualitative sociology: A method to the madness.* New York, NY: Free Press.

Schwartz, P., and Ogilvy, J. (1980, June). *The emergent paradigm: Toward an aesthetic of life.* Paper presented at the ESOMAR meeting, Barcelona, Spain.

Scriven, M. (1972). Pros and cons about goal-free evaluation. *Evaluation Comment, 3*, 1-7.

Seidel, J.V., and Clark, A. (1984). Ethnograph. *Qualitative Sociology, 7*(1/2), 110-125.

Shaffir, W. B., Stebbins, R. A., and Turowetz, A. (Eds.). (1980). *Fieldwork experience: Qualitative approaches to social research.* New York, NY: St. Martin's Press.

Shank, J.W. (1986). An exploration of leisure in the lives of dual career women. *Journal of Leisure Research, 18*(4), 300-319.

Shaw, S. (1985). The meaning of leisure in everyday life. *Leisure Sciences, 7*(1), 1-24.

Sheffield, E. (1988, March). *Trustworthiness and new paradigm research.* Paper presented at the SPRE Research Institute, Saratoga Springs, NY.

Simpson, S., and McAvoy, L. (1983, October). *Legislative intent: Potential source for directives to establish appropriate recreational use on river segments within the National Park system.* Paper presented at the NRPA Leisure Research Symposium, Anaheim, CA.

Smith, A.A. (1985). A participant observer study of a "rough" working-class pub. *Leisure Studies, 4*, 293-306.

Smith, J.K. (1983). Quantitative verses qualitative research: An attempt to clarify the issues. *Educational Researcher, 12*(3), 6-13.

Smith, L.M. (1978). An evolving logic of participant observation, educational ethnography, and other case studies. *Review of Research in Education, 6*, 316-317.

Smith, M.L. (1987). Publishing qualitative research. *American Educational Research Journal, 42*(2), 173-184.

Smith, P.L. (1980). On the distinction between quantitative and qualitative research. *CEDR Quarterly, 13*(3), 3-6.

Smith, J.K., and Heshusius, L. (1986). Closing down the conversation: The end of the quantitative-qualitative debate among educational inquirers. *Educational Researcher, 15*(1), 4-12.

Smith, S.L.J., and Haley, A.J. (1979). Ratio ex machina: Notes on leisure research. *Journal of Leisure Research, 11*(2), 139-143.

Spiegelberg, H. (1975). *Doing phenomenology.* The Hague, Netherlands: Martinus Nijhoff.

Spindler, G. (Ed.). (1982). *Doing the ethnography of schooling.* New York, NY: Holt, Rinehart, and Winston.

Spradley, J.P. (1979). *The ethnographic interview.* New York, NY: Holt, Rinehart and Winston.

Spradley, J. P. (1980). *Participant observation.* New York, NY: Holt, Rinehart and Winston.

Sproull, L. S., and Sproull, R. F. (1982). Managing and analyzing behavioral records: Explanation in non-numeric data analysis. *Human Organizations, 41*(4), 283-290.

Stake, R.E. (1978). The case study method in social inquiry. *Educational Researcher, 7*(2), 5-8.

Stanley, L., and Wise, S. (1983). *Breaking out: Feminist consciousness and feminist research.* London, England: Routledge and Kegan Paul.

Stebbins, R.A. (1979). *Amateurs: On the margin between work and leisure.* Beverly Hills, CA: Sage Publications.

Stebbins, R.A. (1982). Serious leisure: A conceptual statement. *Pacific Sociological Review, 25,* 251-272.

Stoddart, K. (1987). The Corpus: A data-based device for teaching field methods. *Teaching Sociology, 15*(2), 197-199.

Strauss, A. (1987). *Qualitative analysis.* New York, NY: Cambridge University Press.

Stumbo, N. J. (1983). Systematic observation as a research tool for assessing client behavior. *Therapeutic Recreation Journal, 17*(4), 53-63.

Talbot, M. (1986). *Beyond the quantum.* New York, NY: Macmillan Publishing Co.

Taylor, S. J., and Bogdan, R. (1984). *Introduction to qualitative research methods: The search for meaning* (2nd ed.). New York, NY: John Wiley and Sons.

Thorne, B. (1979). Political activist as participant observer. *Symbolic Interaction, 2,* 73-88.

Tinsley, H.E.A. (1984). Limitations, explorations, aspirations: A confession of fallibility and a promise to strive for perfection. *Journal of Leisure Research, 16*(2), 93-98.

Tokarski, W. (1983). The situation of leisure research in Western Germany with an emphasis on the methodological aspects. *Society and Leisure, 6*(2), 493-506.

Tokarski, W. (1987). Leisure and life-styles of the elderly: Outline of a research paradigm. *European Journal of Education, 22*(3-4), 327-333.

Turner, T. (1983). *An ethnography of the organization Basic Choices.* Unpublished master's thesis. University of Wisconsin, Madison, WI.

Tuthill, D. and Ashton, P. (1983). Improving the educational research through the development of educational paradigms. *Educational Researcher, 12*(12), 6-14.

Ulrich. R.S., and Addams, D.L. (1981). Psychological and recreational benefits of a residential park. *Journal of Leisure Research, 13*(1), 43-65.

Uzzell, D.L. (1985). Management issues in the provision of countryside interpretation. *Leisure Studies, 4,* 159-174.

Van Maanen, J. (1979). Reclaiming qualitative methods for organizational research: A preface. *Administrative Service Quarterly, 24*(4), 520-526.

Van Maanen. J. (1988). *Tales of the field.* Chicago, IL: The University of Chicago Press.

Vingerhoets, A., and Buunk, B. (1987). Attitudes toward nudist and public beaches: Some evidence of dissonance reduction and gender differences. *Journal of Leisure Research, 19*(1), 13-21.

Warder, D.S. (1979). *Analysis of visitor use in BLM lands in Wyoming.* Paper presented at the NRPA Leisure Research Symposium, New Orleans, LA.

Warren, C. A. B., and Rasmussen, P. (1977). Sex and gender in field research. *Urban Life, 6,* 349-369.

Wax, R. H. (1971). *Doing fieldwork: Warnings and advice.* Chicago, IL: The University of Chicago Press.

Weatherman, R., and Swenson, K. (1974). Delphi techniques. In S.H. Hedley and J.R. Yates (Eds.), *Futurism in Education.* Berkeley, CA: McCutcheon Publishing Co.

Webb, E. T., Campbell, D. T., Schwartz, R. D., Sechrest, L., and Grove, J. B. (1981). *Nonreactive measures in the social sciences.* Boston, MA: Houghton Mifflin.

Weber, M. (1968). *Economy and society.* New York, NY: Bedminster Press.

Werner, O. and Schoepfle, G.M. (1987). *Systematic fieldwork Vol. 1 and 2.* Newbury Park, CA: Sage Publications.

West, P.C. (1982). Organizational stigma in metropolitan park and recreation agencies. *Therapeutic Recreation Journal, 16*(4), 35-41.

West, P.C. (1984). Social stigma and community recreation participation by the mentally and physically handicapped. *Therapeutic Recreation Journal, 18*(1), 40-49.

West, P.C. (1986). Interorganizational linkage and outdoor recreation for persons with physical and mental disabilities. *Therapeutic Recreation Journal, 20*(1), 63-75.

Westover, T.N. (1986). Park use and perception: Gender differences. *Journal of Park and Recreation Administration, 4*(2), 1-8.

Whyte, W.F. (1984). *Learning from the field.* Beverly Hills, CA: Sage Publications.

Wilkinson, P.F. (1983). Disabled children and integrated play environments. *Recreation Research Review, 10*(1), 20-28.

Wilson, S. (1977). The use of ethnographic techniques in educational research. *Review of Educational Research, 47*(1), 245-265.

Wilson, S. (1979). Exploration of the usefulness of case study evaluations. *Evaluation Quarterly, 3*(3), 446-459.

Wimbush, E.J., and Duffield, B.S. (1985). Integrating education and leisure: Conflict and the community school. *Leisure Studies, 4,* 69-84.

Woodward, D., Green, E., and Hebron, S. (1988). The Sheffield study of gender and leisure: Its methodological approach. *Leisure Studies, 7*, 95-101.

Wuthnow, R., Hunter, J.D., Bergesen, A., and Kurzweil, E. (1984). *Cultural analysis*. London, England: Routledge and Kegan Paul.

Wyman, M. (1985). Nature experiences and outdoor recreation planning. *Leisure Studies, 4*, 175-183.

Yin, R.K. (1984). *Case study research*. Design and methods. Beverly Hills, CA: Sage Publications.

Zelditch, M. (1962). Some methodological problems of field studies. *American Journal of Sociology, 67*, 566-576.

Znaniecki, F. (1934). *The method of sociology*. New York, NY: Farrow and Rinehart.

Zukav, G. (1979). *The dancing wu-li masters*. New York, NY: William Morrow and Company, Inc.

INDEX BY SUBJECT

INDEX BY AUTHOR